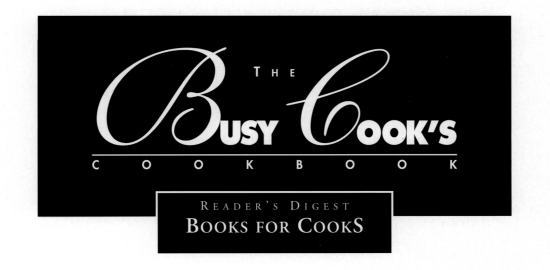

THE **BUSY COOK'S** COOKBOOK

READER'S DIGEST
BOOKS FOR COOKS

THE BUSY COOK'S

COOKBOOK

READER'S DIGEST
BOOKS FOR COOKS

The Reader's Digest Association, Inc.
Pleasantville, New York/Montreal

Edited and designed by Media Projects Incorporated

Portions of this book were previously published in
Reader's Digest Creative Cooking Club.

The credits that appear on page 144 are hereby made a part of this copyright page.

Library of Congress Cataloging in Publication Data
The Busy cook's cookbook.
          p.   cm.—(Books for cooks)
     Includes index.
     ISBN 0-89577-489-5
     1. Quick and easy cookery.   I. Series.
TX833.5.B873 1993
641.5′55—dc20   92-43506

TABLE OF CONTENTS

For many people, getting appealing home-cooked meals on the table can be a daily challenge. The truth is there are not enough hours in the day to devote to lengthy stints in the kitchen. And, not every person has the expertise of a professional chef. But with *The Busy Cook's Cookbook*, help is at hand.

With *The Busy Cook's Cookbook*, the harried career person or overextended homemaker (or both) can beat the kitchen clock again and again and still produce wonderful meals. The carefully selected recipes produce results that not only look and taste delicious, but are fast to make. Working at a reasonable pace, even novice cooks can prepare most of the dishes in under 45 minutes. In some cases, allow a little extra time for marinating, chilling, and other do-ahead tasks. And, over half of the recipes are illustrated by gorgeous color photographs to show cooks what the finished dishes will look like—a real bonus.

From mouthwatering starters to scrumptious desserts, these pages offer possibilities for every occasion. Expecting a few friends for brunch? Serve Bacon and Gruyère Quiche (page 39) and a basketful of Strawberry Muffins (page 117). Or, on the lookout for something new for a weekend barbecue? Fire up the grill for Lemon-Thyme Salmon Steaks (page 58) or Peppered Beef and Vegetable Kebabs (page 43)—either choice will be ready in a flash. Want to throw a casual cocktail party? Garlic-Stuffed Mussels (page 13) and Herbed Smoked Salmon and Cream Cheese Roll (page 17) make perfect party food.

All the recipes have been kitchen-tested to ensure that they are easy to follow, speedy to prepare, truly delectable, and will yield perfect results every time. Each recipe includes at-a-glance serving quantities, preparation and cooking times, and times for do-ahead tasks. Each step in the recipes is clearly numbered. To make the cooking process more organized, each recipe is accompanied by an equipment list of appliances and utensils. And, in a special section, there's a nutritional information listing for each recipe.

What's more, many of the recipes contain helpful hints for preparation and cooking, including choosing the best skewers for barbecuing, how to prevent sliced avocados from discoloring, and a simple method for achieving perfectly poached fish. And, many of the recipes contain serving suggestions, so no time is wasted having to worry about accompaniments. Finally, there are three complete special occasion menus that guide cooks through the organizational minefield with time-saving ideas.

Slaving over a hot stove is the last thing anyone wants to do when preparing food for a cocktail or dinner party or brunch. That's why Herbed Smoked Salmon and Cream Cheese Roll (page 17) is just the dish to serve. Although it looks sophisticated, it requires no cooking, can be made hours in advance, and can be doubled or tripled if greater quantities are required.

Kitchen Planning

Organizing the kitchen is the first step to turning out quick meals. For maximum efficiency, keep the cooking area uncluttered and well equipped with appliances and good utensils, such as a set of high-quality knives and heavy-bottomed pots and pans, which conduct heat more evenly. While the initial investment may seem expensive, good kitchen tools last a lifetime. Arrange like equipment together for easy access and also closest to its primary area of use. For example, store all pots and pans in one spot next to the range and sets of dishes by the dining area. Frequently used equipment such as the blender or food processor belongs on the kitchen counter—not under the sink. If the kitchen is small, explore creative storage solutions, such as overhead pot racks or wall grids.

A special occasion demands special food but it need not call for hours of complicated preparation. Taking only minutes to make, Poached Red Snapper with Wine and Vegetables (page 59) is a treat for the eyes and the palate.

Anyone can put together a meal from pantry staples, but putting together a great meal is another matter altogether. So when time is especially tight or unexpected guests descend, it's vital to have a wide selection of ingredients on hand. Spaghetti Puttanesca (pages 100-101) can be created from shelf food but it's so tasty that no one would ever know it. So stock up now—it will pay dividends in the end.

Pantry Pointers

Next, take steps to achieve a well-stocked pantry. Having available a good selection of canned, dried, and frozen foods is a way to expand dining options without wasting time stopping at the supermarket every day. Often it's possible to create a great meal entirely from on-hand staples. Spaghetti Puttanesca (pages 100-101) and Pasta Carbonara (page 101) are two such choices that are both flavorful and just the ticket for last-minute guests!

What constitutes basic pantry ingredients depends largely on personal preference. However, a spontaneous meal can always be made from items such as pasta, beans, grains, tomato and specialty sauces, dried herbs and spices, assorted condiments, and canned fish—tuna, salmon, sardines, mackerel, and anchovies. Keep a few special pantry foods for impromptu entertaining. Jarred pesto sauce, frozen phyllo dough and puff pastry, and sun-dried tomatoes are ideal for fast hors d'oeuvres. Remember, too, that canned broths and fruit and vegetable juices add flavor to dishes without any extra work needed.

When arranging the pantry, be sure to put similar foods together: oils with vinegars; beans with pasta and grains; jars of condiments; and all the dried herbs and spices, with an assigned place on the shelves. This will minimize scrambling around when dinner is needed in a hurry.

Tools of the Trade for the Busy Cook's Kitchen

Listed below is all the equipment used in this cookbook. It is not essential to own every item. A blender can often double as a food processor; a large, heavy skillet can replace a wok. To improvise a double boiler, use a heatproof bowl set over a saucepan of simmering water. To make a baking pan substitution, choose one with the same volume and a similar depth. To determine volume, measure the amount of water the pan holds when filled to the rim. Allow more baking time when using a deeper pan than the one called for in the recipe.

EQUIPMENT
Small bowl, 2 cups to 1½ quarts
Medium-size bowl, 2 to 3 quarts
Large bowl, 4 to 5 quarts
Blender
Electric hand mixer
Food processor with metal blades
6-cup ring mold
Shallow glass dish, 11″ x 7″ to 9″ x 13″
Toaster oven or toaster
Vegetable steamer
Waffle iron

BAKING
Baking pan, 9″ x 13″
Baking pan, 8″ square
Baking sheets, 12″ x 18″ or 11″ x 15″
Bundt pan, 10″
Jelly roll pan, 15½″ x 10½″
2 layer cake pans, 9″
2 loaf pans, 9″ x 5″
Pie pan, 9″
Tube pan, 9″
Cookie cutters, 2″ and 3″, round and other assorted shapes
Muffin pan, standard size (12-cup)
Pastry bag with plain, star, and other assorted tips
Pastry blender
Pie weights
Rolling pin, 10″ to 12″
Sifter
Wire racks

MEASURING
Glass measuring cups for liquids, 1 to 4 cups
Measuring cups for dry ingredients: ¼ cup, ⅓ cup, ½ cup, and 1 cup
Measuring spoons: ¼ teaspoon, ½ teaspoon, 1 teaspoon, and 1 tablespoon
Kitchen scale

POTS, PANS, AND CASSEROLES
Small saucepan with lid, 2 cups to 1½ quarts
Medium-size saucepan with lid, 2 to 4 quarts
Large saucepan with lid, 5 to 6 quarts
Double boiler
Stockpot with lid, 8 quarts
Small skillet, 6″ to 8″
Medium-size skillet with lid, 8″ to 10″
Large skillet with lid, 10″ to 12″
Nonstick skillet, 8″ to 10″
Crêpe pan, 8″
Broiler pan
Griddle
Deep-fat fryer with removable basket
Paella dish
Wok
Baking dishes, 1½, 2, and 3 quarts
Casserole with lid, 2 quarts
Dutch oven, 4 to 6 quarts
Individual gratin dishes, 1 to 2 cups
Roasting pan with rack, 16″ x 11″ x 5″
Soufflé dish, 1½ quarts

UTENSILS
Apple corer
Bulb baster
Cake testers
Can opener
Candy thermometer
Carving board
Citrus juicer
Colander, 8″ to 10″
Corkscrew
Cutting board
Fine wire mesh sieve, 2″ to 3″
Grater
Kitchen scissors
Kitchen timer
Kitchen tongs
Long-handled fork
Meat mallet
Meat thermometer
Melon-ball cutter
Mortar and pestle
Oven thermometer
Pastry brushes
Pepper mill
Potato masher
Poultry shears
Salad servers
Salt shaker
Skewers, metal or wooden, 10″ to 12″
Spaghetti fork
Vegetable brush
Vegetable peeler
Wire mesh strainer, 6″ to 8″
Wire whisk, stainless steel, 8″ to 12″
Yeast thermometer

KNIVES
Paring knife, 3″ to 4″ blade
Boning knife, 5″ to 6″ blade
Utility knife, 6″ to 8″ blade
Serrated knife, 8″ to 9″ blade
Chef's knife, 8″ to 10″ blade
Carving knife and fork, 10″ blade
Knife sharpening steel

SPATULAS
Large, metal spatula
Rubber spatula
Thin, metal spatula

SPOONS
Long-handled metal kitchen spoons
Slotted stainless steel spoon
Soup ladle
Wooden spoons

SUPPLIES
Airtight plastic containers in assorted sizes
Aluminum foil
Cheesecloth
Kitchen twine
Muffin pan liners, paper or foil
Paper towels
Plastic food storage bags
Plastic wrap
Pot holders
Toothpicks
Wax paper

Two meals from one main course—what better way is there to cut down time spent in the kitchen? The way to do it is with leftovers which are given a new lease on life. Sweet and Savory Chicken Salad (page 70) is proof of how roast chicken (or turkey) leftovers can be transformed into a marvelous and very fresh-tasting salad by adding only a few ingredients and a superb dressing.

Shopping Shortcuts

To avoid time-wasting daily shopping, plan meals on a weekly basis. First decide how many meals will be needed, then select the main dishes, and choose foods that go well with the rest of the menu. Think of buying foods that can be used for more than one meal. For instance, the leftovers from a roast chicken can form the basis of Sweet and Savory Chicken Salad (page 70).

Jot down a shopping list and stick to it. Abiding by the list reduces the temptation to buy on impulse and also lessens the chance of duplicating items. A caveat: Be flexible when it comes to fresh produce. Fruits and vegetables are always best in their season, so buy only the freshest varieties and work them into the menu plans. Shopping in one or two places where the layout is familiar will go much faster. Another advantage of same-store shopping is getting to know the market personnel, who can help with special requests.

Getting Ready

Before beginning to cook, read through the recipe carefully to get a feel for the preparation and an idea of the ingredients and utensils. Check the recipe equipment list to see what appliances and utensils will be required and then refer to the general equipment list on page 8 for specifics on pan sizes and the like. By setting out the ingredients in order of use and gathering the equipment together, preparation will become streamlined and time saved.

While some ingredients perform an essential function, such as egg whites in a soufflé, quite a few are not that critical. Liquids substitute for one another, as long as the choice is similarly sweet or savory—tomato juice for chicken broth or molasses for honey. If a seasonal vegetable is unavailable, use frozen or canned—recipes usually give one or the other, with the appropriate quantities. Dried herbs can almost always stand in for fresh herbs but, since they are more concentrated in flavor, use only one-third as much.

When a substitute for fish is required, use a fish of a similar fat content. Lean, firm-fleshed fish include scrod, haddock, pollack, pike, and hake; lean fish with more delicate flesh are flounder, fluke, and sole. Salmon, tuna, swordfish, and shark have a moderately high fat content. High-fat bluefish is interchangeable with mullet, trout, and mackerel. However, in Soft-Shell Crabs with Ginger Sauce (page 63), the main ingredient is strictly seasonal so there is no substitute.

Whenever possible, include seasonal fruits and vegetables in menu plans and always choose the freshest. One vegetable with a fairly brief season is Brussels sprouts which in Sweet and Sour Marinated Brussels Sprouts (page 84) forms the basis of a quick and crunchy side dish with a pungent flavor. Making this dish out of season is also a snap because The Busy Cook's Cookbook provides a frozen Brussels sprouts alternative.

Beating the Kitchen Clock

Planning ahead clearly saves time and effort. Get into the habit of preparing extra food and reserving some for a jump-start on another meal. Slice extra meat, dice more vegetables, grate another chunk of cheese, then wrap tightly and refrigerate or freeze. Cooked rice and pasta also keep well and can be added to soups, salads, and stews for later in the week. Salad dressings, sauces, and many desserts can be prepared ahead and kept in the refrigerator until they are needed.

The Busy Cook's Cookbook offers many recipes that can be made one day and served the next, from cold salads and room-temperature frittatas to reheatable soups and casseroles. Some good examples are Harvest Festival Pumpkin-Cheese Soup (page 22), Quick Turkey and White Bean Chili (page 74), and Pasta Frittata with Fontina Cheese (page 36). Always cover food securely; plastic wrap stretched over the dish, plus aluminum foil on top is a good method to prevent food from drying out. Thaw frozen soups and casseroles in the refrigerator overnight and reheat them, covered with a lid or aluminum foil, in a moderate oven or over low heat on the rangetop, stirring occasionally, until completely warmed.

To simplify meal planning during the week, figure on an occasional dinner that is based on leftovers. Barbecued chicken, meatloaf, chili, and many other foods taste even better the next day! For almost-instant lunches and dinners, purchase precut meats and poultry, such as beef for stir-frying and boneless, skinless chicken and turkey breasts. The expense is worth the time saved.

To solve the weekday morning rush, have some ready-to-go-foods available, which can be prepared the night before. Try halving grapefruits and oranges, hard boiling some eggs, or mixing up a batch of Rise and Shine Muesli (page 31). Wrap these breakfast foods in plastic wrap and put them in a special section of the refrigerator to avoid hunting around at 7:00 a.m. On long weekends, plan to make more than one casserole to set aside for freezing. Soups and stews freeze beautifully, too, so it pays to make a big batch. By keeping these strategies in mind, less time will be spent in the kitchen.

COOKING TIME-SAVERS

- **THINK SMALL:**
  The smaller the food, the faster it cooks. So buy thin cuts or small pieces of meat, fish, and poultry.

- **THINK FAST:**
  Use quick-cooking methods, such as grilling, broiling, sautéing, and stir-frying.

- **THINK EASY:**
  When time is really tight, select recipes that require the least amount of ingredients, cooking utensils, and appliances. It's possible to put dinner on the table in under 30 minutes . . . and still get rave reviews.

Not all soups have to simmer for hours as evidenced by Harvest Festival Pumpkin-Cheese Soup (page 22), which takes only 40 minutes from start to finish. But that's not all. Robust enough to serve as a main course, this vibrant soup can be prepared a day ahead and then reheated the next, and that way there's no need to spend time cooking.

Quick and Easy Entertaining Ideas

When company is coming, minimize stress by keeping food simple. For example, serve Caribbean Steak (page 43) marinated in lime juice or Pork Tenderloin with Mushrooms and Rosemary (page 44). Or, prepare a freezable one-dish meal such as Pasta al Forno (page 107). Once in the freezer, just forget it until it is time to defrost. Many of the recipes can be made ahead, enabling the cook to avoid a last-minute time crunch and feel relaxed when the guests arrive.

Always do as much as possible beforehand, from cutting up vegetables and storing them in damp paper towels to making croutons for the salad. Prepare the ingredients needed for each recipe a day or so before the party, then refrigerate. When it is time to cook, everything will be set to go. Finally, don't forget the finishing touches that make dishes visually appealing. Simple garnishes are best and they can be done in seconds. Float thin lemon slices on a bowl of soup or make a bed of kale or other greenery for a plate of sliced cold meats. Place sprigs of fresh herbs on a serving platter or decorate with fresh flowers.

Love to have dinner parties but never have time to prepare all the food? Easy entertaining is possible—the solution lies in the choice of dishes that combine speed with flavor and an attractive presentation. Pork Tenderloin with Mushrooms and Rosemary (page 44) is one such dish that fits all three requirements and then some. Try it once and see!

APPETIZERS

*S*peedy and simple appetizers are unbeatable. Fresh ingredients and a little creativity will produce varied and appealing dishes to get meals off to a great start. This chapter offers elegant stuffed shellfish, flavorful mini pizzas, and spicy quesadillas, to name a few dishes.

Herb-Stuffed Shrimp.

Herb-Stuffed Shrimp

1 pound large uncooked shrimp, peeled and deveined, tails intact (16-20 shrimp)

HERB STUFFING (1½ CUPS)

1 cup dry unseasoned bread crumbs
2 large cloves garlic, finely chopped
½ teaspoon dried thyme leaves, crumbled
2 tablespoons chopped fresh parsley
¼ cup (½ stick) unsalted butter, softened
3 drops hot pepper sauce
1 tablespoon fresh lemon juice
⅛ teaspoon salt, or to taste
Freshly ground black pepper

Shrimp are one of the most succulent shellfish and in this recipe they are made even juicier by an herb stuffing. Served with plenty of napkins, this dish makes fabulous finger food. Mop up any juices with slices of crusty French bread.

1 Rinse the shrimp under cold running water and pat dry with paper towels. With a sharp knife, cut along the channel where the vein was removed, taking care not to cut through completely. Set aside.

2 Preheat the oven to 400° F. Lightly grease 4 individual gratin dishes or a 1½-quart baking dish.

3 To make the Herb Stuffing: In a small bowl, mix together the bread crumbs, garlic, thyme, parsley, butter, hot pepper sauce, and lemon juice until well blended. Season to taste with the salt and pepper.

4 Open each shrimp so the cut edges spread out slightly. Fill the curve of the shrimp with some stuffing. Place, stuffing-side up, in the prepared dishes. Repeat filling the remaining shrimp as directed. Sprinkle the remaining stuffing over the top.

5 Bake for 15 minutes, or until the shrimp are opaque and the stuffing is golden. Transfer the shrimp to a serving platter and serve immediately.

4 SERVINGS
PREP TIME: 30 MINUTES
COOKING TIME: 15 MINUTES

EQUIPMENT LIST

Utility knife
Citrus juicer
Pepper mill
Paper towels
4 individual gratin dishes
Small bowl
Kitchen spoon
Teaspoon

Garlic-Stuffed Mussels

½ cup water
2 pounds mussels

GARLIC STUFFING (½ CUP)

2 tablespoons unsalted butter, softened
1 large clove garlic, finely chopped
2 tablespoons finely chopped yellow onion
1 tablespoon chopped fresh parsley
2 tablespoons fresh bread crumbs
¼ teaspoon salt, or to taste
Freshly ground black pepper

The rules of thumb for mussels are: Discard open- or broken-shelled mussels before cooking and closed-shell mussels after cooking.

1 To clean the mussels: Drop them into lightly salted water to cover and let stand for 15 minutes, to rid them of sand. Scrub the mussels thoroughly with a stiff brush and remove the fuzzy "beards." Discard any mussels with broken or open shells.

2 In a large saucepan, bring the water to a boil over high heat. Add the mussels and cook, covered, for 2 to 3 minutes, or until the shells open. Gently stir the mussels once or twice to ensure even cooking.

3 Remove the pan from the heat and drain the mussels. Discard any unopened mussels. Break off the empty half of each mussel shell and discard. Preheat the broiler.

4 To make the Garlic Stuffing: In a small bowl, mix together the butter, garlic, onion, parsley, and bread crumbs. Season to taste with the salt and pepper. Using a thin, metal spatula, spread the stuffing evenly over the mussels.

5 Line a broiler pan with crumpled aluminum foil and carefully arrange the mussels, stuffing-side up, on the foil, 3″ from the heat source. Broil the mussels for 3 minutes, or until the stuffing is golden. Transfer the mussels to a serving platter and serve immediately.

4 SERVINGS
PREP TIME: 20 MINUTES PLUS
15 MINUTES TO STAND
COOKING TIME: 6 MINUTES

EQUIPMENT LIST

Utility knife
Pepper mill
Large bowl
Small bowl
Vegetable brush
Large saucepan
Broiler pan
Kitchen spoon
Colander
Thin, metal spatula
Aluminum foil

Broiled Oysters with Cilantro Pesto

Rock or coarse salt
12 large oysters on the half shell
1 ounce feta cheese, crumbled (¼ cup)
¼ cup chopped red bell pepper

CILANTRO PESTO (½ CUP)

2 cups lightly packed cilantro (coriander leaves) or fresh parsley
2 large cloves garlic, finely chopped
2 ounces walnut pieces (½ cup)
1 tablespoon fresh lime juice
¼ cup olive oil
½ teaspoon salt, or to taste
Freshly ground black pepper

To save time, make the pesto a day ahead and store it in an airtight container in the refrigerator until ready to broil the oysters. Have the fishmonger open the oysters, but do this as close to cooking time as possible.

1 To make the Cilantro Pesto: Place the cilantro, garlic, walnuts, lime juice, and oil in a blender or food processor fitted with the metal blade. Blend or process for 1 minute, or until smooth, scraping down the side of the bowl whenever necessary. Season to taste.

2 Preheat the broiler. Fill a large, flameproof baking dish with a thick layer of rock salt. Arrange the oysters on top, bedding them in the salt. Spoon ½ teaspoon of pesto on each oyster, then sprinkle with the cheese and bell pepper. Place the oysters under broiler 4″ from heat source. Broil for 2 to 3 minutes, or until the cheese begins to melt and the oysters are just warmed through.

3 Transfer the broiled oysters to a large serving platter and serve immediately.

12 OYSTERS
PREP TIME: 30 MINUTES
COOKING TIME: 3 MINUTES

EQUIPMENT LIST

Utility knife
Citrus juicer
Pepper mill
Blender or food processor with metal blade
Rubber spatula
Teaspoon
Large, flameproof baking dish

This colorful Mediterranean trio of hors d'oeuvres will be a party highlight.

Sicilian Mini Pizzas

2 tablespoons yellow cornmeal
1 pound frozen bread dough, thawed
Olive oil

MEDITERRANEAN TOPPING

12 pitted calamata or other black olives
2 tablespoon olive oil
¼ cup finely chopped yellow onion
¼ cup chopped green bell pepper
½ cup chopped eggplant
½ cup chopped zucchini
1 medium-size tomato, seeded and chopped (½ cup)
1 small clove garlic, finely chopped
¼ teaspoon salt, or to taste
¼ teaspoon coarsely ground black pepper
Freshly grated Parmesan cheese (optional)

1 To make the Mediterranean Topping: Place the olives in a blender or food processor fitted with the metal blade. Blend or process for 1 minute, scraping down the side of the bowl whenever necessary. Add 1 tablespoon of the oil and blend or process for 30 seconds, or until smooth. Set aside.

2 In a large skillet, heat the remaining 1 tablespoon of oil over moderate heat for 1 minute. Add the onion and sauté for 5 minutes, or until translucent. Add the bell pepper and eggplant and sauté for 3 minutes, or until softened. Add the zucchini, tomato, garlic, salt, and pepper and cook for 2 minutes more. (Do not overcook the vegetables as they should hold their shape.) Remove the skillet from the heat and keep warm.

3 Preheat the oven to 375° F. Sprinkle 2 baking sheets with the cornmeal. On a lightly floured work surface, knead the dough gently and divide into 24 equal pieces. Using your fingertips, press each piece into a 4″ circle ¼″ thick. Place the dough circles on the baking sheets and brush each one lightly with oil.

4 Bake the pizzas, 1 baking sheet at a time, for 12 minutes, or until golden around the edges. Remove the baking sheet from the oven. Using a large, metal spatula, transfer the pizzas to a wire rack to cool slightly. Repeat as directed with the remaining pizzas.

5 Spread 1 teaspoon of the olive mixture on each pizza. Top with 1 tablespoon of the vegetable mixture. Sprinkle with Parmesan cheese, if desired, and serve immediately.

24 PIZZAS
PREP TIME: 20 MINUTES
COOKING TIME: 32 MINUTES

EQUIPMENT LIST

Utility knife
Blender or food processor with metal blade
Rubber spatula
Large, metal spatula
Large skillet
Kitchen spoon
2 baking sheets
Pastry brush
Wire rack

Prosciutto-Mozzarella Balls

18 small mozzarella balls
2 tablespoons olive oil
¼ teaspoon salt, or to taste
¼ teaspoon coarsely ground black pepper
⅛ teaspoon crushed red pepper flakes
1 teaspoon grated lemon rind
½ teaspoon chopped fresh thyme, or ¼ teaspoon dried thyme leaves, crumbled
4 ounces thinly sliced prosciutto (9 slices)
18 fresh basil leaves, rinsed
Sprigs of fresh basil (optional)

As a substitute for a package of small mozzarella balls, cut a 9-ounce whole piece of mozzarella cheese into eighteen 1″ pieces.

1 Drain the mozzarella balls and place them in a medium-size bowl. Add the oil, salt, pepper, red pepper flakes, lemon rind, and thyme, tossing to coat. Cover with plastic wrap and marinate in the refrigerator for 1 hour, or overnight.

2 Meanwhile, on a work surface, cut each slice of prosciutto lengthwise into 2 equal pieces. Transfer the pieces to a plate, cover with plastic wrap, and chill in the refrigerator for 1 hour.

3 Pat the basil leaves dry with paper towels. Place 1 basil leaf and 1 mozzarella ball on a strip of prosciutto. Lightly wrap the prosciutto around the cheese to make flower petals. Continue wrapping the remaining mozzarella and basil leaves with the prosciutto as directed. Arrange on a serving platter. Garnish with sprigs of fresh basil, if desired, and serve with toothpicks on the side.

4 Alternatively, cover with plastic wrap and chill in the refrigerator for up to 1 hour before serving.

18 PIECES
PREP TIME: 30 MINUTES PLUS
1 HOUR TO MARINATE AND CHILL

EQUIPMENT LIST

Grater
Utility knife
Colander
Medium-size bowl
Kitchen spoon
Plastic wrap
Paper towels

Goat Cheese and Herb Spread

6 ounces chèvre or other goat cheese (1½ cups)

1 8-ounce package cream cheese, softened

1 small red onion, finely chopped (¾ cup)

2 tablespoons vegetable oil

1 tablespoon white wine vinegar

½ teaspoon dried sage leaves, crumbled

½ teaspoon dried thyme leaves, crumbled

¾ teaspoon cracked black pepper, or to taste

Sprigs of fresh sage (optional)

Crusty breads, crackers, or hot toast (optional)

For a simple but stylish appetizer, this spread fits the bill. It can be prepared ahead and takes only minutes to make.

For a special variation that will please the most discerning palate, serve the spread with pears and lettuce leaves. Peel and halve 4 firm, ripe pears. Scoop out the cores and fill the centers with the spread. Place 2 lettuce leaves each on 4 serving plates and arrange 2 pear halves on top. Drizzle with herbed vinaigrette dressing.

1 Place goat cheese, cream cheese, onion, oil, vinegar, sage, thyme, and ½ teaspoon of the pepper in a blender or food processor fitted with the metal blade. Blend or process for 1 minute, or until smooth, scraping down the side of the bowl whenever necessary.

2 Spoon the spread into a serving bowl and sprinkle with the remaining ¼ teaspoon of pepper. Cover the bowl with plastic wrap and chill in the refrigerator for 1 hour, or overnight.

3 Remove the spread from the refrigerator, discard the plastic wrap, and garnish with sprigs of fresh sage, if desired. Serve with crusty breads, crackers, or hot toast.

2 CUPS
PREP TIME: 5 MINUTES PLUS
1 HOUR TO CHILL

EQUIPMENT LIST

Utility knife
Blender or food processor with metal blade
Rubber spatula
Kitchen spoon
Plastic wrap

Delight guests with this smooth spread that has just enough bite. Present it on a wicker tray for a rustic arrangement.

Herbed Smoked Salmon
and Cream Cheese Roll

1	3-ounce package cream cheese, softened
3	tablespoons unsalted butter, softened
8	ounces smoked salmon pieces, finely chopped (1 cup)
¼	teaspoon grated lemon rind
1	tablespoon fresh lemon juice
⅛	teaspoon ground red pepper (cayenne)
½	cup chopped fresh parsley
Lemon slices	

Kick off a dinner party with this easy-to-prepare but impressive smoked salmon appetizer. It can be made at least three hours in advance, and the quantities can easily be doubled. To give the log its neat shape, pack it into a clean, empty can and chill it. After the log is turned out, coat it with chopped parsley. Serve the log with melba toast.

1 In a medium-size bowl, mix together the cream cheese and butter until smooth. Add the smoked salmon, the lemon rind and juice, and ground red pepper and stir until well blended.

2 Spoon the mixture into a clean 14-ounce can, with the bottom intact. Press the mixture firmly into the can (it will not fill it completely), cover with plastic wrap, and chill in the refrigerator for at least 3 hours, or overnight.

3 Spread the chopped parsley on a small sheet of wax paper. Remove the salmon log from the refrigerator and discard the plastic wrap. Using a can opener, open the base of the can and use the base to push the log out of the opposite end. Gently roll the log in the parsley, coating it evenly.

4 Slice the log into 8 slices and arrange on individual serving plates. Garnish with lemon slices and serve immediately.

Elegance and simplicity of preparation are the keynotes of this appetizer. It teams the ever-popular smoked salmon and cream cheese in an unusual way.

6 SERVINGS
PREP TIME: 10 MINUTES PLUS
3 HOURS TO CHILL

EQUIPMENT LIST

Utility knife
Grater
Citrus juicer
Medium-size bowl
Kitchen spoon
14-ounce clean, empty can
Plastic wrap
Wax paper
Can opener

Festive Brie in Phyllo Pastry

4 sheets frozen phyllo pastry, thawed
1 ounce sliced almonds (¼ cup)
¼ cup (½ stick) unsalted butter
1 12-ounce wheel Brie
2 tablespoons chopped fresh dill
3 ounces lump crabmeat
Whole almonds (optional)
Red seedless grapes (optional)
Sprigs of fresh dill (optional)

1 Preheat the oven to 375° F. Grease a baking sheet. Lay the phyllo sheets flat on a work surface, cover with plastic wrap, and then with a damp kitchen towel.

2 To toast the sliced almonds: Spread almonds in a thin layer on an ungreased baking sheet. Toast in the oven for 6 to 8 minutes, or until golden brown. Stir the almonds occasionally to prevent burning. Remove the baking sheet from the oven and cool slightly.

3 In a small saucepan over moderate heat, melt the butter. Remove the pan from the heat. Remove the towel and plastic wrap from 1 sheet of phyllo and place it in front of you on the work surface. Brush with some melted butter. Lay a second sheet of phyllo on top and brush with some butter. Lay a third sheet crosswise over the first 2 sheets and brush with butter. Repeat as directed for the third sheet with the last sheet of phyllo.

4 Place the Brie in the center of the phyllo. Sprinkle the toasted almonds over the Brie, then sprinkle the dill and crabmeat over the almonds. Carefully gather up the edges of the phyllo around the Brie to form a package and pinch firmly at the neck to seal. Transfer to the prepared baking sheet. Brush all over with the remaining butter.

5 Bake for 15 to 20 minutes, or until the phyllo is lightly golden. (If the top browns too quickly, cover it loosely with aluminum foil and continue to bake.) Remove from the oven and let stand for 15 minutes.

6 Transfer the Brie to a serving platter. Garnish with the whole almonds, grapes, and sprigs of fresh dill, if desired. Cut into wedges and serve warm.

Make this Brie in phyllo pastry a celebratory centerpiece.

8 SERVINGS
PREP TIME: 10 MINUTES PLUS
15 MINUTES TO STAND
COOKING TIME: 20 MINUTES

EQUIPMENT LIST

Utility knife
Kitchen towel
2 baking sheets
Plastic wrap
Kitchen spoon
Small saucepan
Pastry brush

Cheese and Crabmeat Quesadillas

4 ounces shredded sharp Cheddar cheese (1 cup)

4 ounces shredded Monterey Jack cheese (1 cup)

6 tablespoons salted butter or margarine

12 8″ flour tortillas

1½ teaspoons coarsely ground black pepper

6 tablespoons fresh, thawed, or canned crabmeat, drained

4 small jalapeño peppers, cored, seeded, and thinly sliced (4 tablespoons) (optional)

Quesadillas—"sandwiches" of cooked flour tortillas—make quick and easy appetizers. For a party, make up batches with different fillings. Serve these quesadillas warm, cut into wedges, with guacamole (see recipe below) or with plain lowfat yogurt or sour cream.

1 Preheat the oven to 200° F. In a medium-size bowl, combine the Cheddar and Monterey Jack cheeses.

2 To make the Cheese Quesadillas: In a large skillet over moderate heat, melt 1 tablespoon of the butter. Place 1 flour tortilla in the skillet and sprinkle with ⅓ cup of the cheese mixture, then ¼ teaspoon of the pepper. Place another tortilla on top and cook for 2 to 3 minutes on each side, or until the cheese begins to melt. Using a large, metal spatula, transfer the quesadilla to a baking sheet and keep warm in the oven. Cook and fill 4 of the remaining tortillas as directed, adding 1 tablespoon of melted butter to the skillet for each quesadilla.

3 Meanwhile, make the Crabmeat Quesadillas. In another large skillet over moderate heat, melt 1 tablespoon of the butter. Place 1 flour tortilla in the skillet and sprinkle with 2 tablespoons of the crabmeat, then with ⅓ cup of the cheese mixture and ¼ teaspoon of the pepper. Place another tortilla on top and cook for 2 to 3 minutes on each side, or until the cheese begins to melt. Using a large, metal spatula, transfer the quesadilla to a second baking sheet and keep warm in the oven. Cook and fill the 4 remaining tortillas as directed, adding 1 tablespoon of melted butter to the skillet for each quesadilla.

4 Cut each quesadilla into 4 wedges and arrange on a serving platter or individual serving plates. Garnish with the jalapeño pepper slices, if desired. Serve immediately.

24 WEDGES
PREP TIME: 15 MINUTES
COOKING TIME: 30 MINUTES

EQUIPMENT LIST

Grater
Utility knife
Medium-size bowl
Kitchen spoon
2 large skillets
Large, metal spatula
2 baking sheets

Fresh From the Garden Guacamole

2 medium-size ripe tomatoes, chopped (2 cups)

1 medium-size yellow, red, or green bell pepper, cored, seeded, and finely chopped (1 cup)

1 small carrot, peeled and finely chopped (½ cup)

½ cup frozen, thawed, or canned corn kernels, drained

3 tablespoons chopped fresh cilantro (coriander leaves) or fresh parsley

1 small jalapeño pepper, cored, seeded, and finely chopped (1 tablespoon)

2 tablespoons fresh lemon juice

2 medium-size ripe avocados

Most cooks have a favorite version of guacamole, the classic Mexican dip that usually contains mashed avocados mixed with tomatoes, onion, lemon juice, and jalapeño peppers. Those living on the west coast prefer a creamier, spicier version and often add mayonnaise, garlic, and hot pepper sauce to the basic recipe. Here is a refreshing and healthful alternative, using an array of fresh vegetables for texture and color. Serve it with quesadillas or on its own as a salad.

1 In a large glass or ceramic bowl, mix the tomatoes, bell pepper, carrot, corn, cilantro, jalapeño pepper, and lemon juice. Cover the bowl with plastic wrap and chill in the refrigerator for at least 1 hour, or overnight to allow the flavors to blend.

2 Just before serving, cut the avocados in half lengthwise and remove the pits. Peel and finely chop the avocados. Remove the plastic wrap from the bowl and discard. Stir the avocados into the vegetable mixture until well blended. Serve immediately.

4 CUPS
PREP TIME: 15 MINUTES PLUS
1 HOUR TO CHILL

EQUIPMENT LIST

Utility knife
Vegetable peeler
Colander
Citrus juicer
Large glass bowl
Kitchen spoon
Plastic wrap

SOUPS

*W*hether the occasion calls for a light starter or a hearty main dish, homemade soups needn't take hours to prepare. A wide range of ingredients can be used to create smooth or chunky, boldly or subtly flavored, hot or chilled soups—all in a matter of minutes.

Chilled Tomato and Avocado Soup.

Chilled Tomato and Avocado Soup

1	28-ounce can whole tomatoes, drained and juice reserved
1	large ripe avocado, peeled, pitted, and cut in 1″ cubes (1 cup)
1	cup tomato juice
1	large clove garlic, finely chopped
2	green onions (including tops), finely chopped (¼ cup)
1	tablespoon finely chopped yellow onion
2	tablespoons fresh lime juice
¼	cup finely chopped fresh cilantro (coriander leaves) or fresh parsley
¼	teaspoon salt, or to taste
Freshly ground black pepper	
Sprigs of fresh cilantro (coriander leaves) (optional)	

Simple and refreshing, chilled vegetable soups should be made in advance so that they have time to chill thoroughly and the flavors have a chance to develop and combine. Selecting the freshest vegetables and herbs available will ensure that the soups have a good color and a superb flavor.

This soup makes a memorable first course or luncheon main course. Serve it with tortilla chips for a southwestern summer lunch.

1 Place the tomatoes in a blender or food processor fitted with the metal blade. Blend or process for 1 minute, or until almost smooth. Add the avocado and process by pulsing on and off for 1 minute, or until the mixture is almost smooth, scraping down the side of the bowl whenever necessary.

2 Transfer the mixture to a large bowl. Add the reserved canned juice, tomato juice, garlic, green and yellow onions, lime juice, and the ¼ cup of cilantro. Season to taste with the salt and pepper. Stir well, cover the bowl with plastic wrap, and chill in the refrigerator for 2 hours.

3 Ladle the soup into chilled individual soup bowls and garnish with sprigs of fresh cilantro, if desired. Serve immediately.

4 SERVINGS
PREP TIME: 25 MINUTES PLUS
2 HOURS TO CHILL
COOKING TIME: 30 MINUTES

EQUIPMENT LIST

Strainer
Small bowl
Large bowl
Paring knife
Utility knife
Citrus juicer
Pepper mill
Blender or food processor with metal blade
Rubber spatula
Kitchen spoon
Plastic wrap

Pasta e Fagioli

2	tablespoons olive oil
1	medium-size red onion, finely chopped (1½ cups)
1	medium-size red or green bell pepper, cored, seeded, and finely chopped (1 cup)
2	large cloves garlic, finely chopped
1	small zucchini, halved lengthwise and thinly sliced (1 cup)
8	ounces fresh spinach, stemmed, rinsed, and torn in pieces (2 cups)
1	14½-ounce can whole tomatoes
1	10½-ounce can cannellini beans, drained and rinsed
¼	cup chopped fresh parsley
⅛	teaspoon salt, or to taste
Freshly ground black pepper	
8	ounces ditalini or small pasta shells (2 cups)
Grated Romano cheese (optional)	

This hearty Tuscan soup, full of pasta and white beans, as its name says, makes a great nutritious one-dish meal in less than an hour. Improvise and change the vegetables according to what's in season. Serve this soup with a mixed green salad and crusty Italian bread.

1 In a large saucepan, heat the oil over moderate heat for 1 minute. Add the onion and bell pepper and sauté for 5 minutes, or until the vegetables are softened. Add the garlic and zucchini and sauté for 2 minutes. Add the spinach and sauté for 2 minutes, or until wilted. Add the tomatoes with their juice, the beans, and parsley. Season to taste with the salt and pepper. Cook, uncovered, stirring occasionally, for 20 minutes.

2 Meanwhile, bring a large saucepan of water to a boil over high heat. Cook the ditalini in the boiling water for 8 to 10 minutes, or until al dente. Drain well.

3 Transfer the ditalini to individual soup bowls. Ladle some bean soup on top of the ditalini. Sprinkle with the grated Romano cheese, if desired, and serve immediately.

6 SERVINGS
PREP TIME: 10 MINUTES
COOKING TIME: 30 MINUTES

EQUIPMENT LIST

Utility knife
Colander
Pepper mill
2 large saucepans
Kitchen spoon

Harvest Festival
Pumpkin-Cheese Soup

1½ pounds pumpkin or frozen winter squash cubes, thawed and drained
¼ cup (½ stick) salted butter or margarine
1 medium-size yellow onion, finely chopped (1 cup)
1 tablespoon peeled, grated fresh ginger, or 1½ teaspoons ground ginger
3½ cups chicken stock or canned broth
½ teaspoon ground white pepper
1 cup half-and-half or milk
6 ounces shredded sharp Cheddar cheese (1½ cups)
Thinly sliced green onions (optional)

Offer this vivid soup for a satisfying one-dish supper on a crisp autumn evening. Accompany it with a fresh fruit salad and plenty of good whole-grain bread. It can be prepared a day ahead up to the point of adding the half-and-half and the cheese and stored, covered, in the refrigerator.

1 To prepare the fresh pumpkin: Using a sharp knife, slice off the top and a little from the bottom of the pumpkin so it will stand flat. Remove the skin by cutting down under the skin from the top to the bottom, working around the pumpkin. After the skin has been removed, cut the pumpkin in half and scrape out the seeds and pulp. Cut the flesh into pieces and set aside.

2 In a large saucepan over moderate heat, melt the butter. Add the yellow onion and ginger and sauté for 5 minutes, or until onion is softened. Add the stock, pepper, and pumpkin. Bring the mixture to a boil over moderately high heat. Reduce the heat to low and simmer, covered, for 15 minutes, or until the pumpkin is tender.

3 Transfer half the soup to a blender or food processor fitted with the metal blade. Blend or process for 1 minute, or until smooth. Return the purée to the saucepan.

4 Stir in the half-and-half and cheese. Cook over low heat, stirring frequently, for 5 to 7 minutes, or until the cheese is melted and the soup is heated through.

5 Ladle the soup into individual soup bowls. Garnish with sliced green onions, if desired, and serve immediately.

6 SERVINGS
PREP TIME: 10 MINUTES
COOKING TIME: 30 MINUTES

EQUIPMENT LIST

Utility knife
Carving knife
Vegetable peeler
Grater
Kitchen spoons
Large saucepan with lid
Blender or food processor with metal blade

Ring in the change of seasons with this hearty autumn soup.

Southwestern Corn Chowder

Heavy cream or milk is called for in most chowders, but this deliciously rich chowder obtains its creamy texture from a vegetable purée.

4 medium-size ears corn, shucked, or 1 20-ounce package frozen corn kernels, thawed and drained
1 tablespoon vegetable oil
1 medium-size yellow onion, finely chopped (1 cup)
¼ teaspoon ground cumin
1 medium-size ripe tomato, seeded and chopped (1 cup)
1 small California white or other boiling potato, peeled and cut in ½" cubes (½ cup)
4 cups chicken stock or canned broth
⅛ teaspoon ground red pepper (cayenne)
⅛ teaspoon salt, or to taste
Freshly ground black pepper
¼ cup sour cream (optional)
Snipped fresh chives or chopped green onion tops (optional)

1 If using fresh corn, hold 1 cob vertically over a shallow dish and, using a small, sharp knife, cut the kernels from the cob. Repeat cutting the kernels from the remaining ears of corn as directed.

2 Bring a small saucepan of water to a boil over high heat. Add ½ cup of the corn. Reduce the heat to moderately high and cook, uncovered, for 3 minutes, or until crisp-tender. Drain well and set aside.

3 In a large saucepan, heat the oil over moderate heat for 1 minute. Add the onion and sauté for 5 minutes, or until translucent. Add the cumin and cook, stirring continuously, for 30 seconds, or until fragrant. Add the tomato, potato, the remaining 3½ cups of corn, and the stock. Bring the mixture to a boil over high heat. Reduce the heat to moderate and cook, uncovered, for 10 minutes, or until the potato is tender when tested with a fork. Stir in the ground red pepper.

4 Transfer half the soup to a blender or food processor fitted with the metal blade. Blend or process for 1 minute, or until smooth. Transfer purée to a large bowl. Purée remaining soup as directed and transfer to the bowl. Stir in reserved corn and season to taste. Return soup to the pan. Cook over moderate heat for 3 minutes, or until heated through. Ladle the soup into individual soup bowls. Garnish with the sour cream and chives, if desired, and serve immediately.

4 SERVINGS
PREP TIME: 15 MINUTES
COOKING TIME: 20 MINUTES

EQUIPMENT LIST

Utility knife
Vegetable peeler
Pepper mill
Shallow dish
Small saucepan
Large saucepan
Colander
Kitchen spoons
Blender or food processor with metal blade
Large bowl

Serve this corn chowder as a starter or light lunch. It will get high grades for flavor—and it's healthy, too.

Chinese Asparagus and Noodle Soup

This delicately flavored soup is surprisingly quick and easy to prepare. Fresh ginger, sesame oil, and cellophane noodles give it a decidedly Chinese flavor. For a heartier version of this soup, stir in 2 cups of chopped, cooked chicken when the noodles are added. Proceed as directed.

Cellophane noodles, also called bean threads, aren't noodles in the traditional sense of the word; rather, they are made from the starch of green mung beans. They can be found in larger supermarkets or in Asian food stores.

2	ounces cellophane noodles
1	cup warm water
8	ounces fresh asparagus spears, or 1 10-ounce package frozen asparagus spears, thawed and drained
4	cups chicken stock or canned broth
1	tablespoon peeled, grated fresh ginger, or 1½ teaspoons ground ginger
2	teaspoons sesame oil
2	green onions (including tops), finely chopped (¼ cup)

1 In a small bowl, combine the cellophane noodles and water and let stand for 15 minutes, or until softened. Drain the noodles. Separate and straighten the long strands and, using scissors, cut the long cellophane noodles in half.

2 Meanwhile, prepare the asparagus. If using fresh asparagus, snap off the woody ends and rinse the spears under cold running water. If the skins seem tough, peel the stalks with a vegetable peeler or sharp knife. Cut the fresh or thawed aspargus spears into 2″ pieces and set aside.

3 In a medium-size saucepan, combine the stock and ginger and bring to a boil over high heat. Stir in the sesame oil. Add the cellophane noodles and cook over moderately high heat for 5 minutes. Add the asparagus and cook, stirring occasionally, for 5 to 8 minutes, or until the asparagus are tender. Stir in the green onions.

4 Ladle soup into individual soup bowls and serve immediately.

The subtle taste of this Chinese-inspired soup makes it a marvelous foil for a spicy main course.

4 SERVINGS
PREP TIME: 10 MINUTES PLUS
15 MINUTES TO STAND
COOKING TIME: 15 MINUTES

EQUIPMENT LIST

Vegetable peeler
Grater
Utility knife
Small bowl
Colander
Kitchen scissors
Medium-size saucepan
Kitchen spoon

Gingered Cream of Carrot Soup

2	tablespoons vegetable oil
2	teaspoons peeled, grated fresh ginger, or 1 teaspoon ground ginger
1	medium-size yellow onion, finely chopped (1 cup)
½	cup long-grain white rice
6	cups chicken stock or canned broth
4	large carrots, peeled and coarsely chopped (4 cups)
2	tablespoons chopped fresh cilantro (coriander leaves) or fresh parsley
¼	teaspoon salt, or to taste

Freshly ground black pepper
Sprigs of fresh cilantro (coriander leaves) (optional)

Puréed carrots and rice give this soup its creamy richness—without using a drop of cream. Serve it as a first course to a roast chicken or pork entrée.

1 In a large saucepan, heat the oil over moderate heat for 1 minute. Add the ginger and onion and sauté for 5 minutes, or until the onion is translucent. Add the rice, stirring to coat with the oil.

2 Add the stock and bring the mixture to a boil over high heat. Add the carrots, reduce the heat to moderately low, and cook, uncovered, for 25 minutes, or until carrots are very tender.

3 Using a slotted spoon, transfer the cooked carrots and rice to a blender or a food processor fitted with the metal blade. Add ¼ cup of the cooking liquid and blend or process for 1 minute, or until smooth, scraping down the side of the bowl whenever necessary.

4 Return the purée to the pan, stirring until well blended. Cook, uncovered, over low heat for 1 to 2 minutes, or until the soup is heated through. Stir in the 2 tablespoons of cilantro and season to taste with the salt and pepper.

5 Ladle the soup into individual soup bowls, garnish with sprigs of fresh cilantro, if desired, and serve immediately.

6 SERVINGS
PREP TIME: 10 MINUTES
COOKING TIME: 35 MINUTES

EQUIPMENT LIST

Vegetable peeler
Grater
Utility knife
Pepper mill
Large saucepan
Kitchen spoon
Slotted spoon
Blender or food processor with metal blade
Rubber spatula

Hot or Not Vegetable Soup

1	tablespoon unsalted butter
1	medium-size yellow onion, coarsely chopped (1 cup)
4	medium-size California white or other boiling potatoes, peeled and chopped (4 cups)
2	cups water
1	cup milk
2	medium-size carrots, peeled and shredded (1½ cups)
1	medium-size zucchini, shredded (2 cups)
1	small green bell pepper, cored, seeded, and chopped (½ cup)
¼	cup chopped fresh parsley
¼	teaspoon salt, or to taste

Freshly ground black pepper
Sprigs of fresh parsley (optional)

¼	cup milk or water (optional)
¼	cup light cream (optional)

This satisfying soup can be served either hot or cold, hence its name. It's quick to prepare and the taste of the fresh vegetables really comes through. For a hearty lunch, add a cup of chopped baked ham to the soup and serve it hot, accompanied by bread and cheese. For an elegant first course, serve it cold, topped with a swirl of cream.

1 In a large saucepan over moderate heat, melt the butter. Add the onion and sauté for 5 minutes, or until translucent. Add the potatoes and the 2 cups of water and bring to a boil over high heat. Reduce the heat to low and cook, partially covered, for 10 minutes, or until the potatoes are tender when tested with a fork. Remove the pan from the heat.

2 In a blender or food processor fitted with the metal blade, blend or process the potato mixture and the 1 cup of milk, in batches, until smooth. Return the purée to the pan and stir in the carrots, zucchini, bell pepper, and parsley. Season to taste with the salt and pepper. Bring the soup to a simmer over low heat and cook, uncovered, stirring frequently, for 5 minutes, or until vegetables have softened slightly.

3 Ladle the soup into individual soup bowls. Garnish with sprigs of fresh parsley, if desired, and serve warm.

4 Alternatively, transfer the soup to a large bowl, cover with plastic wrap, and chill in the refrigerator for 1 hour, or overnight. Stir in the ¼ cup of milk and swirl with ¼ cup of light cream before serving.

4 TO 6 SERVINGS
PREP TIME: 15 MINUTES
COOKING TIME: 30 MINUTES

EQUIPMENT LIST

Utility knife
Vegetable peeler
Grater
Pepper mill
Large saucepan with lid
Kitchen spoons
Fork
Blender or food processor with metal blade

White Gazpacho

1 small yellow onion, quartered
2 large cloves garlic
1 small head fennel (anise), trimmed, peeled, and coarsely chopped, or 2 stalks celery, coarsely chopped (1 cup)
1 small jicama, peeled and coarsely chopped (1 cup), or 1 8-ounce can water chestnuts, drained and chopped
2 medium-size cucumbers, peeled and sliced (2 cups)
1 8-ounce container plain lowfat yogurt (1 cup)
½ cup sour cream
½ cup chicken stock or canned broth
2 tablespoons lemon juice
⅛ teaspoon salt, or to taste
Ground white pepper
2 tablespoons chopped fresh parsley (optional)

Fennel and jicama (pronounced hic-ah-muh) add their distinctive flavors to this unusual version of gazpacho, the classic chilled vegetable soup. Jicama, also called Mexican potato, is a large, round root vegetable with brown skin and sweet and juicy white flesh.

Serve the soup as a light and refreshing first course to a barbecue or a Mexican dinner, accompanied by condiments, such as chopped tomatoes, chopped green onions, chopped green bell peppers, and croutons.

1 Place the onion, garlic, fennel, and jicama in a blender or food processor fitted with the metal blade. Blend or process for 30 seconds, or until finely chopped, scraping down the side of the bowl whenever necessary. Transfer vegetables to a large bowl.

2 Add the cucumbers and yogurt to the blender or food processor and blend or process for 10 seconds, or until smooth, scraping down the side of the bowl whenever necessary. Add the yogurt mixture to the vegetables, stirring until well blended.

3 Stir in the sour cream, stock, and lemon juice until well blended. Season to taste with the salt and pepper. Cover the bowl with plastic wrap and chill in the refrigerator for 2 hours.

4 Ladle the soup into chilled individual soup bowls. Garnish with chopped fresh parsley, if desired, and serve immediately.

4 SERVINGS
PREP TIME: 15 MINUTES PLUS
2 HOURS TO CHILL

EQUIPMENT LIST

Utility knife
Vegetable peeler
Citrus juicer
Blender or food processor with metal blade
Rubber spatula
Large bowl
Kitchen spoon
Plastic wrap

South-of-the-border flavors figure prominently in this version of a classic Mexican soup.

Curried Avocado Soup

2	medium-size ripe avocados
1	teaspoon fresh lemon juice
2	green onions (white parts only), chopped (2 tablespoons)
¼	teaspoon salt, or to taste
½	teaspoon curry powder
⅛	teaspoon hot pepper sauce
1	6-ounce can frozen orange juice concentrate, thawed
1¼	cups chicken stock or canned broth
2	cups half-and-half
1	medium-size orange, sliced
	Snipped fresh chives or chopped green onion tops (optional)

A great way to use avocados that are too soft to serve in salads is to make them the basis of a soup. The result is a splendid chilled soup that is just right for casual summer dining.

1 Cut the avocados in half and remove the pits. Reserve the pits. Sprinkle 1 avocado half with the lemon juice and set aside. Scoop the flesh from the remaining avocado halves and place in a blender or food processor fitted with the metal blade.

2 Add the 2 tablespoons of green onions, salt, curry powder, hot pepper sauce, and the orange juice concentrate. Blend or process for 30 seconds, or until smooth, scraping down the side of the bowl whenever necessary. Slowly add the stock while the motor is running and blend or process for 1 minute, or until smooth. Add the half-and-half and blend or process for 30 seconds, or until smooth.

3 Transfer the soup to a large glass bowl. Add reserved pits, cover the bowl with plastic wrap, and chill in the refrigerator for 1 hour. (Adding the pits ensures that it retains its bright green color.)

4 Peel the remaining avocado half and cut the flesh into thin slices. Remove the pits from the soup and discard. Ladle the soup into chilled individual soup bowls. Garnish with avocado and orange slices, sprinkle with the chives, if desired, and serve immediately.

4 SERVINGS
PREP TIME: 10 MINUTES PLUS
1 HOUR TO CHILL

EQUIPMENT LIST

Citrus juicer
Utility knife
Teaspoon
Kitchen spoon
Blender or food processor with metal blade
Rubber spatula
Large glass bowl
Plastic wrap

Artichoke Vichyssoise

2	tablespoons unsalted butter
2½	pounds leeks (white part only), trimmed, rinsed, and sliced (3½ cups)
1	medium-size California white or other boiling potato, peeled and chopped (1 cup)
1	pound Jerusalem artichokes, peeled and chopped (2 cups)
6	cups chicken stock or canned broth
¼	teaspoon salt, or to taste
	Freshly ground black pepper
½	cup heavy cream
2	tablespoons snipped fresh chives or chopped green onion tops

Traditional vichyssoise combines leeks and potatoes with cream. In this version, Jerusalem artichokes have been added, giving the soup an even richer flavor and a wonderful silky texture.

1 In a medium-size saucepan over moderate heat, melt the butter. Add the leeks and sauté for 5 minutes, or until they start to soften.

2 Add the potato, artichokes, and stock to the pan and bring to a boil over high heat. Reduce the heat to low and simmer, uncovered, for 20 minutes, or until the vegetables are tender when tested with a fork.

3 Remove the pan from the heat and transfer half the vegetable mixture to a blender or food processor fitted with the metal blade. Blend or process for 1 minute, or until smooth. Transfer the purée to a large bowl. Repeat as directed with the remaining mixture and transfer to the bowl.

4 Season the purée to taste with the salt and pepper and cool to room temperature. Cover the bowl with plastic wrap and chill in the refrigerator for at least 1 hour.

5 Ladle the soup into chilled individual soup bowls. Swirl a little heavy cream on top of each, sprinkle with the chives, and serve immediately.

6 SERVINGS
PREP TIME: 10 MINUTES PLUS
1 HOUR 20 MINUTES TO
COOL AND CHILL
COOKING TIME: 25 MINUTES

EQUIPMENT LIST

Utility knife
Vegetable peeler
Pepper mill
Kitchen scissors
Medium-size saucepan
Kitchen spoon
Fork
Blender or food processor with metal blade
Large bowl
Plastic wrap

From a weekday lunch on the run to a lazy Sunday brunch, this chapter has easy recipes that are sure to fit the bill. Choose from a new way with waffles, up-to-the-minute granola and muesli, and French bread sandwiches with a difference.

Waffles with Blueberry-Spice Sauce.

Waffles with Blueberry-Spice Sauce

¼ cup (½ stick) unsalted butter
1½ cups milk
3 large eggs, separated
1½ cups all-purpose flour
1 tablespoon granulated sugar
2 teaspoons baking powder
½ teaspoon salt

BLUEBERRY-SPICE SAUCE (2 CUPS)

¼ cup granulated sugar
1 tablespoon cornstarch
½ teaspoon cinnamon
¼ teaspoon ground nutmeg
½ cup water
½ teaspoon grated lemon rind
2 cups fresh blueberries, stemmed or 2 cups frozen blueberries, thawed and drained

1 To make the Blueberry-Spice Sauce: In a small saucepan, combine sugar, cornstarch, cinnamon, nutmeg, water, and lemon rind. Cook over moderate heat, stirring continuously, until the mixture comes to a boil. Add the blueberries and cook, stirring continuously, until the mixture returns to a boil. Reduce the heat to low and cook, stirring continuously, for 5 minutes, or until the sauce has thickened slightly. Remove the pan from the heat and set aside.

2 Preheat the oven to 200° F. To make the waffles: Heat a waffle iron according to the manufacturer's instructions.

3 In a medium-size saucepan over low heat, melt the butter. Remove pan from the heat and cool slightly. Stir in the milk and egg yolks. In a medium-size bowl, combine the flour, sugar, baking powder, and salt. Slowly add the liquid, stirring until just mixed. In a medium-size bowl, using an electric mixer set on high speed, beat egg whites to stiff peaks. Gently and thoroughly fold the egg whites into the batter.

4 Ladle or pour enough batter over the hot waffle iron to cover two thirds of the grid. Using a thin, metal spatula, spread batter to the edges of the grid. Close lid and cook for 3 to 5 minutes, or until the steam stops. Transfer waffles to a platter, cover with aluminum foil, and place in the oven to keep warm while you prepare the remaining batter.

5 Place 3 waffles on individual serving plates and spoon some sauce over them. Serve immediately.

4 TO 6 SERVINGS OR 12 WAFFLES
PREP TIME: 15 MINUTES
COOKING TIME: 25 MINUTES

EQUIPMENT LIST

2 small bowls
2 medium-size bowls
Grater
Small saucepan
Medium-size saucepan
Kitchen spoons
Waffle iron
Electric mixer
Rubber spatula
Thin, metal spatula
Ladle
Aluminum foil

Corn Pancakes with Cherry Sauce

1 cup yellow cornmeal
½ cup all-purpose flour
2 teaspoons baking powder
¼ teaspoon salt
2 tablespoons unsalted butter
1 cup milk
2 large eggs, lightly beaten
Vegetable oil

CHERRY SAUCE (1 CUP)

1 8-ounce can dark pitted cherries in syrup
2 teaspoons fresh lemon juice
2 2″ strips lemon rind
⅛ teaspoon ground cinnamon
1 tablespoon granulated sugar
1½ teaspoons cornstarch
1 tablespoon water

1 To make the Cherry Sauce: Drain the cherry syrup into a small saucepan and reserve. Halve or quarter the cherries, depending on size, and set aside. Add lemon juice and rind, cinnamon, and sugar to the reserved syrup. Cook over moderate heat, stirring continuously, for 5 minutes, or until sugar dissolves. In a small bowl, combine cornstarch and water and stir until smooth. Remove the lemon rind from syrup mixture and discard. Stir cornstarch mixture into syrup. Cook, stirring continuously, for 2 to 3 minutes, or until thickened. Remove the pan from the heat. Stir in reserved cherries. Partially cover and set aside.

2 To make the pancakes: In a medium-size bowl, combine the cornmeal, flour, baking powder, and salt. In a small saucepan over moderate heat, melt the butter. Add the melted butter to the cornmeal mixture with the milk and eggs. Stir until just mixed.

3 Heat a griddle or large, heavy skillet and lightly brush with oil. For each pancake, drop 1 tablespoonful of the batter onto the griddle and cook for 1 minute, or until bubbles appear on the surface. Using a large, metal spatula, flip the pancakes over and cook for 1 minute more, or until golden. Transfer the pancakes to a serving platter and keep warm. Repeat as directed with remaining batter, brushing the griddle with oil if needed.

4 Place 4 pancakes on individual serving plates and spoon some sauce over them. Serve immediately.

4 SERVINGS OR 16 3″ PANCAKES
PREP TIME: 10 MINUTES
COOKING TIME: 16 MINUTES

EQUIPMENT LIST

Citrus juicer
Paring knife
Strainer
2 small saucepans with 1 lid
Small bowl
Medium-size bowl
Kitchen spoons
Rubber spatula
Large, metal spatula
Griddle or large, heavy skillet
Pastry brush
Tablespoon

Fruit and Nut Granola Parfait

1 small ripe kiwi, peeled and sliced (¼ cup)

¾ cup strawberries, hulled and sliced or ¾ cup frozen strawberries, thawed, drained, and sliced

1 small ripe banana, sliced (½ cup)

1 16-ounce container plain lowfat yogurt (2 cups)

GRANOLA (3 CUPS)

3 tablespoons vegetable oil

3 tablespoons honey

2 cups old-fashioned rolled oats

⅓ cup wheat germ

⅛ teaspoon salt, or to taste

⅛ teaspoon ground nutmeg

1 ounce sliced almonds (¼ cup)

1 ounce unsalted cashews (¼ cup)

¼ cup dark or golden raisins

Granola fans will be partial to this scrumptious version that adds a twist to this fiber-rich dish. Make several batches of granola and store them in covered containers in the freezer. It will stay fresh for up to a month, and it will be available at a moment's notice to use as a topping for muffins or coffee cakes, served over ice cream, or eaten plain with milk.

1 Preheat the oven to 300° F. Line a baking sheet or jelly-roll pan with aluminum foil.

2 To make the granola: In a large bowl, mix together the oil and honey until well blended. Add the oats, wheat germ, salt, nutmeg, and almonds, stirring to coat.

3 Spread the oat mixture evenly on the prepared baking sheet. Bake, stirring occasionally, for 15 to 20 minutes, or until golden brown. Remove the baking sheet from the oven. Stir in the cashews and raisins and cool for 1 hour.

4 To assemble: In a medium-size bowl, combine kiwi, strawberries, and banana. Spoon 2½ cups of the granola into the bottom of a medium-size glass bowl. Top with half of the fruit. Spoon the yogurt over the fruit and top with the remaining half of the fruit. Sprinkle with the remaining ½ cup of granola. Serve immediately.

6 SERVINGS
PREP TIME: 15 MINUTES PLUS
1 HOUR TO COOL
COOKING TIME: 20 MINUTES

EQUIPMENT LIST

Utility knife
Baking sheet
Aluminum foil
Large bowl
Medium-size bowl
Medium-size glass bowl
Kitchen spoon

Get the day off to a great start with this pretty bowl full of health.

Rise and Shine Muesli

½	cup old-fashioned rolled oats
3	tablespoons dark raisins
½	cup light cream or half-and-half
⅔	cup milk
1	ounce chopped walnuts (¼ cup)
1	medium-size Granny Smith or other tart apple
1	medium-size orange
1	medium-size ripe banana
8	teaspoons firmly packed light brown sugar
¼	teaspoon ground cinnamon

Muesli is a German word meaning "mixture," and this one includes oats, raisins, walnuts, cream, and fruit. It is a great breakfast dish to serve to weekend guests because it can be made the night before and the fruit added just before serving. Try substituting other dried fruits such as chopped dried apricots or apples for the raisins.

1 In a medium-size bowl, combine the oats, raisins, cream, and milk. Cover the bowl with plastic wrap and chill in the refrigerator for at least 4 hours, or overnight.

2 Preheat the oven to 350° F. To toast the walnuts: Spread the walnuts in a thin layer on a baking sheet. Toast in the oven for 7 to 10 minutes, or until golden brown. Stir the walnuts occasionally while toasting to prevent burning. Remove the baking sheet from the oven and cool completely.

3 Core the apple and finely chop. Peel the orange, divide it into sections, and finely chop. Thinly slice the banana. Add the apple, orange, banana, and walnuts to the muesli mixture, stirring until it is well blended.

4 Spoon the muesli into individual serving bowls. Sprinkle each one with 2 teaspoons of the sugar and some of the cinnamon and serve immediately.

4 SERVINGS
PREP TIME: 15 MINUTES PLUS
4 HOURS TO CHILL
COOKING TIME: 10 MINUTES

Equipment List

Medium-size bowl
Kitchen spoons
Plastic wrap
Baking sheet
Paring knife
Utility knife

Spiced Oatmeal with Honeyed Orange Sections

¼	cup orange juice
1	tablespoon honey
1	medium-size orange, peeled and sectioned (1 cup)
⅓	cup dark or golden raisins
2⅔	cups water
1⅓	cups quick-cooking rolled oats
2	tablespoons toasted bran
¼	teaspoon ground cinnamon
¼	teaspoon ground nutmeg
1	tablespoon firmly packed light brown sugar (optional)
⅓	cup milk (optional)
⅛	teaspoon salt, or to taste

Orange sections add vitamin C and a bright touch of color to this satisfying hot cereal. For a summertime treat, use a fresh peach, peeled, pitted, and chopped instead of the orange and proceed as directed.

1 In a small saucepan, combine the orange juice and honey. Add the orange sections and raisins, stirring to coat. Cook over moderately low heat, stirring occasionally, for 3 minutes, or until heated through. Remove the pan from the heat.

2 In a large saucepan, bring the water to a boil over high heat. Add the oats, bran, cinnamon, and nutmeg. Reduce the heat to moderate and cook for 1 minute, stirring occasionally. Remove the pan from the heat. Cover and let stand for 2 minutes, or until the oatmeal reaches the desired consistency.

3 Stir in the sugar and milk, if desired, and season to taste with the salt. Spoon the oatmeal into individual serving bowls.

4 Spoon some of the orange sections and raisins on top of the oatmeal and serve immediately.

4 SERVINGS
PREP TIME: 10 MINUTES PLUS
2 MINUTES TO STAND
COOKING TIME: 4 MINUTES

Equipment List

Utility knife
Small saucepan
Large saucepan with lid
Kitchen spoons

Swiss Cheese Gougère

In its native Burgundy, gougère, a cheese pastry ring, is served by itself and is eaten hot or cold. Here the basic recipe is varied with two different fillings. Be sure to have the filling ready to add as soon as the gougère is baked. (Both fillings can be prepared ahead, stored, covered, in the refrigerator, and reheated just before serving.) Accompany this dish with small, pungent black olives, such as Niçoise.

⅔ cup water
¼ cup (½ stick) salted butter or margarine
¾ cup all-purpose flour
2 large eggs
2 ounces shredded Gruyère or other Swiss cheese (½ cup)
⅛ teaspoon dry mustard
Sprigs of fresh thyme (optional)

1 Preheat the oven to 425° F. Lightly grease a 9″ pie pan. In a medium-size saucepan over high heat, bring the water and butter to a boil. Add the flour all at once and stir with a wooden spoon until mixture forms a ball and pulls away from the side of the pan. Remove the pan from the heat, add 1 egg, and beat until fully incorporated. Add the second egg and beat until well combined. Stir in the cheese and mustard.

2 Spoon the cheese mixture around the edges of the pie pan. Bake for 20 minutes. Reduce the oven temperature to 375° F. Bake the gougère for 10 minutes more, or until puffy and golden.

3 Spoon the filling into the center of the gougère. Garnish with sprigs of fresh thyme, if desired, and serve immediately.

4 SERVINGS
PREP TIME: 5 MINUTES
COOKING TIME: 30 MINUTES

EQUIPMENT LIST

Grater
9″ pie pan
Medium-size saucepan
Wooden spoon
Kitchen spoon

Three Pepper Filling

THREE PEPPER FILLING

1 tablespoon olive oil
1 small yellow onion, sliced (1 cup)
1 large clove garlic, finely chopped
1 medium-size green bell pepper, cored, seeded, and sliced (1 cup)
1 medium-size red bell pepper, cored, seeded, and sliced (1 cup)
1 medium-size yellow bell pepper, cored, seeded, and sliced (1 cup)
2 tablespoons water
⅛ teaspoon salt, or to taste
Freshly ground black pepper

1 In a large skillet, heat the oil over moderate heat for 1 minute. Add the onion and garlic and sauté for 5 minutes, or until the onion is translucent.

2 Add the green, red, and yellow bell peppers and sauté for 3 minutes. Add the water. Cook, covered, for 4 minutes, or until bell peppers are tender. Season to taste with the salt and pepper. Spoon the filling into the center of the gougère. Serve immediately.

2½ CUPS
PREP TIME: 10 MINUTES
COOKING TIME: 13 MINUTES

EQUIPMENT LIST

Utility knife
Pepper mill
Large skillet with lid
Kitchen spoon

Spinach-Tomato Filling

SPINACH-TOMATO FILLING

2 tablespoons olive oil
¼ cup chopped yellow onion
1 large clove garlic, finely chopped
1 pound fresh spinach, stemmed, rinsed, and chopped (4 cups)
1 large tomato, peeled and chopped (1½ cups)
⅛ teaspoon salt, or to taste
Freshly ground black pepper

1 In a large skillet, heat the oil over moderate heat for 1 minute. Add the onion and sauté for 5 minutes, or until translucent.

2 Add the garlic and sauté for 30 seconds, or until fragrant. Add the spinach. Cook, stirring occasionally, for 1 minute, or until wilted. Stir in the tomato. Cook, stirring occasionally, for 4 minutes, or until the juices have evaporated and the pan is almost dry. Season to taste with the salt and pepper. Spoon the filling into the center of the gougère. Serve immediately.

2½ CUPS
PREP TIME: 10 MINUTES
COOKING TIME: 12 MINUTES

EQUIPMENT LIST

Utility knife
Pepper mill
Large skillet
Kitchen spoon

Peach Blintzes

3 tablespoons unsalted butter
1 cup all-purpose flour
¼ teaspoon salt
⅔ cup milk
⅔ cup water
3 large eggs
Vegetable oil
Seedless red grapes (optional)
Mint leaves (optional)

PEACH FILLING/SAUCE (2½ CUPS)

½ cup water
3 tablespoons granulated sugar
2 tablespoons fresh lemon juice
2 teaspoons cornstarch
¼ teaspoon almond extract
2 large ripe peaches, peeled and thinly sliced (2 cups), or 2 cups frozen sliced peaches, thawed and drained
1 cup lowfat cottage cheese
½ cup plain lowfat yogurt

1 Preheat the oven to 375° F. Grease a 9″ x 13″ baking dish. To make the blintzes: In a small saucepan over moderate heat, melt the butter. Remove the pan from the heat. In a blender or food processor fitted with the metal blade, combine the flour, salt, milk, the ⅔ cup of water, eggs, and melted butter. Blend or process for 1 minute, or until thoroughly blended.

2 Heat a crêpe pan or 8″ nonstick skillet over moderate heat for 1 minute, then lightly brush with some oil. Pour in 3 tablespoons of batter and tilt the pan in all directions to spread batter evenly over the surface. Cook for 45 seconds, or until bottom is lightly browned. Using a large, metal spatula, turn blintze over and cook for 45 seconds more, or until spotty brown. Transfer the blintze to a wire rack to cool. Repeat as directed with remaining batter, adding oil to the pan if needed.

3 To make Peach Filling/Sauce: In a medium-size saucepan, mix the ½ cup of water, 2 tablespoons of the sugar, the lemon juice, cornstarch, and almond extract until well blended. Bring to a boil over moderately high heat, stirring frequently. Stir in half the peaches and reserve remainder. Reduce the heat to low and cook, covered, for 8 minutes, or until peaches are tender. Remove pan from heat.

4 In a small bowl, stir together the cottage cheese, yogurt, and the remaining 1 tablespoon of sugar until well blended.

5 Place 1 blintze on a work surface. Spoon 3 tablespoons of the cheese mixture down the middle of the blintze. Spoon 2 to 3 tablespoons of the reserved peaches over the cheese. Roll the blintze into a cylinder and place, seam-side up, in the prepared baking dish. Repeat filling the remaining blintzes as directed and place them in the baking dish.

6 Cover the baking dish with aluminum foil. Bake for 10 minutes, or until blintzes are heated through. Remove baking dish from oven. Transfer blintzes to individual serving plates and top with the Peach Sauce. Garnish with grapes and mint leaves, if desired. Serve immediately.

This gorgeous dish will add a touch of class to the brunch table.

4 SERVINGS OR 8 BLINTZES
PREP TIME: 10 MINUTES
COOKING TIME: 31 MINUTES

EQUIPMENT LIST

Citrus juicer
Vegetable peeler
Utility knife
9″ x 13″ baking dish
Small saucepan
Medium-size saucepan with lid
Crêpe pan or 8″ nonstick skillet
Blender or food processor with metal blade
Pastry brush
Large, metal spatula
Wire rack
Small bowl
Kitchen spoons
Aluminum foil

Molded Spanish Salad

This colorful and refreshing molded salad which is chock-full of fresh vegetables makes an attractive brunch centerpiece. It can be made and chilled the night before. Unmold just before serving. Fill the center of the ring with chicken or turkey salad and serve it with French rolls.

4	cups tomato juice, chilled
2	envelopes (¼ ounce each) unflavored gelatin
¼	cup red wine vinegar
1	large clove garlic, finely chopped
3	drops hot pepper sauce
⅛	teaspoon ground cumin
¼	teaspoon salt, or to taste
	Freshly ground black pepper
1	large ripe tomato, peeled, seeded, and chopped (1½ cups)
¼	cup finely chopped yellow onion
¼	cup finely chopped green bell pepper
⅓	cup peeled, seeded, and finely chopped cucumber

1 Place 1 cup of the tomato juice in a small saucepan. Sprinkle the gelatin over the tomato juice and let stand for 3 minutes to soften. Cook, uncovered, over moderate heat, stirring continuously, until the mixture simmers and the gelatin completely dissolves.

2 Transfer the tomato juice to a large bowl and stir in the remaining 3 cups of tomato juice, the vinegar, garlic, hot pepper sauce, and cumin. Season to taste with the salt and pepper. Chill the mixture for 1½ hours, or until it begins to set and has the consistency of unbeaten egg whites.

3 Lightly grease a 6-cup ring mold. Fold the tomato, onion, bell pepper, and cucumber into the chilled mixture. Pour into the mold. Chill in the refrigerator for 3½ hours, or until firm. Unmold the salad onto a serving platter. (Be sure that the mixture is really firm before unmolding the salad.) Serve immediately.

6 SERVINGS
PREP TIME: 15 MINUTES PLUS
5 HOURS TO CHILL
COOKING TIME: 5 MINUTES

EQUIPMENT LIST

Utility knife
Pepper mill
Vegetable peeler
Small saucepan
Kitchen spoons
Large bowl
6-cup ring mold
Rubber spatula

Broccoli-Ham Rolls
with Cheese Sauce

Simple to prepare, these rolls can be served for brunch or for a light lunch, accompanied by a fruit salad. They can be assembled the night before and kept, covered, in the refrigerator. Make the sauce just before baking.

1	10-ounce package frozen chopped broccoli, thawed and drained (2 cups)
1	3-ounce package cream cheese, softened
½	cup plain lowfat yogurt
⅛	teaspoon salt, or to taste
	Freshly ground black pepper
8	thin slices baked ham (4 ounces)

CHEESE SAUCE (1 CUP)

1	tablespoon unsalted butter
1	tablespoon all-purpose flour
⅛	teaspoon ground red pepper (cayenne)
¾	cup milk
2	ounces shredded Monterey Jack cheese (½ cup)

1 Preheat the oven to 375° F. Grease a 2-quart shallow baking dish or casserole. Squeeze the excess liquid from the broccoli. In a medium-size bowl, combine the broccoli, cream cheese, and yogurt until well blended. Season to taste with the salt and pepper.

2 Place a slice of ham on a work surface and spread with ¼ cup of the broccoli mixture. Starting with a short end, roll up the ham jelly-roll style and place, seam-side down, in the prepared baking dish. Repeat filling and rolling the remaining ham slices as directed and transfer to the dish.

3 To make the Cheese Sauce: In a small saucepan over moderate heat, melt the butter. Stir in the flour and ground red pepper and cook, stirring continuously, for 30 seconds. Slowly add the milk and cook, stirring continuously, for 5 minutes, or until thickened slightly. Add the Monterey Jack cheese and stir until melted. Remove the pan from the heat and pour the sauce over the ham rolls.

4 Bake, covered, for 10 minutes. Uncover and bake for 10 minutes more, or until the sauce is bubbly and lightly browned.

5 Remove the baking dish from the oven. Transfer the ham rolls to individual serving plates and serve immediately.

4 SERVINGS
PREP TIME: 10 MINUTES
COOKING TIME: 26 MINUTES

EQUIPMENT LIST

Colander
Pepper mill
Grater
2-quart shallow baking dish with lid
Medium-size bowl
Kitchen spoons
Small saucepan

Pasta Frittata with Fontina Cheese

Frittata, the Italian word for omelet, is a thick, open-faced pancake. Its texture is firmer than an omelet because it is cooked slowly and then either flipped and finished on the stove top or broiled for a few minutes.

Frittatas are ideal for unexpected guests because they can be cooked a few hours ahead of time and served at room temperature. Another plus is that they can usually be assembled with any ingredients that are on hand. For example, in place of the noodles, tomatoes, and zucchini in this recipe, use 1½ cups of sliced, cooked potatoes, 1 cup of chopped baked ham, and 2 teaspoons of chopped fresh rosemary. Add these ingredients to the sautéed onions and proceed as directed.

4	ounces medium-width dried egg noodles (2 cups)
7	large eggs
¼	cup milk
¼	teaspoon salt, or to taste
¼	teaspoon coarsely ground black pepper
2	teaspoons unsalted butter
2	teaspoons olive oil
1	small yellow onion, finely chopped (½ cup)
1	small clove garlic, finely chopped
3	plum tomatoes, seeded and chopped (1 cup)
½	cup finely chopped zucchini
4	ounces Fontina or Gruyère cheese, cut in thin slices (1 cup)
2	tablespoons grated Parmesan cheese
Chopped fresh parsley (optional)	

1 Bring a medium-size saucepan of water to a boil over high heat. Cook the noodles in the boiling water for 6 to 8 minutes, or until al dente. Drain well, rinse under cold running water, and drain again.

2 Meanwhile, in a medium-size bowl, whisk together the eggs, milk, salt, and pepper.

3 In a 10″ skillet or a paella dish with ovenproof handles, heat the butter and oil over moderate heat for 1 minute. Add the onion and garlic and sauté for 5 minutes, or until the onion is translucent. Add the tomatoes and zucchini and sauté for 5 minutes, or until softened. Stir in the noodles, spreading the mixture to cover the bottom of the skillet evenly.

4 Whisk the egg mixture and pour it over the filling. Cook, uncovered, over moderately low heat for 10 to 13 minutes, or until the bottom and side are set and the top surface is still liquid.

5 Meanwhile, preheat the broiler. Gently place the slices of Fontina cheese over the frittata and sprinkle with Parmesan cheese. Place the skillet under the broiler 6″ from the heat source. Broil for 1 to 2 minutes, or until the surface is puffed and lightly golden. Remove the skillet from the broiler and let stand for 2 minutes.

6 Gently run a knife around the side to loosen the frittata from the skillet. Cut into wedges and, using a large, metal spatula, transfer the wedges to individual serving plates. Garnish the frittata with the chopped fresh parsley, if desired, and serve warm or at room temperature.

6 SERVINGS
PREP TIME: 15 MINUTES
COOKING TIME: 26 MINUTES

EQUIPMENT LIST

Utility knife
Medium-size saucepan
Colander
Medium-size bowl
Wire whisk
10″ ovenproof skillet
Kitchen spoons

Chilled Picnic Baguette

1	small French or Italian loaf
¼	cup extra virgin olive oil
4	large cloves garlic, finely chopped
4	large iceberg lettuce leaves
1	medium-size yellow onion, thinly sliced (1½ cups)
3	small ripe tomatoes, thinly sliced (1½ cups)
½	cup chopped, pitted black olives
4	ounces chèvre or other goat cheese, crumbled (1 cup)
¼	cup finely shredded fresh basil, or 4 teaspoons dried basil leaves, crumbled
¼	cup red wine vinegar
⅛	teaspoon salt, or to taste
	Freshly ground black pepper

This recipe is an adaptation of pain bagna, the French version of the American "sub." Perfect for picnics, the ingredients mingle to produce a heady blend of flavors. Take lots of napkins as the baguette is juicy to eat.

1 Split the loaf in half lengthwise. Remove half of the crumbs from both halves, leaving the crust intact. (Reserve the crumbs for another use.) Brush the inside of each loaf half with the oil.

2 Sprinkle the garlic over the inside of the bottom half of the loaf. Place the lettuce leaves on top, then the onion and tomato slices. Arrange the olives, goat cheese, and basil over the top and sprinkle with the vinegar. Season to taste with the salt and pepper.

3 Place the top half of the loaf over the filling, pressing firmly to flatten. Wrap the loaf tightly in plastic wrap and transfer to a serving platter. Place a second platter on top and weigh it down with 3 unopened 28-ounce cans. Chill in the refrigerator for 2 hours.

4 Remove the weights and plastic wrap and cut the loaf into 4 pieces. Serve immediately.

4 SERVINGS
PREP TIME: 20 MINUTES PLUS
2 HOURS TO CHILL

EQUIPMENT LIST

Utility knife
Serrated knife
Pepper mill
Pastry brush
Plastic wrap
3 28-ounce cans or weights

Hot Vegetable Baguette

1	large French or Italian loaf
¼	cup olive oil
4	large cloves garlic, finely chopped
1	medium-size red onion, chopped (1½ cups)
1	medium-size zucchini, trimmed and chopped (2 cups)
1	medium-size red or green bell pepper, cored, seeded, and chopped (¾ cup)
½	large ripe tomato, chopped (¾ cup)
1	tablespoon dried basil leaves, crumbled
2	teaspoons dried oregano leaves, crumbled
2	tablespoons chopped fresh parsley
½	teaspoon crushed red pepper flakes
2	tablespoons grated Parmesan cheese
2	ounces shredded Swiss cheese (½ cup)

This vegetable-filled bread, with its blend of Mediterranean flavors, is perfect for a buffet or Sunday night supper. Store any leftovers, wrapped in plastic wrap, in the refrigerator. Bring to room temperature before serving.

1 Prepare the loaf as directed in Salad Baguette and reserve the crumbs. Brush the inside of each loaf half with 2 tablespoons of the oil. Sprinkle one-quarter of the garlic over the inside of the bottom half of the loaf. Using a sharp knife, cut 1″ slits at 2″ intervals along the top half of the loaf. Set aside.

2 In a large skillet, heat the remaining 2 tablespoons of oil over moderate heat for 1 minute. Add half of the remaining garlic and the onion and cook, stirring continuously, for 3 minutes, or until softened. Add the zucchini, bell pepper, and tomato and cook, stirring continuously, for 5 minutes, or until the vegetables are crisp-tender. Add the basil, oregano, parsley, and red pepper flakes. Sprinkle with the Parmesan cheese and reserved bread crumbs, stirring to combine. Cook, stirring occasionally, for 10 to 15 minutes more, or until the juices are absorbed.

3 Meanwhile, preheat the oven to 350° F. In a small bowl, combine the remaining garlic with the Swiss cheese.

4 Spoon the vegetable mixture into the bottom half of the loaf. Place the top half of the loaf over the filling—do not flatten. Spoon garlic mixture into the slits. Wrap the loaf in aluminum foil.

5 Bake for 10 to 15 minutes, or until the cheese has melted. Remove the foil and cut the loaf into 1″ slices. Serve immediately.

8 SERVINGS
PREP TIME: 35 MINUTES
COOKING TIME: 15 MINUTES

EQUIPMENT LIST

Utility knife
Serrated knife
Grater
Pastry brush
Large skillet
Kitchen spoons
Small bowl
Aluminum foil

Puffy Pancake
with Greek-Style Filling

½ cup all-purpose flour
½ cup milk
2 large eggs
⅛ teaspoon salt, or to taste
1 tablespoon vegetable oil

GREEK-STYLE FILLING (3½ CUPS)

1 tablespoon vegetable oil
6 ounces mushrooms, trimmed,
  cleaned, and sliced (1¾ cups)
1 medium-size yellow onion,
  sliced (1½ cups)
1 large carrot, peeled and
  shredded (1 cup)
¾ cup vegetable juice
1 teaspoon cornstarch
½ teaspoon dried basil leaves,
  crumbled
4 ounces feta cheese, crumbled
  (1 cup)
2 tablespoons sliced, pitted
  black olives
2 tablespoons chopped flat-leaf
  parsley (optional)

This light pancake features a tangy vegetable and cheese filling. Serve it for a quick, low-calorie lunch or supper dish.

1 Preheat the oven to 450° F. Heat a 10″ ovenproof skillet in the oven for 5 minutes.

2 In a medium-size bowl, using an electric mixer set on medium speed, beat the flour, milk, eggs, and salt until well blended.

3 Remove the skillet from the oven. Add the 1 tablespoon of oil to the skillet, tilting to coat the bottom and side. Pour the batter into the skillet and bake for 10 minutes. Reduce the oven temperature to 350° F. and bake the pancake for 10 minutes more, or until puffed and lightly golden.

4 Meanwhile, make the Greek-Style Filling. In a large saucepan, heat the 1 tablespoon of oil over moderate heat for 1 minute. Add the mushrooms, onion, and carrot and sauté for 5 minutes, or until the vegetables are softened.

5 In a small bowl, stir together the vegetable juice, cornstarch, and basil until well blended. Add the juice mixture to the vegetables and cook, stirring continuously, for 3 to 4 minutes, or until thickened slightly.

6 Remove the pancake from the oven. Sprinkle half the cheese over the pancake and spoon the vegetable mixture on top. Sprinkle the remaining cheese and the olives over the filling. Garnish with the flat-leaf parsley, if desired. Cut the pancake into wedges and serve immediately.

6 SERVINGS
PREP TIME: 25 MINUTES
COOKING TIME: 20 MINUTES

EQUIPMENT LIST

Utility knife
Vegetable peeler
Grater
10″ ovenproof skillet
Medium-size bowl
Small bowl
Electric mixer
Large saucepan
Kitchen spoon

The great flavors of Greek cooking are captured in this simple dish.

Bacon and Gruyère Quiche

1   9″ unbaked pie shell

SAVORY FILLING

8   strips lean bacon, chopped
1½   cups light cream
4   large eggs
¼   teaspoon salt, or to taste
Freshly ground black pepper
⅛   teaspoon ground nutmeg
4   ounces shredded Gruyère
     cheese (1 cup)
2   medium-size tomatoes, cut in
     wedges (optional)

This quiche is simple to prepare and packs a flavorful punch.

8 SERVINGS
PREP TIME: 15 MINUTES PLUS
30 MINUTES TO CHILL
COOKING TIME: 26 MINUTES

EQUIPMENT LIST

Utility knife
Pepper mill
Grater
Fork
Aluminum foil
Paper towels
Pie weights or dried beans
Medium-size skillet
Slotted spoon
Plate
Small bowl
Wire whisk
Wire rack

Quiche, a savory custard pie, can be served as a light main course and is also great for picnics and tailgate spreads. Any number of ingredients can be added to this basic recipe. Try a combination of 1 cup of sliced, sautéed mushrooms and 2 tablespoons each of chopped red and green bell peppers, or 1 cup lump crabmeat and ¼ cup sautéed chopped red onion.

1   Preheat the oven to 375° F. Prick the bottom of the pie shell with a fork, line with aluminum foil, and fill with pie weights or dried beans. Bake the shell for 6 to 7 minutes. Remove the weights and foil and bake the shell for 2 to 4 minutes more, or until golden brown.

2   Meanwhile, make the Savory Filling: In a medium-size skillet over moderate heat, cook the bacon for 8 to 10 minutes, or until crisp. Using a slotted spoon, transfer the bacon to a plate lined with paper towels to drain.

3   In a small bowl, whisk together the cream, eggs, salt, pepper, and nutmeg. Pour the mixture into the baked pie shell and sprinkle the bacon and the cheese on top.

4   Bake the quiche for 12 to 15 minutes, or until the filling has set. Remove the quiche from the oven and transfer to a wire rack to cool slightly. Garnish with the tomato wedges, if desired, and serve warm.

Lean cuts of meat
are now the rule, rather
than the exception, and
the faster and healthier
cooked the better. This
chapter provides an array
of dishes—homey,
elegant, classically
inspired, and ethnically
based, that can be served
for everyday or more
formal occasions.

*Beef and Mushroom
Stir-Fry.*

Beef and Mushroom Stir-Fry

1	pound flank steak
2	tablespoons low-sodium soy sauce
1	tablespoon rice wine vinegar
1	teaspoon granulated sugar
1	tablespoon ground coriander
1	tablespoon cornstarch
3	tablespoons vegetable oil
2	large cloves garlic, chopped
1	small yellow onion, thinly sliced (1 cup)
6	green onions (including tops), sliced (¾ cup)
1	medium-size red or green bell pepper, cored, seeded, and thinly sliced (1 cup)
4	ounces mushrooms, trimmed, cleaned, and sliced (1¼ cups)
4	ounces bean sprouts (1½ cups)

SOY-SHERRY SAUCE (1 CUP)

1	tablespoon cornstarch
½	cup beef stock or canned broth
1	tablespoon low-sodium soy sauce
1	tablespoon dry sherry
1	teaspoon granulated sugar
2	teaspoons sesame oil

Stir-frying is an ideal way to preserve the fresh taste and crunchy texture of vegetables. Serve this Asian-inspired dish with Chinese noodles.

Rice wine vinegar can be found in most large supermarkets and Asian food stores, but if it is unavailable, substitute cider vinegar.

1 Using a sharp knife, cut flank steak across the grain into thin slices. In a large, shallow glass dish, combine the 2 tablespoons of soy sauce, vinegar, 1 teaspoon of sugar, coriander, 1 tablespoon of cornstarch, and 1 tablespoon of vegetable oil. Add the steak slices, tossing to coat. Cover the dish with plastic wrap and let stand for 30 minutes at room temperature to allow the flavors to blend.

2 Meanwhile, make the Soy-Sherry Sauce. In a small bowl, dissolve the 1 tablespoon of cornstarch in 2 tablespoons of the stock. Stir in the remaining stock, the 1 tablespoon of soy sauce, sherry, the 1 teaspoon of sugar, and sesame oil and set aside.

3 In a preheated wok or large, heavy skillet, heat 1 tablespoon of the remaining vegetable oil for 1 minute, or until very hot. Add the beef with any marinade left in the dish and stir-fry for 2 minutes, or until browned. Using a slotted spoon, transfer the beef to a plate.

4 Heat the remaining 1 tablespoon of vegetable oil in the wok for 1 minute. Add the garlic and stir-fry for 30 seconds. Add the yellow and green onions, bell pepper, mushrooms, and bean sprouts. Stir-fry for 2 to 3 minutes, or until the vegetables are crisp-tender. Stir in the Soy-Sherry Sauce and stir-fry for 1 minute, or until sauce thickens slightly. Return the beef to the wok with any juices and stir-fry for 1 minute, or until heated through. Serve immediately.

4 SERVINGS
PREP TIME: 15 MINUTES PLUS
30 MINUTES TO STAND
COOKING TIME: 10 MINUTES

EQUIPMENT LIST

Utility knife
Chef's knife
Large, shallow glass dish
Kitchen spoons
Slotted spoon
Plastic wrap
Small bowl
Wok or large, heavy skillet
Plate

Greek Beef in a Pita Pocket

12	ounces boneless beef chuck, sirloin, or flank steak
4	large pita pockets
4	tablespoons olive oil
2	tablespoons fresh lemon juice
2	large cloves garlic, chopped
½	teaspoon dried oregano leaves, crumbled
1	medium-size green bell pepper, cored, seeded, and thinly sliced (1 cup)
1	small yellow onion, thinly sliced (1 cup)
¼	teaspoon salt, or to taste
	Freshly ground black pepper
¼	cup plain lowfat yogurt

1 Preheat the oven to 250° F. To prepare the beef: For easy slicing, wrap beef in aluminum foil or plastic wrap and place it in freezer for 15 to 20 minutes. Remove meat from freezer and cut it across the grain into slices about ⅛″ thick. Place it in a large, shallow glass dish.

2 Split the pita pockets, wrap in foil, and place in oven to warm. In a small bowl, whisk together 2 tablespoons of the oil, the lemon juice, garlic, and oregano. Pour mixture over the beef, tossing to coat.

3 In a large skillet, heat 1 tablespoon of oil over moderately high heat for 1 minute. Add the beef and stir-fry for 3 minutes, or until browned and cooked through. Transfer beef to a plate and keep warm.

4 Heat the remaining 1 tablespoon of oil in the skillet for 1 minute. Add the bell pepper and onion and stir-fry for 3 minutes, or until the vegetables are crisp-tender. Return the beef to the skillet and cook for 1 to 2 minutes, or until heated through. Season to taste.

5 Remove pita pockets from the oven. Fill each with some of the beef mixture. Top with 1 tablespoon of yogurt. Serve immediately.

4 SERVINGS
PREP TIME: 15 MINUTES PLUS
20 MINUTES TO FREEZE
COOKING TIME: 10 MINUTES

EQUIPMENT LIST

Citrus juicer
Utility knife
Chef's knife
Pepper mill
Aluminum foil
Large, shallow glass dish
Small bowl
Wire whisk
Large skillet
Kitchen spoon
Plate

Beef Tostadas

The chili that is the basis of this Mexican-style dish can also be served over steamed rice, or wrapped in a warm flour tortilla and accompanied by guacamole, salsa, and sour cream.

1   tablespoon vegetable oil
1   small yellow onion, finely chopped (½ cup)
12   ounces lean ground beef
1   tablespoon chili powder
1   teaspoon ground cumin
2   6-ounce cans vegetable juice (1½ cups)
1   16-ounce can red kidney beans, drained and rinsed
½   teaspoon hot pepper sauce
4   ounces shredded Monterey Jack cheese (1 cup)
1   small green bell pepper, finely chopped (½ cup)
1   medium-size ripe tomato, seeded and chopped (1 cup)
½   small head iceberg lettuce, shredded (2½ cups)

TOSTADAS

Vegetable oil
6   8″ flour tortillas

6 SERVINGS
PREP TIME: 10 MINUTES
COOKING TIME: 35 MINUTES

EQUIPMENT LIST

Utility knife
Colander
Grater
Large skillet
Medium-size skillet
Kitchen spoon
Aluminum foil
Baking sheet
Pastry brush
Tongs
Wire rack

1 In a large skillet, heat the 1 tablespoon of oil over moderate heat for 1 minute. Add the onion and sauté for 5 minutes, or until translucent. Add the beef and cook, stirring frequently, for 5 minutes, or until no pink color remains. Add the chili powder and cumin and cook, stirring continuously, for 1 minute more.

2 Stir in the vegetable juice, kidney beans, and hot pepper sauce. Bring the mixture to a boil over high heat. Reduce the heat to low and simmer, uncovered, stirring frequently, for 10 minutes. Stir in ¾ cup of the cheese, the bell pepper, and tomato. Remove the skillet from the heat and keep warm.

3 Preheat the oven to 400° F. To make the tostadas: Crumple up pieces of aluminum foil to form six 4″ balls. Place balls on a baking sheet, spacing them evenly apart.

4 Lightly brush a medium-size skillet with oil and heat over moderate heat for 30 seconds. Place one tortilla in the skillet and cook for 5 seconds on each side, or until softened. Using tongs, remove the tortilla from the skillet and place over 1 of the balls of foil, pressing it gently. Repeat cooking and forming the remaining tortillas as directed, lightly brushing the skillet with oil and heating it each time.

5 Bake tostadas in the oven for 10 minutes, or until golden.

6 Remove the baking sheet from the oven and set on a wire rack to cool slightly. Invert the tostadas and discard the foil. Transfer the tostadas to individual serving plates. Place some shredded lettuce in each one and spoon the filling on top. Sprinkle some of the remaining ¼ cup of cheese on top of the filling and serve immediately.

Caribbean Steak

Accompany this dish with herbed rice and a mixed green salad.

1½ pounds flank steak
Lime wedges (optional)
Sprigs of fresh parsley (optional)

LIME MARINADE (1 CUP)

⅓ cup fresh lime juice
¼ cup vegetable oil
2 tablespoons molasses
2 tablespoons prepared mustard
2 large cloves garlic, finely chopped
½ teaspoon grated lime peel
Freshly ground black pepper

1 Using a sharp knife, score the flank steak at 1″ intervals to ensure that the meat stays flat while cooking. Set aside.

2 To make the Lime Marinade: In a large, shallow glass dish, combine the lime juice, oil, molasses, mustard, garlic, lime peel, and pepper. Add the steak, turning to coat. Cover the dish with plastic wrap and marinate in the refrigerator for 2 hours, turning occasionally.

3 Thirty minutes before cooking, remove the steak from refrigerator and let stand at room temperature.

4 Preheat the broiler. Place the steak under the broiler 4″ from the heat source. Broil for 5 to 6 minutes on each side for medium-rare meat. Remove pan from the broiler and transfer steak to a carving board. Cover with aluminum foil and let stand for 5 minutes.

5 Cut the steak across the grain into thin slices. Transfer the steak slices to individual serving plates. Garnish with lime wedges and sprigs of fresh parsley, if desired. Serve immediately.

4 SERVINGS
PREP TIME: 10 MINUTES PLUS
2 HOURS 35 MINUTES TO MARINATE
COOKING TIME: 12 MINUTES

EQUIPMENT LIST

Citrus juicer
Utility knife
Carving knife
Grater
Pepper mill
Large, shallow glass dish
Large, metal spatula
Plastic wrap
Aluminum foil
Broiler pan
Carving board

Peppered Beef and Vegetable Kebabs

These beef kebabs are a quick and versatile way to enjoy outdoor cooking, and can easily be transferred to the broiler if the weather turns foul. Serve them with a grain pilaf, such as bulgur, couscous, or barley.

For cooking the kebabs, choose skewers made of metal or wood. The best are 12″ long and square and oval instead of round. These will keep the pieces of food from revolving while cooking. Soak wooden skewers in water for 1 to 2 hours before using to prevent them from burning on the grill.

1 pound sirloin tip, cut in 1″ pieces
2 teaspoons coarsely ground black pepper
2 medium-size yellow onions, cut in wedges (3 cups)
1 large green bell pepper, cored, seeded, and cut in 2″ pieces (1½ cups)
1 large red bell pepper, cored, seeded, and cut in 2″ pieces (1½ cups)
2 small yellow squash, cut in 1″ thick slices (2 cups)
12 medium-size mushroom caps, cleaned

VINEGAR MARINADE (½ CUP)

1 tablespoon Dijon-style mustard
2 tablespoons red wine vinegar
1 large clove garlic, chopped
¼ cup olive oil

1 To make the Vinegar Marinade: In a large, shallow glass dish, combine the mustard, vinegar, garlic, and oil until well blended. Add the beef, turning to coat. Set aside.

2 Prepare a charcoal grill until the coals form white ash, preheat a gas grill to high, or preheat the broiler.

3 Strain the marinade into a small bowl and reserve. Sprinkle pepper over the beef, gently pressing it into the surface of the meat. Thread the meat pieces, onion wedges, bell peppers, squash, and mushroom caps alternately onto four 12″ metal or wooden skewers.

4 Place the kebabs on the grill or under the broiler 4″ from the heat source. Grill or broil, turning and brushing frequently with the reserved marinade, for 12 to 15 minutes for medium-rare meat.

5 Transfer the kebabs to individual serving plates and serve immediately.

4 SERVINGS
PREP TIME: 15 MINUTES
COOKING TIME: 15 MINUTES

EQUIPMENT LIST

Carving knife
Utility knife
Large, shallow glass dish
Kitchen spoon
Charcoal or gas grill or broiler pan
Strainer
Small bowl
4 12″ metal or wooden skewers
Pastry brush

Pork Tenderloin
with Mushrooms and Rosemary

Mushrooms, perfumed by fresh rosemary and with just a hint of vermouth, turn plain pork tenderloin into a meal that is stylish enough for entertaining, but also quick and easy enough for a mid-week meal. Serve this dish with steamed snow peas or sugar snap peas and carrots.

1½   pounds pork tenderloin, trimmed and cut in 8 slices
2   tablespoons unsalted butter
4   ounces mushrooms, trimmed, cleaned, and sliced (1¼ cups)
1   small yellow onion, finely chopped (½ cup)
1   large clove garlic, finely chopped
1   tablespoon chopped fresh rosemary, or 1 teaspoon dried rosemary leaves, crumbled
¼   teaspoon coarsely ground black pepper
¼   teaspoon celery salt (optional)
2   tablespoons dry vermouth or chicken stock or canned broth
Sprigs of fresh rosemary (optional)
Sprigs of fresh thyme (optional)
Fresh whole mushrooms (optional)

1 Place half the pork medallions on a sheet of wax paper, spacing them 2″ apart. Cover with a second sheet of wax paper and, using a meat mallet or a rolling pin, flatten the pork medallions to 1″ thick. Repeat flattening the remaining pork medallions as directed.

2 In a large skillet over moderate heat, melt 1 tablespoon of the butter. Add half the pork medallions and cook for 3 to 4 minutes on each side, or until tender. Using a slotted spoon, transfer the pork medallions to a plate. Melt the remaining 1 tablespoon of butter in the skillet over moderate heat. Cook the remaining pork medallions as directed and transfer to the plate. Keep warm.

3 Add the sliced mushrooms, onion, garlic, 1 tablespoon of chopped rosemary, pepper, and celery salt, if desired, to the juices in the skillet. Cook over low heat, stirring continuously, for 1 to 2 minutes, or until thickened slightly. Stir in the vermouth.

4 Return the pork slices to the skillet and spoon the mushroom mixture over them. Cook, covered, for 4 minutes, or until the juices run clear when the meat is pierced with a knife.

5 Spoon some of the sliced mushrooms onto individual serving plates. Arrange 2 pork slices on top. Spoon some sauce over the meat. Garnish with sprigs of fresh rosemary and thyme and whole mushrooms, if desired, and serve immediately.

4 SERVINGS
PREP TIME: 10 MINUTES
COOKING TIME: 22 MINUTES

EQUIPMENT LIST

Carving knife
Utility knife
Wax paper
Meat mallet or rolling pin
Large skillet with lid
Large, metal spatula
Slotted spoon
Kitchen spoon
Plate

Mushrooms and rosemary make this pork tenderloin dish pleasing to the eye and palate.

Pork Medallions
with Artichokes and Capers

Serve this enchanting and easily-prepared dish with egg noodles tossed in a little oil or butter.

1	pound pork tenderloin, trimmed and cut in 8 slices
2	tablespoons olive oil
1	large clove garlic, finely chopped
¼	cup finely chopped yellow onion
¼	cup chicken stock or canned broth
2	tablespoons fresh lemon juice
1	9-ounce package frozen artichoke hearts, thawed, drained, and halved
1	medium-size red or green bell pepper, cored, seeded, and cut in narrow strips (1 cup)
2	tablespoons unsalted butter, cut in small pieces
1	tablespoon capers, drained and rinsed
⅛	teaspoon salt, or to taste
Freshly ground black pepper	
Pitted black olives (optional)	

1 Place half the pork medallions on a sheet of wax paper, spacing them 2″ apart. Cover with a second sheet of wax paper and, using a meat mallet or a rolling pin, flatten the pork medallions to 1″ thick. Repeat flattening the remaining pork medallions as directed.

2 In a large skillet, heat 1 tablespoon of the oil over moderate heat for 1 minute. Add half the pork medallions and cook for 3 to 4 minutes on each side, or until tender. Using a slotted spoon, transfer the pork medallions to a plate. Heat the remaining 1 tablespoon of oil in the skillet over moderate heat for 1 minute. Cook the remaining pork medallions as directed and transfer to the plate. Keep warm.

3 Add the garlic and onion to the skillet and sauté for 1 minute. Add stock and lemon juice, stirring to scrape up the browned bits from the bottom of the pan. Add the artichokes and bell pepper and cook, covered, for 5 minutes, or until the vegetables are tender. Uncover and cook for 2 to 3 minutes more, or until the sauce has thickened slightly.

4 Reduce the heat to low and stir in the butter, piece by piece, until melted and well blended. Stir in the capers. Season to taste with the salt and pepper.

5 Transfer the pork medallions to individual serving plates. Spoon some vegetables and sauce over the medallions. Garnish with the olives, if desired, and serve immediately.

4 SERVINGS
PREP TIME: 10 MINUTES
COOKING TIME: 27 MINUTES

EQUIPMENT LIST

Carving knife
Utility knife
Citrus juicer
Colander
Pepper mill
Wax paper
Meat mallet or rolling pin
Large skillet with lid
Large, metal spatula
Slotted spoon
Kitchen spoon
Plate

Lemon-Pecan Pork Chops

This pork chop dish is simplicity itself and flavorful too. Serve it with buttered boiled potatoes and steamed fresh spinach.

4	boneless pork loin chops (6 ounces each), cut ½″ thick
⅛	teaspoon salt, or to taste
Freshly ground black pepper	
1	tablespoon salted butter or margarine
2	tablespoons finely chopped pecans
1	small clove garlic, finely chopped
¼	cup fresh lemon juice
1	teaspoon grated lemon rind
Lemon slices (optional)	

1 Pat the pork chops dry with paper towels and sprinkle both sides with the salt and pepper.

2 In a large skillet over moderate heat, melt the butter. Add the pork chops and cook for 5 to 7 minutes on each side, or until the meat is browned and tender. Using a slotted spoon, transfer the pork chops to a serving platter, sprinkle with the pecans, and keep warm.

3 Add the garlic and the lemon juice and rind to the skillet, stirring to scrape up the browned bits from the bottom of the pan. Cook over moderate heat, stirring continuously, for 1 minute. Remove the pan from the heat.

4 Transfer the pork chops to individual serving plates. Spoon the sauce over the pork chops. Garnish with the lemon slices, if desired, and serve immediately.

4 SERVINGS
PREP TIME: 10 MINUTES
COOKING TIME: 15 MINUTES

EQUIPMENT LIST

Pepper mill
Paring knife
Citrus juicer
Grater
Paper towels
Large skillet
Large, metal spatula
Slotted spoon
Kitchen spoon

Bavarian Pork Chops

2 tablespoons vegetable oil
8 boneless pork loin chops (3 ounces each), cut ½″ thick
⅔ cup chicken stock or canned broth
2 tablespoons unsalted butter
4 green onions (including tops), thinly sliced (½ cup)
2 teaspoons all-purpose flour
¼ cup dry sherry (optional)
6 ounces mushrooms, trimmed, cleaned, and thinly sliced (1¾ cups)
1 tablespoon chopped fresh thyme, or 1 teaspoon dried thyme leaves, crumbled
¾ teaspoon chopped fresh sage, or ¼ teaspoon dried sage leaves, crumbled
2 teaspoons Dijon-style mustard
1 tablespoon chopped fresh parsley
⅛ teaspoon salt, or to taste
Freshly ground black pepper
Sprigs of fresh parsley (optional)

Enhance lean and tender boneless pork loin chops with an herb sauce spiced with mustard. Serve the chops with buttered spaetzle (dumplings) and sweet and sour red cabbage for a meal with German flair.

1 In a large skillet, heat 1 tablespoon of the oil over moderately high heat for 1 minute. Add half the pork chops and cook for 2 minutes on each side, or until browned. Using a slotted spoon, transfer the pork chops to a plate. Heat the remaining 1 tablespoon of oil in the skillet over moderately high heat for 1 minute. Cook the remaining pork chops as directed and transfer to the plate.

2 Add the stock to the skillet, stirring to scrape up the browned bits from the bottom of the pan. Bring to a boil over high heat. Remove from the heat, then pour the stock into a small bowl and reserve.

3 In the same skillet over moderate heat, melt the butter. Add the green onions and sauté for 2 minutes, or until softened. Stir in the flour and cook, stirring continuously, for 1 minute. Add the sherry, if desired, the reserved stock, mushrooms, thyme, and sage and cook, stirring continuously, for 2 minutes, or until well blended.

4 Return the pork chops with any accumulated juices to the skillet. Cook, covered, over moderately low heat for 5 minutes, or until the pork chops are tender. Uncover and cook the pork chops for 1 minute more, stirring occasionally.

5 Transfer the pork chops to individual serving plates. Add the mustard and chopped parsley to the skillet, stirring until the sauce is well blended. Season to taste with the salt and pepper. Spoon the sauce over the pork chops. Garnish with sprigs of fresh parsley, if desired, and serve immediately.

Enjoy the best of German cuisine with these pork chops.

4 SERVINGS
PREP TIME: 10 MINUTES
COOKING TIME: 20 MINUTES

EQUIPMENT LIST

Utility knife
Pepper mill
Large skillet with lid
Large, metal spatula
Slotted spoon
Kitchen spoon
Plate
Small bowl

Ginger-Lime Pork

Grated fresh ginger and lime juice lend a zesty flavor to lean pork tenderloin and the fast cooking of the vegetables ensures that they retain their vitamins, vivid colors, and crunchy texture. Serve this dish with steamed white rice or Chinese-style noodles.

1   pound pork tenderloin, partially frozen until firm

12   fresh asparagus spears or 12 frozen asparagus spears, thawed and drained

2   tablespoons vegetable oil

4   medium-size carrots, peeled and cut in narrow strips (2 cups)

6   tablespoons dry white wine or chicken stock or canned broth

2   tablespoons fresh lime juice

1   teaspoon low-sodium soy sauce

⅛   teaspoon coarsely ground black pepper

1½   teaspoons peeled, grated fresh ginger

½   teaspoon grated lime peel

Strips of lime peel (optional)

Lettuce leaves (optional)

Kiwi slices (optional)

Plum slices (optional)

Sprigs of fresh mint (optional)

4 SERVINGS
PREP TIME: 15 MINUTES
COOKING TIME: 20 MINUTES

EQUIPMENT LIST

Vegetable peeler
Utility knife
Carving knife
Citrus juicer
Grater
Wok or large, heavy skillet with lid
Kitchen spoon
Slotted spoon
Plate

1 Slice the pork tenderloin into ¼″ thick slices. Cut each slice into thin strips. Set aside.

2 To prepare the asparagus: If using fresh asparagus, snap off the woody ends and rinse the spears under cold running water. If the skins seem tough, peel the stalks with a vegetable peeler or sharp knife. Cut the fresh or thawed asparagus diagonally into 1″ pieces.

3 In a preheated wok or large, heavy skillet, heat 1 tablespoon of the oil over high heat until very hot. Add the carrots and cook, stirring frequently, for 5 minutes. Add the asparagus and cook, stirring, for 1 minute. Reduce the heat to moderately low. Add 1 tablespoon of the wine to the wok, cover, and cook for 4 to 5 minutes, or until the vegetables are crisp-tender. With a slotted spoon, transfer vegetables to a plate. Keep warm.

4 Heat the remaining 1 tablespoon of the oil in the wok over moderate heat. Add the pork strips and cook, stirring frequently, for 4 to 5 minutes, or until no pink color remains. Reduce the heat to low. Add the remaining 5 tablespoons of the wine, the lime juice, soy sauce, pepper, ginger, and grated lime peel to the wok. Cook, stirring, for 2 minutes. Return the vegetables to the wok, stir well, and cook for 1 minute.

5 Transfer the stir-fry to a serving platter. Sprinkle with the strips of lime peel and garnish with the lettuce leaves, kiwi and plum slices, and sprigs of fresh mint, if desired, and serve immediately.

This pork dish offers a delightful melange of flavors.

Double-Sauced Lamb Chops

4   loin lamb chops (4-6 ounces each), cut 1½" thick
Sprigs of flat-leaf parsley (optional)
Strips of pimento (optional)

CREAMY PIMENTO SAUCE (1 CUP)

2   teaspoons vegetable oil
1   tablespoon finely chopped white onion
1   tablespoon finely chopped pimento
½   cups chicken stock or canned broth
½   cup heavy cream

RED WINE SAUCE (1 CUP)

2   teaspoons cornstarch
2   teaspoons water
2   teaspoons vegetable oil
1   tablespoon finely chopped white onion
2   ounces mushrooms, trimmed, cleaned, and finely chopped (¾ cup)
¼   cup dry red wine
½   cup beef stock or canned broth
Freshly ground black pepper

Serve these beautifully presented lamb chops with a wild rice salad. For an accompaniment, bake four individual round frozen puffed pastry shells according to package directions and fill with creamed spinach.

1   To make the Creamy Pimento Sauce: In a small saucepan, heat the 2 teaspoons of oil over moderately high heat for 1 minute. Add the onion and sauté for 1 minute. Add the pimento and sauté for 30 seconds. Add the chicken stock and bring to a boil over high heat. Reduce heat to low and simmer, uncovered, for 10 minutes, or until the sauce is reduced by half. Whisk in the cream and simmer, stirring continuously, for 5 minutes, or until the sauce has thickened slightly. Remove the pan from the heat and keep warm.

2   To make the Red Wine Sauce: In a small bowl, combine the cornstarch and water until well blended. In a small saucepan, heat the 2 teaspoons of oil over moderately high heat for 1 minute. Add the onion and sauté for 1 minute. Add the mushrooms and sauté for 2 minutes, or until softened. Add the wine and cook, stirring continuously, for 1 minute, or until almost dry. Add the beef stock and bring to a boil over high heat. Reduce the heat to low, stir in the cornstarch mixture, and simmer, stirring continuously, for 1 minute, or until the sauce has thickened slightly. Season to taste with the pepper. Remove the pan from the heat and keep warm.

3   Preheat the broiler. Place chops under the broiler 4" from the heat source. Broil for 7 minutes, then turn and broil for 4 to 5 minutes more for medium-rare meat. Remove the pan from the broiler.

4   Spoon 2 tablespoons of each of the sauces onto individual serving plates and place a chop on top. Garnish with the sprigs of flat-leaf parsley and strips of pimento, if desired, and serve immediately.

4 SERVINGS
PREP TIME: 15 MINUTES
COOKING TIME: 26 MINUTES

EQUIPMENT LIST

Utility knife
Pepper mill
2 small saucepans
Kitchen spoons
Wire whisk
Small bowl
Broiler pan
Large, metal spatula

Broiled Lamb Chops with Blue Cheese Butter

2   tablespoons Worcestershire sauce
2   teaspoons dry mustard
2   tablespoons olive oil
4   loin lamb chops (4-6 ounces each), cut 1½" thick

BLUE CHEESE BUTTER (¼ CUP)

2   tablespoons unsalted butter, softened
2   tablespoons soft blue cheese

1   Preheat the broiler. In a small bowl, combine the Worcestershire sauce, mustard, and oil. Place chops under the broiler 4" from the heat source and brush with half of the Worcestershire sauce mixture. Broil for 7 minutes, then turn, brush with the remaining mixture, and broil for 4 to 5 minutes more for medium-rare meat.

2   Meanwhile, make the Blue Cheese Butter. In a small bowl, mix together the butter and blue cheese until well blended.

3   Remove the pan from the broiler. Transfer the chops to individual serving plates. Place 1 tablespoon of the Blue Cheese Butter on top of each chop and serve immediately.

4 SERVINGS
PREP TIME: 10 MINUTES
COOKING TIME: 12 MINUTES

EQUIPMENT LIST

2 small bowls
Kitchen spoons
Broiler pan
Pastry brush
Large, metal spatula

Lamb and White Bean Salad

12   slices cooked leg of lamb, trimmed (12 ounces)
1   16-ounce can cannellini or other white beans, drained and rinsed
1   small red onion, finely chopped (¾ cup)
¼   cup chopped fresh parsley
⅛   teaspoon salt, or to taste
⅛   teaspoon ground white pepper
¼   cup sun-dried tomatoes in oil, drained and cut in narrow strips
1   small red onion, thinly sliced and separated into rings (1 cup)
Sprigs of fresh mint (optional)
Curly endive or escarole (optional)

MINT DRESSING (1¼ CUPS)

¼   cup red wine vinegar
¼   cup chopped fresh mint, or 4 teaspoons dried mint leaves, crumbled
1   tablespoon chopped fresh thyme, or 1 teaspoon dried thyme leaves, crumbled
¾   cup olive oil
⅛   teaspoon salt, or to taste
⅛   teaspoon ground white pepper

This delectable main dish salad is the perfect summertime meal. It requires no cooking, it uses leftover leg of lamb, and it can be prepared hours ahead and refrigerated until ready to assemble.

1 To make the Mint Dressing: In a small bowl, combine the vinegar, chopped mint, and thyme. Slowly add the oil, whisking vigorously until well blended, or place the ingredients in a small jar with a tight-fitting lid and shake to blend. Season to taste with ⅛ teaspoon each of the salt and pepper.

2 Pour ¾ cup of the dressing into a large, shallow glass dish. Add the lamb slices, turning to coat. Cover the dish with plastic wrap and marinate in the refrigerator for 4 hours, or overnight, turning the lamb occasionally.

3 Meanwhile, in a medium-size bowl, combine the beans and chopped red onion. Pour the remaining ½ cup of dressing over the salad, stirring to coat. Cover the bowl with plastic wrap and let stand at room temperature for 2 hours to allow the flavors to blend.

4 Stir the parsley into the beans. Season to taste with ⅛ teaspoon each of the salt and pepper.

5 Drain the lamb slices and discard the marinade. Spoon the beans onto individual serving plates. Arrange the lamb slices, sun-dried tomatoes, and red onion rings over the beans. Garnish with sprigs of fresh mint and curly endive, if desired, and serve at room temperature.

4 SERVINGS
PREP TIME: 20 MINUTES PLUS
4 HOURS TO MARINATE

EQUIPMENT LIST

Carving knife
Utility knife
Colander
Small bowl
Medium-size bowl
Kitchen spoon
Slotted spoon
Wire whisk
Large, shallow glass dish
Plastic wrap

Spicy Lamb Stir-Fry

2 tablespoons vegetable oil
1 pound boneless leg of lamb, well trimmed and cut in 1½" strips
1 medium-size yellow onion, thinly sliced (2 cups)
10 ounces snow peas, trimmed and strings removed, or 1 10-ounce package frozen snow peas, thawed and drained
1 large Winesap or other tart cooking apple, peeled, cored, and chopped (1 cup)
1 2-ounce jar chopped pimento, drained
1 8-ounce can sliced water chestnuts, drained
1 8-ounce can bamboo shoots, drained
⅓ cup dark raisins
1 ounce unsalted peanuts (¼ cup)
Shredded coconut (optional)

SOY-GINGER SAUCE (¾ CUP)

2 tablespoons low-sodium soy sauce
2 tablespoons curry powder
½ cup beef stock or canned broth
2 tablespoons cornstarch
1 tablespoon water
½ teaspoon granulated sugar
¼ teaspoon ground ginger

This cross-cultural stir-fry represents the best of two cuisines. The traditional Indian combination of lamb and curry powder is mixed with crisp, stir-fried vegetables for a dish that is as attractive as it is flavorful. Be sure to have all the ingredients ready before starting to cook as the cooking time is very brief. Serve over pasta or brown rice.

1 To make the Soy-Ginger Sauce: In a small bowl, whisk together the soy sauce, curry powder, stock, cornstarch, water, sugar, and ginger until well blended. Set aside.

2 In a preheated wok or large, heavy skillet, heat the oil over high heat for 1 minute, or until very hot. Add the lamb strips and stir-fry for 2 minutes, or until they are cooked through. Using a slotted spoon, transfer the lamb strips to a plate.

3 Add the onion and snow peas and stir-fry for 2 minutes, or until crisp-tender. Transfer the vegetables to the plate with the lamb.

4 Pour the sauce into the wok and cook, stirring continuously, for 2 minutes, or until the sauce has thickened.

5 Return the lamb strips and vegetables to the wok and stir to coat with the sauce. Add the apple, pimento, water chestnuts, bamboo shoots, raisins, and peanuts and stir-fry for 1 minute, or until heated through. Sprinkle with the coconut, if desired, and serve immediately.

Add an ethnic touch to mid-week suppers with this interesting marriage of Indian spices and Chinese cooking techniques.

4 SERVINGS
PREP TIME: 20 MINUTES
COOKING TIME: 8 MINUTES

EQUIPMENT LIST

Carving knife
Utility knife
Vegetable peeler
Strainer
Small bowl
Wire whisk
Wok or large, heavy skillet
Kitchen spoon
Slotted spoon
Plate

Veal Cutlets
with Tomatoes and Mushrooms

1 tablespoon olive oil
4 veal cutlets (4 ounces each), cut ¼" thick
½ cup dry white wine
8 ounces mushrooms, trimmed, cleaned, and very thinly sliced (2½ cups)
2 medium-size tomatoes, seeded and chopped (2 cups)
¼ cup finely chopped fresh basil
¼ teaspoon salt, or to taste
Freshly ground black pepper

This recipe is one that all cooks should have at their fingertips. It's perfect for a special family occasion, great for company, and it can be prepared in next to no time. Serve the veal cutlets with spinach rotelli pasta tossed in olive oil and sprinkled with Parmesan cheese.

1 In a large skillet, heat the oil over moderately high heat. Add the veal and cook for 3 minutes on each side, or until cooked through. Using a slotted spoon, transfer cutlets to a serving platter. Keep warm.

2 Add wine and mushrooms to the skillet, stirring to scrape up the browned bits from the bottom of the pan. Cook over moderately high heat, stirring continuously, for 3 minutes, or until the mushrooms are softened. Stir in the tomatoes and basil and cook for 2 minutes, or until heated through. Season to taste with the salt and pepper.

3 Spoon the tomato and mushroom sauce over the veal cutlets and serve immediately.

4 SERVINGS
PREP TIME: 15 MINUTES
COOKING TIME: 15 MINUTES

EQUIPMENT LIST

Utility knife
Pepper mill
Large skillet
Large, metal spatula
Slotted spoon
Kitchen spoon

Sample the delights of veal with this versatile dish.

Veal Patties with Cream Sauce

Ground veal is a less expensive way to enjoy a sometimes costly meat. Accompany this dish with steamed asparagus and a rice pilaf.

1 pound ground veal
½ cup fresh bread crumbs
¼ cup chopped yellow onion
1 tablespoon grated lemon rind
1 tablespoon chopped fresh parsley
1 teaspoon dried tarragon leaves, crumbled
⅛ teaspoon hot pepper sauce
¼ teaspoon salt, or to taste
Freshly ground black pepper
2 tablespoons vegetable oil
Chopped fresh tarragon (optional)

CREAM SAUCE (½ CUP)

½ cup dry white wine or water
½ cup light cream
1 tablespoon fresh lemon juice
1 teaspoon dried tarragon leaves, crumbled

1 In a large bowl, combine the ground veal, bread crumbs, onion, lemon rind, parsley, the 1 teaspoon of tarragon, hot pepper sauce, salt, and pepper until well blended. Form the mixture into four ¾″ thick patties.

2 In a large skillet, heat the oil over moderately high heat for 1 minute. Add the veal patties and cook for 5 minutes on each side, or until no pink color remains. Using a slotted spoon, transfer the patties to a serving platter and keep warm.

3 To make the Cream Sauce: Add the wine to the skillet, stirring to scrape up the browned bits from the bottom of the pan. Cook over moderately high heat, stirring occasionally, for 5 minutes, or until reduced by one-half. Add the cream, lemon juice, and the 1 teaspoon of tarragon. Bring to a boil over moderately high heat and cook, stirring occasionally, for 5 minutes more, or until reduced by one-half.

4 Spoon the sauce over the patties. Garnish with chopped fresh tarragon, if desired, and serve immediately.

4 SERVINGS
PREP TIME: 15 MINUTES
COOKING TIME: 21 MINUTES

EQUIPMENT LIST

Utility knife
Grater
Pepper mill
Citrus juicer
Large bowl
Kitchen spoons
Slotted spoon
Large skillet
Large, metal spatula

Grilled Herbed Veal Chops

This is a great dish to serve to guests because it is quick to prepare and has an elegant presentation. If shallots are unavailable, substitute finely chopped white onion. Serve it with roasted potatoes.

½ teaspoon dried rosemary leaves, crumbled
½ teaspoon dried sage leaves, crumbled
½ teaspoon dried savory leaves, crumbled
½ teaspoon dried thyme leaves, crumbled
4 veal rib chops (8 ounces each), trimmed
1 tablespoon vegetable oil
4 small carrots, peeled and cut in narrow strips (2 cups)
8 ounces thin green beans, trimmed (2 cups), or 8 ounces frozen French-cut green beans, thawed and drained
2 tablespoons unsalted butter
4 shallots, finely chopped (¼ cup)
½ teaspoon fresh lemon juice
⅛ teaspoon salt, or to taste
Freshly ground black pepper

1 Prepare a charcoal grill until the coals form white ash, preheat a gas grill to high, or preheat the broiler. In a small bowl, combine the rosemary, sage, savory, and thyme leaves. Set aside.

2 Pat the veal chops dry with paper towels. Rub the chops on both sides with the oil and then with the herb mixture. Place the veal chops on the grill or under the broiler 4″ from the heat source. Grill or broil for 5 to 7 minutes on each side for medium meat. Using a large, metal spatula, transfer the chops to a serving platter and keep warm.

3 Meanwhile, bring a medium-size saucepan of water to a boil over high heat. Cook the carrots and green beans in the boiling water for 5 minutes, or until tender. Drain the vegetables, rinse under cold running water, and drain again.

4 In a large skillet over moderate heat, melt the butter. Add the shallots and sauté for 3 minutes, or until softened. Add the carrots and green beans and sauté for 2 minutes, or until heated through. Sprinkle with the lemon juice and season to taste with the salt and pepper. Remove the skillet from the heat.

5 Arrange the sautéed vegetables around the veal chops on the serving platter and serve immediately.

4 SERVINGS
PREP TIME: 20 MINUTES
COOKING TIME: 19 MINUTES

EQUIPMENT LIST

Utility knife
Vegetable peeler
Citrus juicer
Pepper mill
Charcoal or gas grill or broiler pan
Small bowl
Kitchen spoons
Paper towels
Large, metal spatula
Medium-size saucepan
Colander
Large skillet

*F*ish and shellfish

offer endless scope as a

main course. And here

the choice is so varied:

From broiled trout to

poached red snapper to

scallop kebabs to shrimp

salad with a twist.

Goodness is their essence,

and they're quick to

prepare, too.

*Broiled Trout with
Provençale Relish.*

Broiled Trout
with Provençale Relish

Trout, simply broiled with oil and a little seasoning, is a perfect light entrée. Serve it with Provençale Relish and sautéed potato balls.

2   brook or rainbow trout
     (1 pound each), cleaned,
     boned, cut in 4 fillets, rinsed,
     and patted dry
1   tablespoon olive oil
¼   teaspoon salt, or to taste
Ground white pepper
Lemon slices (optional)
Sprigs of flat-leaf parsley (optional)

PROVENÇALE RELISH (2½ CUPS)

3   tablespoons olive oil
2   large cloves garlic, cut in half
1   small eggplant, chopped
     (1½ cups)
¼   teaspoon salt, or to taste
¼   teaspoon coarsely ground
     black pepper
1   small zucchini, cut in ¼″
     pieces (1 cup)
2   medium-size tomatoes,
     peeled, seeded, and chopped
     (2 cups)
1   tablespoon fresh lemon juice

1 To make Provençale Relish: In a large skillet, heat 2 tablespoons of the oil over moderate heat for 1 minute. Add garlic and sauté for 2 minutes, or until golden. Add eggplant and season with ¼ teaspoon of the salt and pepper. Sauté for 2 to 3 minutes, or until softened.

2 Using a slotted spoon, transfer the garlic and eggplant to a medium-size bowl. In the same skillet, heat the remaining 1 tablespoon of oil over moderate heat for 1 minute. Add the zucchini and sauté for 2 minutes, or until crisp-tender.

3 Transfer zucchini to the bowl with the eggplant. Add the tomatoes and lemon juice. Stir well, cover the bowl with plastic wrap, and chill in the refrigerator for 1 hour.

4 Preheat the broiler. Line a broiler pan with aluminum foil. Arrange trout, flesh-side up, on broiler pan. Lightly brush with the 1 tablespoon of oil and season with ¼ teaspoon of the salt and the pepper. Place trout under the broiler 4″ from the heat source. Broil for 3 to 4 minutes, or until fish flakes easily when tested with a fork.

5 Transfer the trout to individual serving plates and garnish with lemon slices and sprigs of flat-leaf parsley, if desired. Serve immediately with the Provençale Relish.

4 SERVINGS
PREP TIME: 20 MINUTES PLUS
1 HOUR TO CHILL
COOKING TIME: 13 MINUTES

EQUIPMENT LIST

Utility knife
Paper towels
Plastic wrap
Aluminum foil
Citrus juicer
Large skillet
Kitchen spoon
Slotted spoon
Medium-size bowl
Broiler pan
Pastry brush
Fork

Grilled Lemon Halibut

2   halibut or swordfish steaks
     (1 pound each), cut 1″ thick
1   large carrot, peeled and cut in
     narrow strips (1 cup)
1   medium-size red or green bell
     pepper, cored, seeded, and
     cut in narrow strips (1 cup)
2   green onions (including tops),
     sliced diagonally (¼ cup)

LEMON DRESSING (⅔ CUP)

2   tablespoons fresh lemon juice
2   shallots, finely chopped
     (2 tablespoons)
1   teaspoon dried oregano
     leaves, crumbled
½   cup olive oil
⅛   teaspoon salt, or to taste
Freshly ground black pepper

1 Prepare a charcoal grill until the coals form white ash, preheat a gas grill to high, or preheat the broiler. Cut the halibut steaks in half crosswise. Rinse under cold running water and pat dry with paper towels. Place the halibut steaks on a large plate.

2 To make the Lemon Dressing: In a small bowl, whisk together the lemon juice, shallots, and oregano. Slowly add the oil, whisking vigorously until well blended, or place the ingredients in a small jar with a tight-fitting lid and shake to blend. Season to taste with the salt and pepper.

3 In a medium-size bowl, combine the carrot, bell pepper, and green onion. Pour ½ cup of the Lemon Dressing over the vegetables, tossing gently to coat.

4 Brush the halibut steaks with the remaining 2 tablespoons of dressing. Place the fish on the grill or under the broiler 4″ from the heat source. Grill or broil for 4 minutes, then turn the fish, brush again with the remaining dressing, and grill or broil for 3 to 4 minutes more, or until the fish flakes easily when tested with a fork.

5 Transfer the halibut steaks and the vegetables to individual serving plates and serve immediately.

4 SERVINGS
PREP TIME: 20 MINUTES
COOKING TIME: 8 MINUTES

EQUIPMENT LIST

Vegetable peeler
Utility knife
Citrus juicer
Pepper mill
Charcoal or gas grill or broiler pan
Paper towels
Large plate
Small bowl
Medium-size bowl
Wire whisk
Kitchen spoon
Pastry brush
Large, metal spatula
Fork

Sole Véronique

Véronique is the term used to describe dishes that are garnished with seedless white grapes, of which Sole Véronique is the most popular. Serve it with steamed red-skinned new potatoes sprinkled with parsley and a lettuce and tomato salad.

6 SERVINGS
PREP TIME: 20 MINUTES
COOKING TIME: 18 MINUTES

6 lemon or grey sole or flounder fillets (5-6 ounces each)
2 tablespoons unsalted butter
2 shallots, finely chopped (2 tablespoons)
½ cup dry white wine or water
¼ cup fish stock or bottled clam juice
½ cup light cream or half-and-half
2 teaspoons fresh lemon juice
6 ounces seedless white grapes, peeled (1 cup)
⅛ teaspoon salt, or to taste
Ground white pepper
Lime slices (optional)
Seedless white grapes (optional)

1 Rinse the sole fillets under cold running water and pat dry with paper towels. Starting with the wide end, roll up each fillet jelly-roll style, skin-side in, and secure with toothpicks.

2 In a large skillet over moderate heat, melt the butter. Add the shallots and sauté for 1 minute, or until slightly softened. Place the rolled fillets on top of shallots. Pour the wine and stock over fillets. Lay a 12″ circle of wax paper on the fillets. Bring to a boil over moderately high heat. Reduce the heat to moderately low and cook, covered, for 10 to 12 minutes, or until the fish flakes easily when tested with a fork. Remove the lid and the paper from the fillets. Using a large, metal spatula, transfer the fillets to a plate, remove the toothpicks, and keep warm.

3 Add the cream and lemon juice to the skillet and cook over moderate heat, stirring continuously, for 5 minutes, or until reduced by one-half. (Do not boil.) Gently stir in the 1 cup of grapes. Season to taste. Remove skillet from the heat.

4 Transfer the fillets to individual serving plates and spoon the sauce over them. Garnish with the lime slices and grapes, if desired, and serve immediately.

EQUIPMENT LIST

Utility knife
Citrus juicer
Paper towels
12″ circle wax paper
Toothpicks
Large skillet with lid
Kitchen spoon
Fork
Large, metal spatula
Plate

Poached Shark Steaks
with Cucumber-Dill Sauce

4   Mako shark or swordfish
     steaks (8 ounces each), cut
     ½″ thick
½   cup dry white wine or water
2   cups chicken stock or canned
     broth
½   cup water
2   shallots, finely chopped
     (2 tablespoons)

CUCUMBER-DILL SAUCE (2 CUPS)

2   large cucumbers, peeled,
     seeded, and chopped
1   teaspoon superfine sugar
¼   teaspoon salt, or to taste
2   tablespoons white vinegar
1   shallot, finely chopped
     (1 tablespoon)
1   8-ounce container plain
     lowfat yogurt (1 cup)
½   cup sour cream
3   tablespoons chopped fresh
     dill

In this recipe, greased wax paper is laid on top of the fish in the skillet before it is covered with a lid to protect the delicate flesh and retain moisture and flavor. Serve with herbed white rice or oven-roasted potatoes.

1 To make the Cucumber-Dill Sauce: Place the cucumbers in a medium-size bowl with the sugar, salt, vinegar, and the 1 tablespoon of shallots. Stir in the yogurt, sour cream, and dill. Spoon the sauce into a sauceboat or serving dish, cover with plastic wrap, and chill in the refrigerator for 1 hour.

2 Rinse the shark steaks under cold running water and pat dry with paper towels. Grease a 12″ circle of wax paper.

3 In a large, nonstick skillet, bring the wine, stock, water, and the 2 tablespoons of shallots to a boil over high heat. Reduce the heat to moderately high and cook, covered, for 4 to 5 minutes, or until the shallots are softened.

4 Arrange the shark steaks in the skillet. Lay the wax paper, greased-side down, on the shark steaks. Cook, covered, over moderate heat for 5 minutes, or until the fish flakes easily when tested with a fork.

5 Remove the lid and the paper from the shark steaks. Using a large, metal spatula, transfer the shark steaks to a serving platter. Serve immediately with the Cucumber-Dill Sauce.

4 SERVINGS
PREP TIME: 10 MINUTES PLUS
1 HOUR TO CHILL
COOKING TIME: 10 MINUTES

EQUIPMENT LIST

Utility knife
Vegetable peeler
Medium-size bowl
Kitchen spoon
Plastic wrap
Paper towels
12″ circle wax paper
Large, nonstick skillet with lid
Fork

Baked Scrod

½   cup dry unseasoned bread
     crumbs
⅓   cup corn flake crumbs
2   tablespoons toasted wheat
     germ
2   tablespoons chopped fresh
     parsley
½   teaspoon dried thyme leaves,
     crumbled
¼   teaspoon dried oregano
     leaves, crumbled
¼   teaspoon salt
Freshly ground black pepper
¼   cup (½ stick) unsalted butter
1   tablespoon fresh lemon juice
4   scrod or flounder fillets
     (6 ounces each)
Lemon wedges (optional)

Here, scrod, which is young cod, is coated with an herbed crumb mixture, then baked. The result is a crisp, delicious, and lower-calorie alternative to fried fish. Serve with creamy coleslaw from the deli and corn on the cob for an effortless supper.

1 Preheat the oven to 450° F. Grease a baking sheet. In a shallow dish, combine the bread crumbs, corn flake crumbs, wheat germ, chopped parsley, thyme, oregano, salt, and pepper.

2 In a small saucepan over moderate heat, melt the butter with the lemon juice. Transfer to a shallow bowl.

3 Rinse the scrod fillets under cold running water and pat dry with paper towels. Dip each fillet in the butter mixture, then roll in the crumb mixture to coat evenly, shaking off the excess.

4 Arrange the scrod fillets on the baking sheet. Bake for 12 to 14 minutes, or until the coating is golden brown and the fish flakes easily when tested with a fork.

5 Using a large, metal spatula, transfer the baked scrod fillets to individual serving plates. Garnish with lemon wedges, if desired, and serve immediately.

4 SERVINGS
PREP TIME: 10 MINUTES
COOKING TIME: 14 MINUTES

EQUIPMENT LIST

Utility knife
Pepper mill
Citrus juicer
Baking sheet
Shallow dish
Small saucepan
Shallow bowl
Paper towels
Fork

Lemon-Thyme Salmon Steaks

4   salmon steaks (6 ounces
     each), cut 1" thick
¼   teaspoon salt, or to taste
Freshly ground black pepper
Sprigs of fresh thyme (optional)
Lemon twists (optional)
Zucchini curls (optional)

LEMON-THYME MARINADE
(⅓ CUP)

3   tablespoons olive oil
2   tablespoons fresh lemon juice
1½   teaspoons chopped fresh
     thyme, or ½ teaspoon dried
     thyme leaves, crumbled

To ensure even cooking and prevent the salmon from disintegrating, the belly flaps of the salmon steaks are curled in and secured against the solid piece of fish before they are marinated and cooked. Serve with steamed green beans and a mixture of boiled wild and white rice.

1 Rinse the salmon steaks under cold running water and pat dry with paper towels. Place a salmon steak on a work surface. Curl 1 belly flap into the center bone of the fish. Wrap the second flap around the outside of the first flap to form a neat oval. Secure the flaps with a 4" wooden skewer. Repeat as directed with the remaining salmon steaks. Season with the salt and pepper.

2 To make the Lemon-Thyme Marinade: In a large, shallow glass dish, combine the oil, lemon juice, and 1½ teaspoons of thyme. Place the salmon steaks in the marinade, turning to coat. Cover with plastic wrap and marinate in the refrigerator for 30 minutes.

3 Prepare a charcoal grill until the coals form white ash, preheat a gas grill to high, or preheat the broiler. Place the salmon steaks on the grill or under the broiler 4" from the heat source. Discard the marinade. Grill or broil for 4 minutes on each side, or until the flesh is opaque and flakes easily when tested with a fork.

4 Using a large, metal spatula, transfer the salmon steaks to individual serving plates and garnish with sprigs of fresh thyme, lemon twists, and zucchini curls, if desired. Serve immediately.

4 SERVINGS
PREP TIME: 10 MINUTES PLUS
30 MINUTES TO MARINATE
COOKING TIME: 8 MINUTES

EQUIPMENT LIST

Pepper mill
Citrus juicer
Utility knife
Paper towels
Plastic wrap
4 4" wooden skewers
Large, shallow glass dish
Kitchen spoon
Charcoal or gas grill or broiler pan
Large, metal spatula
Fork

Citrus Halibut with Herbs

4   halibut steaks (8 ounces
     each), cut 1" thick
8   large green cabbage leaves,
     thick stalks removed
Orange rind, cut in thin strips
     (optional)

CITRUS-HERB MARINADE
(⅔ CUP)

¼   cup orange juice
2   tablespoons fresh lemon juice
1   teaspoon grated orange rind
1   shallot, finely chopped (1
     tablespoon)
¼   cup chopped fresh parsley
2   teaspoons dried rosemary
     leaves, crumbled
2   tablespoons olive oil
¼   teaspoon salt, or to taste
Freshly ground black pepper

The aromatic combination of herbs and orange juice gives this baked fish exceptional flavor.

1 Rinse the halibut steaks under cold running water and pat dry with paper towels. Set aside.

2 To make the Citrus-Herb Marinade: In a large, shallow glass dish, combine the orange and lemon juices, grated orange rind, shallot, parsley, rosemary, oil, salt, and pepper. Place the halibut steaks in the marinade, turning to coat. Cover the dish with plastic wrap and marinate in the refrigerator, turning the fish once, for 30 minutes.

3 Preheat the oven to 425° F. Transfer the fish and marinade to a large baking dish. Bake for 15 minutes. Remove dish from the oven, uncover, and spoon the juices over fish. Bake, uncovered, for 5 minutes more, or until fish flakes easily when tested with a fork.

4 Meanwhile, place cabbage leaves in a steamer set over boiling water in a medium-size saucepan. Steam, covered, over high heat for 5 to 7 minutes, or until crisp-tender.

5 Transfer 2 cabbage leaves to each individual serving plate and top with the fish steaks. Garnish with the orange rind, if desired. Serve immediately.

4 SERVINGS
PREP TIME: 15 MINUTES PLUS
30 MINUTES TO MARINATE
COOKING TIME: 20 MINUTES

EQUIPMENT LIST

Utility knife
Paring knife
Citrus juicer
Pepper mill
Paper towels
Plastic wrap
Large, shallow glass dish
Large baking dish
Kitchen spoons
Large, metal spatula
Fork
Steamer
Medium-size saucepan

Poached Red Snapper
with Wine and Vegetables

4 red snapper fillets with skin (6 ounces each)
¼ teaspoon salt, or to taste
Freshly ground black pepper
2 tablespoons unsalted butter
½ cup chicken stock or canned broth
½ cup dry white wine or water
2 medium-size carrots, peeled and cut in narrow strips (1½ cups)
2 green onions (including some tops), halved lengthwise and cut in narrow strips (¼ cup)
1 tablespoon chopped fresh parsley
1 tablespoon chopped fresh tarragon, or 1 teaspoon dried tarragon leaves, crumbled
Lemon wedges (optional)
Sprigs of fresh tarragon (optional)

Red snapper, so named because of its reddish skin and eyes, is the best known member of the large snapper family. It is found primarily in the Gulf of Mexico and is available year round, with its peak season in the summer months. Its delicate flesh is firm-textured and contains very little fat. If red snapper fillets are unavailable, other firm, white-fleshed fish fillets, such as halibut, sole, or different snappers, can be substituted.

Poaching is one of the best ways to prepare red snapper fillets. The fish absorbs the flavors of the stock as well as its own juices. To further enhance the flavor, add fresh vegetables, as in this recipe. A first course of creamy mushroom soup will complement the fish, as will a side dish of oven-roasted potatoes and French dinner rolls.

1 Rinse the red snapper fillets under cold running water and pat dry with paper towels. Season the fish fillets on both sides with the salt and pepper.

2 In a large skillet over moderate heat, melt the butter. Place the fish fillets in the skillet, skin-sides down, and cook for 2 minutes.

3 Using a large, metal spatula, carefully turn the fish fillets skin-sides up. Add the stock, wine, carrots, green onions, parsley, and the 1 tablespoon of tarragon to the skillet. Cover and cook over moderately low heat for 10 to 12 minutes, or until fish flakes easily when tested with a fork.

4 Transfer fish fillets, skin-side down, to a serving platter. Spoon the vegetables and sauce over the fish fillets. Garnish with the lemon wedges and sprigs of fresh tarragon, if desired, and serve immediately.

Perfectly poached red snapper will provide a main course with panache.

4 SERVINGS
PREP TIME: 15 MINUTES
COOKING TIME: 15 MINUTES

Equipment List

Pepper mill
Vegetable peeler
Utility knife
Paper towels
Large skillet with lid
Large, metal spatula
Fork

Linguine with Herbed Clam and Tomato Sauce

4	dozen littleneck clams
1	tablespoon white vinegar
¾	cup dry red wine or water
1	large clove garlic, unpeeled
¼	cup olive oil
2	large cloves garlic, finely chopped
1	tablespoon tomato paste
1	28-ounce can whole tomatoes, drained and chopped
1	tablespoon chopped fresh oregano, or 1 teaspoon dried oregano leaves, crumbled
1	tablespoon chopped fresh parsley
1½	teaspoons crushed red pepper flakes
⅛	teaspoon salt, or to taste

Freshly ground black pepper
12 ounces dried linguine
Sprigs of flat-leaf parsley
      (optional)

Try this robust and delicious clam sauce with almost any pasta. Serve it with crusty Italian bread.

1 Scrub the clams under cold running water and place them in a large bowl with lightly salted water to cover. Add the vinegar and let stand for 20 minutes. (The vinegar acts as an irritant and causes the clams to flush out any sand.) Drain the clams well.

2 In a stockpot, combine the clams, wine, and whole garlic clove. Bring to a boil over high heat. Reduce the heat to moderate and cook, covered, for 6 to 9 minutes, or just until the shells open. Gently stir the clams once or twice to ensure even cooking.

3 Using a slotted spoon, transfer the clams to a large bowl, discarding any that haven't opened. Remove the clams from the shells. Cut large clams into smaller pieces. Set aside. Strain the cooking liquid through a fine sieve lined with cheesecloth or a paper towel into a small bowl. Discard the garlic.

4 In a large skillet, heat the oil over moderate heat for 1 minute. Add the chopped garlic and tomato paste and sauté for 1 minute. Add reserved cooking liquid, tomatoes, oregano, chopped parsley, and red pepper flakes. Cook, stirring frequently, for 4 to 5 minutes, or until the sauce has thickened slightly. Add the clams and cook, stirring frequently, for 5 minutes more. Season to taste with the salt and pepper. Remove the skillet from the heat and keep warm.

5 Meanwhile, bring a large saucepan of water to a boil over high heat. Cook the linguine in the boiling water for 8 to 10 minutes, or until al dente. Drain the linguine and transfer to a large, shallow serving bowl. Spoon the sauce over the pasta. Garnish with the sprigs of flat-leaf parsley, if desired, and serve immediately.

The fresh clam and tomato sauce transforms any pasta into an exceptional dish.

4 SERVINGS
PREP TIME: 15 MINUTES PLUS
20 MINUTES TO STAND
COOKING TIME: 20 MINUTES

EQUIPMENT LIST

Utility knife
Colander
Pepper mill
Vegetable brush
2 large bowls
Small bowl
Stockpot with lid
Kitchen spoon
Slotted spoon
Fine sieve
Cheesecloth or paper towels
Large skillet
Large saucepan

Southwest Shrimp Salad
with Roasted Red Pepper Sauce

1 pound large uncooked
   shrimp, peeled and deveined
   (24 shrimp)
¾ cup orange juice
¼ cup vegetable oil
1 tablespoon finely chopped
   fresh parsley
1 small jalapeño pepper, cored,
   seeded, and finely chopped
   (1 tablespoon)
1 large clove garlic, finely
   chopped
18 cherry tomatoes
1 small head iceberg lettuce,
   leaves separated and rinsed

ROASTED RED PEPPER SAUCE
(1¼ CUPS)

2 medium-size red bell peppers,
   cored, seeded, and halved
½ cup vegetable oil
1 large clove garlic, quartered
¼ teaspoon ground red pepper
   (cayenne)

When handling jalapeño peppers remember that the seeds and veins are extremely hot and contain oils that can burn sensitive skin. Wear rubber gloves and take care to avoid rubbing the eyes, mouth, or nose when working with peppers. Wash hands and gloves thoroughly afterwards.

To save time, use 4 roasted and drained bell pepper halves from a jar and place them in the blender with the remaining ingredients for the sauce.

1 To make the salad: Place the shrimp in a large, shallow glass dish. In a small bowl, whisk together the orange juice, oil, parsley, jalapeño pepper, and garlic and pour over the shrimp. Cover the dish with plastic wrap and marinate in the refrigerator for 1 hour.

2 Prepare a charcoal grill until the coals form white ash, preheat a gas grill to high, or preheat the broiler.

3 To make the sauce: Place bell peppers on the grill or under the broiler 4″ from the heat source. Grill or broil for 15 minutes, turning frequently, until charred and blistered on all sides. Cool peppers slightly. Using a small knife, peel off and discard the charred skin. Place the peppers in a blender or food processor fitted with the metal blade. Add the oil, garlic, and ground red pepper and blend or process for 1 minute, or until the mixture is smooth.

4 Remove shrimp from marinade and reserve liquid. Thread shrimp and tomatoes alternately onto six 10″ metal or wooden skewers.

5 Place skewers on grill or under broiler 4″ from the heat source. Grill or broil, brushing frequently with reserved marinade, for 3 to 4 minutes on each side. Remove from the heat.

6 Line individual serving plates with lettuce leaves. Remove shrimp and tomatoes from skewers and arrange on top of lettuce. Spoon some of the sauce over each salad. Serve warm or at room temperature.

6 SERVINGS
PREP TIME: 20 MINUTES PLUS
1 HOUR TO MARINATE
COOKING TIME: 23 MINUTES

EQUIPMENT LIST

Utility knife
Rubber gloves
Large, shallow glass dish
Small bowl
Wire whisk
Plastic wrap
Charcoal or gas grill or broiler pan
Fork
Blender or food processor with
   metal blade
6 10″ metal or wooden skewers
Pastry brush

Honey-Lime Broiled Shrimp

1 pound large uncooked
   shrimp, peeled and deveined
   (24 shrimp)
4 large cloves garlic
1 pound dried linguine

HONEY-LIME MARINADE (⅔ cup)

2 tablespoons honey
1 tablespoon vegetable oil
½ cup fresh lime juice
2 drops hot pepper sauce

1 Place the shrimp in a large, shallow, ovenproof glass dish. In a small bowl, whisk together the honey, oil, lime juice, and the hot pepper sauce and pour over the shrimp. Cover the dish with plastic wrap and marinate in the refrigerator for 1 hour.

2 Preheat the broiler. Place garlic in a large stockpot of water and bring to a boil over high heat. Cook the linguine in the boiling water for 8 to 10 minutes, or until al dente.

3 Meanwhile, place the dish with the shrimp under the broiler 4″ from the heat source. Broil for 6 to 8 minutes, turning and brushing frequently with the marinade.

4 Drain the linguine and discard garlic. Transfer to individual serving plates. Spoon some of the shrimp and marinade over the linguine and serve immediately.

6 SERVINGS
PREP TIME: 10 MINUTES PLUS
1 HOUR TO MARINATE
COOKING TIME: 10 MINUTES

EQUIPMENT LIST

Citrus juicer
Large, shallow, ovenproof glass dish
Small bowl
Wire whisk
Plastic wrap
Large stockpot
Pastry brush
Colander

Mussels Provençale

4 pounds mussels
4 tablespoons unsalted butter
1 medium-size yellow onion, finely chopped (1 cup)
4 large cloves garlic, finely chopped
1 14½-ounce can whole tomatoes, drained and chopped
1 cup fish stock or bottled clam juice
2 tablespoons chopped fresh parsley

"Provençale" refers to dishes prepared in the style of Provence, a region in southeastern France. Characteristic ingredients include tomatoes, garlic, and onions, all of which complement mussels. This easily prepared and economical recipe makes a delicious first course or light supper. Serve it with crusty French bread for dipping into the broth.

1 To clean the mussels: Drop them into lightly salted water to cover and let stand for 15 minutes to rid them of sand. Scrub the mussels thoroughly with a stiff brush and remove the fuzzy "beards." Discard any mussels with broken or open shells.

2 In a 6-quart Dutch oven over moderate heat, melt the butter. Add the onion and garlic and sauté for 5 minutes, or until the onion is translucent.

3 Add the tomatoes, stock, and parsley and bring to a boil over high heat. Reduce the heat to low. Add the mussels and cook, covered, for 3 to 5 minutes, or just until the shells open. Gently stir them once or twice to ensure that the mussels cook evenly.

4 Using a slotted spoon, transfer the mussels to individual large soup bowls, discarding any mussels that haven't opened. Ladle some of the broth into each bowl. Serve immediately.

4 SERVINGS
PREP TIME: 35 MINUTES
COOKING TIME: 15 MINUTES

EQUIPMENT LIST

Utility knife
Colander
Vegetable brush
Large bowl
6-quart Dutch oven
Kitchen spoon

The fine cuisine of Provence is reflected in this mussel dish.

Soft-Shell Crabs with Ginger Sauce

2 teaspoons sesame seeds
8 large soft-shell crabs (5-6 ounces each), cleaned
½ cup all-purpose flour
Freshly ground black pepper
¼ teaspoon ground red pepper (cayenne)
3-4 tablespoons vegetable oil

GINGER SAUCE (2 CUPS)

1 tablespoon cornstarch
3 tablespoons low-sodium soy sauce
3 tablespoons dry sherry (optional)
3 tablespoons vegetable oil
4 shallots, finely chopped (¼ cup), or ¼ cup finely chopped white onion
2 tablespoons peeled, grated fresh ginger, or 1 tablespoon ground ginger
1 cup chicken stock or canned broth
4 green onions (including tops), finely chopped (½ cup)

Soft-shell crabs are crabs that have shed their hard shells. They are generally available in the summer months. Use soft-shell crabs the day they are bought. To save time, have them cleaned at the fish market.

1 To toast the sesame seeds: In a small skillet over moderate heat, toast the seeds, stirring continuously, for 2 minutes, or until fragrant and golden. Remove the skillet from the heat and set aside.

2 In a large, shallow dish, combine the flour with black and red peppers. Dredge crabs lightly in the flour mixture.

3 In a large skillet, heat the 3 tablespoons of oil over moderately high heat for 1 minute. Cook 4 of the crabs for 3 to 4 minutes on each side, or until golden. Using a slotted spoon, transfer crabs to a serving platter and keep warm. Cook remaining crabs as directed, adding more oil to the skillet, if needed.

4 To make the sauce: In a small bowl, combine cornstarch with soy sauce and sherry, if desired, and set aside. Wipe skillet with paper towels and heat the 3 tablespoons of oil over moderately high heat for 1 minute. Add shallots and sauté for 1 minute. Add ginger and sauté 1 minute more. Add stock and green onions and bring mixture to a boil over high heat. Reduce heat to low and simmer for 2 minutes. Slowly stir cornstarch mixture into sauce, bring to a boil over high heat, and cook, stirring continuously, for 2 minutes, or until sauce has thickened slightly.

5 Transfer crabs to individual serving plates and spoon sauce over them. Sprinkle with toasted sesame seeds and serve immediately.

4 SERVINGS
PREP TIME: 30 MINUTES
COOKING TIME: 30 MINUTES

EQUIPMENT LIST

Pepper mill
Utility knife
Vegetable peeler
Grater
Small skillet
Large skillet
Kitchen spoons
Slotted spoon
Large, shallow dish
Large, metal spatula
Small bowl
Paper towels

Cucumber-Scallop Brochettes

2 medium-size cucumbers
1 pound sea scallops, rinsed and patted dry
¼ cup fresh lemon juice
3 tablespoons vegetable oil
¼ teaspoon salt, or to taste
⅛ teaspoon white pepper
⅓ cup finely chopped fresh dill
Sprigs of fresh dill (optional)

1 Preheat the broiler. Peel the cucumbers, cut them in half lengthwise, and scrape out the seeds with a spoon. Trim the ends and cut each half crosswise into 1″ pieces.

2 Beginning with a cucumber piece, alternately thread scallops and cucumber pieces onto four 10″ metal or wooden skewers. Each skewer should have 4 to 5 scallops. Place skewers in a large, shallow dish.

3 In a small bowl, whisk together the lemon juice, oil, salt, and pepper. Brush the mixture over the brochettes. Spread the chopped dill on a plate or work surface. Carefully roll each skewer in the dill to coat evenly.

4 Place the skewers on a lightly greased broiler pan or rack 4″ from the heat source. Broil for 4 to 8 minutes, or until the scallops are opaque throughout. Turn the brochettes every 2 to 3 minutes to ensure even cooking of the fish.

5 Transfer the brochettes to individual serving plates, garnish with sprigs of fresh dill, if desired, and serve immediately.

4 SERVINGS
PREP TIME: 20 MINUTES
COOKING TIME: 8 MINUTES

EQUIPMENT LIST

Paper towels
Citrus juicer
Utility knife
Vegetable peeler
Teaspoon
4 10″ metal or wooden skewers
Large, shallow dish
Small bowl
Wire whisk
Pastry brush
Plate
Broiler pan

POULTRY

*P*oultry's popularity is undeniable. It's healthy and satisfying, fairly inexpensive, and just perfect for speedy preparations. This chapter presents flavorful yet simple recipes—from stir-fries to roasts to salads—that will enhance any cook's poultry repertoire.

Grilled Chicken with Potato Salad.

Grilled Chicken with Potato Salad

2　whole chicken breasts (4 halves), skinned and boned (1½ pounds)
1　bunch watercress, coarse stems removed, rinsed (optional)

CURRY DRESSING (¾ CUP)

1½　teaspoons curry powder
1　tablespoon Dijon-style mustard
¼　cup red wine vinegar
½　cup olive oil

POTATO SALAD

10　small red-skinned potatoes, sliced ¼″ thick (2 cups)
2　medium-size carrots, peeled and cut in ¼″ cubes (1½ cups)
2　cups cantaloupe balls
1　stalk celery, chopped (½ cup)
1　small yellow onion, chopped (½ cup)
1　green onion (including top), chopped (2 tablespoons)
Chopped fresh parsley (optional)

1 Prepare a charcoal grill until the coals form white ash, preheat a gas grill to high, or preheat the broiler. Rinse the chicken breasts under cold running water. Pat dry with paper towels.

2 To make the Curry Dressing: In a small bowl, combine curry powder, mustard, and vinegar. Slowly add oil, whisking vigorously until well blended, or place ingredients in a small jar with a tight-fitting lid and shake to blend. Pour half the dressing into a large, shallow glass dish. Add the chicken breasts to the dish, turning to coat. Set aside.

3 To make the Potato Salad: Bring a large saucepan of water to a boil over high heat. Cook the potatoes in the boiling water, partially covered, for 7 minutes. Add the carrots and cook, partially covered, for 3 minutes more, or until the potatoes and carrots are tender. Drain well, rinse under cold running water, and drain again.

4 Transfer the potatoes and carrots to a large bowl. Add the melon balls, celery, yellow and green onions, and parsley, if desired. Whisk remaining dressing and pour it over the salad, tossing to coat.

5 Place the chicken breasts on the grill or under the broiler 4″ from the heat source. Reserve the dressing. Grill or broil the chicken breasts, brushing occasionally with dressing, for 5 minutes on each side, or until the juices run clear when the meat is pierced with a knife.

6 Transfer the chicken breasts to individual serving plates. Garnish with sprigs of watercress, if desired, and serve immediately with the Potato Salad.

4 SERVINGS
PREP TIME: 20 MINUTES
COOKING TIME: 20 MINUTES

EQUIPMENT LIST

Utility knife
Vegetable peeler
Melon ball cutter
Charcoal or gas grill or broiler pan
Paper towels
Small bowl
Large bowl
Wire whisk
Large, shallow glass dish
Large, metal spatula
Large saucepan with lid
Colander
Kitchen spoon
Pastry brush

Peachy Pistachio Chicken

2　whole chicken breasts (4 halves), skinned and boned (1½ pounds)
Freshly ground black pepper
2　teaspoons Dijon-style or prepared mustard
3　ounces prosciutto, chopped
2　ounces shelled, unsalted pistachio nuts, chopped (½ cup)
3　tablespoons peach preserves
3　medium-size ripe peaches, peeled, pitted, and thinly sliced (2 cups), or 2 cups frozen sliced peaches, thawed and drained
¼　cup dry white wine or water

1 Preheat the oven to 350° F. Grease a large baking dish. Rinse the chicken breasts under cold running water. Pat dry with paper towels.

2 Place 1 chicken breast on a sheet of wax paper, then cover with a second sheet of wax paper. Using a meat mallet or a rolling pin, flatten the chicken breast to ¼″ thick. Flatten remaining chicken breasts as directed. Remove wax paper and sprinkle chicken breasts with the pepper. Spread each chicken breast with ½ teaspoon of mustard, then top each with 1 tablespoon of prosciutto and 1 tablespoon of pistachio nuts. Roll up chicken breasts, lengthwise, and secure with toothpicks. Place chicken breasts, seam-sides down, in the prepared dish.

3 In a small saucepan, heat the preserves over moderately low heat for 2 to 3 minutes, or until melted. Brush the preserves over the chicken breasts and sprinkle each with 1 tablespoon of pistachio nuts. Bake, uncovered, for 15 minutes.

4 Add sliced peaches and wine to the baking dish. Bake the chicken breasts, uncovered, for 10 to 15 minutes more, or until the meat is tender and juices run clear when meat is pierced with a knife.

5 Transfer the chicken breasts and peaches to a serving platter and remove and discard the toothpicks. Serve immediately.

4 SERVINGS
PREP TIME: 15 MINUTES
COOKING TIME: 30 MINUTES

EQUIPMENT LIST

Pepper mill
Utility knife
Vegetable peeler
Large baking dish
Paper towels
Wax paper
Meat mallet or rolling pin
Thin, metal spatula
Toothpicks
Small saucepan
Kitchen spoon
Pastry brush

Baked Chicken
with Spicy Red Pepper Sauce

This crisp baked chicken is enriched with a rosy sauce, which has a piquant hint of vinegar. Raspberry vinegar is available in large supermarkets and specialty food stores. Serve this dish with steamed spinach and a rice pilaf.

1   3-3½ pound chicken, skinned and cut in serving pieces
2   tablespoons olive oil
½   teaspoon salt, or to taste
½   teaspoon coarsely ground black pepper
Chopped green onions (optional)

SPICY RED PEPPER SAUCE
(1½ CUPS)

1   small yellow onion, finely chopped (½ cup)
1   large red bell pepper, cored, seeded, and chopped (1 cup)
½   teaspoon dried tarragon leaves, crumbled
½   cup dry white wine or water
½   cup raspberry vinegar or red wine vinegar
¼   teaspoon ground red pepper (cayenne)
½   teaspoon granulated sugar
½   cup chicken stock or canned broth
¼   cup heavy cream

4 SERVINGS
PREP TIME: 10 MINUTES
COOKING TIME: 35 MINUTES

EQUIPMENT LIST

Utility knife
Paper towels
Wire rack
Roasting pan
Small saucepan
Kitchen spoon
Blender or food processor with metal blade
Rubber spatula

1   Preheat the oven to 350° F. Rinse the chicken pieces under cold running water and pat dry with paper towels.

2   Rub the chicken pieces with the oil and place on a wire rack in a roasting pan. Season with the salt and pepper. Bake for 30 to 35 minutes, or until juices run clear when the meat is pierced with a knife.

3   Meanwhile, make the Spicy Red Pepper Sauce. In a small saucepan, combine the onion, bell pepper, tarragon, wine, and vinegar. Bring to a boil over high heat. Reduce heat to moderately low and simmer, uncovered, stirring occasionally, for 5 to 8 minutes, or until liquid has almost evaporated. (Take care not to let the sauce burn.)

4   Remove the pan from the heat and transfer the mixture to a blender or food processor fitted with the metal blade. Blend or process for 1 minute, or until smooth, scraping down the side of the bowl whenever necessary. Return the purée to the saucepan.

5   Stir in the ground red pepper, sugar, stock, and cream. Simmer over low heat, stirring occasionally, for 4 to 5 minutes, or until thickened slightly.

6   Transfer the chicken pieces to a serving dish and pour the sauce over them. Garnish with the chopped green onions, if desired, and serve immediately.

This colorful chicken dish will brighten any family occasion.

Drunken Chicken

2	whole chicken breasts (4 halves), boned (1½ pounds)
2	tablespoons unsalted butter
6	ounces mushrooms, trimmed, cleaned, and sliced (1¾ cups)
1	cup sour cream or plain lowfat yogurt
	Shredded carrot (optional)
	Shredded celery (optional)

BRANDY MARINADE (⅓ CUP)

¼	cup brandy, light rum, dry sherry, or chicken stock or canned broth
1	tablespoon low-sodium soy sauce
2	teaspoons fresh lime juice
1	teaspoon firmly packed light brown sugar
¼	teaspoon crushed red pepper flakes
1	teaspoon peeled, grated fresh ginger, or ½ teaspoon ground ginger
⅛	teaspoon ground nutmeg

This popular Chinese dish is an adaption of an ancient recipe favored by an empress of the Tang dynasty. Although noted for her great beauty, she was also renowed for her fondness for alcohol—hence this recipe's name.

To make the carrot and celery garnish: With a very sharp knife, cut the vegetables into thin strips and place in a bowl of ice water until needed. Drain well, pat them dry with paper towels.

1 Rinse the chicken breasts under cold running water. Pat dry with paper towels. Pierce the chicken breasts several times with a fork.

2 To make the Brandy Marinade: In a large, shallow glass dish, combine brandy, soy sauce, lime juice, sugar, red pepper flakes, ginger, and nutmeg. Add chicken, turning to coat. Cover with plastic wrap and marinate in refrigerator for 30 minutes, turning occasionally.

3 In a large skillet over moderate heat, melt the butter. Remove the chicken from the marinade and reserve liquid. Add chicken to the skillet and cook for 5 minutes on each side, or until the juices run clear when the meat is pierced with a knife. Transfer chicken to a serving platter and keep warm.

4 Add mushrooms to the skillet and sauté for 2 minutes, or until softened. Add reserved marinade, increase heat to high, and cook, stirring continuously, for 2 minutes. Reduce heat to low and stir in sour cream. Cook for 2 minutes, stirring continuously, until heated through. Spoon the sauce over the chicken. Garnish with the shredded carrot and celery, if desired, and serve immediately.

4 SERVINGS
PREP TIME: 15 MINUTES PLUS
30 MINUTES TO MARINATE
COOKING TIME: 14 MINUTES

EQUIPMENT LIST

Paring knife
Citrus juicer
Vegetable peeler
Grater
Paper towels
Plastic wrap
Fork
Large, shallow glass dish
Large skillet
Large, metal spatula
Kitchen spoon

Chicken and brandy make a spirited recipe in more ways than one!

Grilled Chicken Wings with Lemon and Pepper

16   chicken wings (3½ pounds)
Lemon wedges (optional)
Chopped fresh parsley (optional)

LEMON-PEPPER MARINADE
(⅔ CUP)
½   cup fresh lemon juice
1   tablespoon grated lemon rind
3   large cloves garlic, finely chopped
⅓   cup olive oil
⅛   teaspoon salt, or to taste
½   teaspoon ground white pepper

For a delicious variation on this recipe try Orange-Flavored Chicken Wings. Substitute ½ cup of orange juice and 1 tablespoon of grated orange rind for the lemon juice and rind. Add 3 to 4 drops of hot pepper sauce and 1 teaspoon of dried crumbled rosemary leaves to the marinade. Proceed as directed.

Cut the wings at the joints and serve them as an appetizer or leave them whole and accompany with baked potatoes and coleslaw for an inexpensive dinner.

1   Rinse the chicken wings under cold running water and pat dry with paper towels.

2   To make the Lemon-Pepper Marinade: In a large, shallow glass dish, combine the lemon juice and rind and garlic. Stir in the oil, salt, and pepper. Add the chicken wings, turning to coat. Cover the dish with plastic wrap and marinate at room temperature for 15 minutes, turning occasionally.

3   Prepare a charcoal grill until the coals form white ash, preheat a gas grill to high, or preheat the broiler.

4   Remove the chicken wings from the marinade and place on the grill or under the broiler 4″ from the heat source. Grill or broil the chicken wings, brushing frequently with the marinade, for 5 minutes. Turn the chicken wings, brush with the marinade, and grill or broil for 4 to 5 minutes more, or until the juices run clear when the meat is pierced with a knife.

5   Transfer the chicken wings to a serving platter. Garnish with the lemon wedges and chopped fresh parsley, if desired, and serve immediately.

A citrus marinade adds zest to grilled chicken wings.

4 SERVINGS
PREP TIME: 10 MINUTES PLUS
15 MINUTES TO MARINATE
COOKING TIME: 10 MINUTES

EQUIPMENT LIST

Citrus juicer
Grater
Utility knife
Paper towels
Plastic wrap
Large, shallow glass dish
Kitchen spoon
Charcoal or gas grill or broiler pan
Pastry brush
Large, metal spatula

Chicken Livers
with Marsala and Fresh Sage

Here is a quick sauté dish that could be served over buttered noodles or steamed white rice for a superb but simple weekday meal.

1¼	pounds chicken livers, trimmed and halved
⅔	cup all-purpose flour
½	teaspoon paprika
⅛	teaspoon salt, or to taste
	Freshly ground black pepper
1	tablespoon olive oil
3	tablespoons unsalted butter
4	shallots, finely chopped (¼ cup), or ¼ cup finely chopped white onion
6	ounces mushrooms, trimmed, cleaned, and halved (1¾ cups)
¾	cup Marsala or Madeira wine
2	tablespoons chopped fresh sage, or 2 teaspoons dried sage leaves, crumbled
2	tablespoons chopped fresh parsley

4 SERVINGS
PREP TIME: 10 MINUTES
COOKING TIME: 12 MINUTES

EQUIPMENT LIST

Utility knife
Pepper mill
Paper towels
Large, shallow dish
Large skillet
Kitchen spoon
Slotted spoon
Plate

1 Rinse the chicken livers under cold running water. Pat dry with paper towels. In a large, shallow dish, combine the flour, paprika, salt, and pepper. Dredge the livers in the flour mixture, coating them completely and shaking off the excess.

2 In a large skillet, heat the oil and 1 tablespoon of the butter over moderate heat for 1 minute. Add the chicken livers and sauté for 3 to 5 minutes, or until browned and cooked through. Using a slotted spoon, transfer the livers to a plate lined with paper towels to drain.

3 In the same skillet over moderate heat, melt 1 tablespoon of the remaining butter. Add shallots and sauté for 1 minute, or until softened. Add mushrooms and sauté for 3 to 4 minutes, or until lightly golden. Add Marsala and sage, stirring to scrape up the browned bits from the bottom of the pan. Bring mixture to a boil over high heat. Boil for 1 minute, stirring continuously, or until sauce is slightly reduced. Remove the skillet from the heat. Stir in the remaining 1 tablespoon of butter and the parsley.

4 Transfer the chicken livers to individual serving plates. Spoon some sauce over the livers and serve immediately.

Spicy Chicken and Rice Casserole

Accompany this hearty dish with a fresh spinach salad.

1	chicken breast (2 halves), boned (1¼ pounds)
1	teaspoon paprika
¼	teaspoon ground red pepper (cayenne)
½	teaspoon salt, or to taste
¼	teaspoon coarsely ground black pepper
2	tablespoons olive oil
4	large cloves garlic, finely chopped
2	stalks celery, chopped (1 cup)
1	large green bell pepper, cored, seeded, and chopped (1 cup)
4	green onions (including tops), chopped (½ cup)
2	cups chicken stock or canned broth
1	cup long-grain white rice

4 SERVINGS
PREP TIME: 15 MINUTES
COOKING TIME: 30 MINUTES

EQUIPMENT LIST

Utility knife
Large baking dish
Large, shallow dish
Paper towels
Aluminum foil
Kitchen spoon
Slotted spoon
Large skillet
Plate

1 Preheat the oven to 350° F. Lightly grease a large baking dish. Rinse the chicken breast under cold running water. Pat dry with paper towels. Cut the chicken into 2″ pieces.

2 In a large, shallow dish, combine the paprika, ground red pepper, salt, and black pepper. Add the chicken pieces, turning to coat with the spices.

3 In a large skillet, heat the oil over moderate heat for 1 minute. Add the chicken and sauté for 2 to 3 minutes, or until lightly browned. Using a slotted spoon, transfer the chicken to a plate lined with paper towels to drain.

4 Add the garlic, celery, bell pepper, and green onions to the skillet and sauté for 4 to 5 minutes, or until the vegetables begin to soften. Add the rice, stirring to coat with the oil. Add the stock. Increase the heat to high and bring the mixture to a boil. Stir in the reserved chicken pieces.

5 Transfer mixture to the prepared dish and cover tightly with aluminum foil. Bake for 25 to 30 minutes, or until the rice is tender and the liquid is absorbed. Remove the baking dish from the oven, discard the foil, and serve immediately.

Sweet and Savory Chicken Salad

This recipe is delectable enough to justify cooking a chicken especially for it. However leftover chicken will taste equally good as will leftover turkey, making it an excellent way to use up the Thanksgiving bird.

Try varying the types of dried fruit. Substitute 2 ounces (¼ cup) of dried apples and 2 ounces (¼ cup) of golden raisins for the apricots and figs and proceed as directed.

2 cups chopped cooked chicken
2 ounces dried apricots, cut in slivers (¼ cup)
2 ounces dried figs, cut in slivers (¼ cup)
2 stalks celery, chopped (1 cup)
2 ounces sharp Cheddar cheese, cut in small cubes (½ cup)
2 ounces coarsely chopped pecans (½ cup)
Red cabbage leaves (optional)
Belgian and curly endive leaves (optional)

ORANGE-MUSTARD DRESSING (¾ CUP)
1 tablespoon grated orange rind
2 tablespoons orange juice
1 tablespoon white wine vinegar
1 teaspoon Dijon-style mustard
1 tablespoon honey
2 tablespoons olive oil
⅛ teaspoon salt, or to taste
Freshly ground black pepper
1 small red onion, finely chopped (¾ cup)
1 teaspoon poppy seeds (optional)

1 To make the Orange-Mustard Dressing: In a small bowl, whisk together the orange rind and juice, vinegar, mustard, and honey. Slowly add the oil, whisking vigorously until well blended, or place the ingredients in a small jar with a tight-fitting lid and shake to blend. Season to taste with the salt and pepper. Stir in the onion and the poppy seeds, if desired. Cover the bowl with plastic wrap and let stand for 1 hour to allow the flavors to blend.

2 To make the chicken salad: In a large bowl, mix together the chicken, apricots, figs, celery, Cheddar cheese, and pecans. Pour the dressing over chicken salad, tossing gently to combine. Cover the bowl with plastic wrap and chill in the refrigerator for 3 hours, or overnight.

3 Line individual serving plates with the cabbage and endive leaves, if desired. Spoon the chicken salad on top of the leaves. Serve immediately.

4 SERVINGS
PREP TIME: 20 MINUTES PLUS
4 HOURS TO STAND AND CHILL

EQUIPMENT LIST
Utility knife
Grater
Pepper mill
Small bowl
Large bowl
Wire whisk
Kitchen spoon
Plastic wrap

Pretty and piquant, this chicken dish will be a hit any time of year.

Warm Smoked Chicken Salad
with Plums and Walnuts

4	ounces snow peas, trimmed and strings removed (1¼ cups)
2	ounces walnut pieces (½ cup)
¼	cup olive oil
¼	cup red wine vinegar
1	large clove garlic, finely chopped
1½	teaspoons ground ginger
8	ounces smoked chicken breast, cut in narrow strips (1½ cups)
4	medium-size ripe plums, pitted and sliced (2 cups)
1	8-ounce can baby corn, drained and rinsed (1 cup)
6	green onions (including tops), sliced diagonally (¾ cup)
1	head Romaine lettuce, rinsed and torn in pieces (optional)

Smoked poultry, which is available in the deli section of most large supermarkets, has become increasingly popular. The subtle flavor comes from the wood chips used in the smoking process. Serve this flavorful salad as a summertime main dish.

1 Bring a medium-size saucepan of salted water to a boil over high heat. Add the snow peas and cook for 1 minute, or until crisp-tender. Drain snow peas well, rinse under cold running water, and drain again. Set aside.

2 In a large skillet over moderate heat, toast the walnuts for 5 minutes, or until fragrant. Stir the walnuts occasionally while toasting to prevent burning. Remove the skillet from the heat and transfer the walnuts to a plate lined with paper towels. Set aside.

3 Return the skillet to the heat and add the oil, vinegar, garlic, and ginger. Bring to a boil over high heat, then reduce the heat to moderately low. Add the chicken, plums, corn, green onions, snow peas, and walnuts. Cook, stirring frequently, for 2 minutes, or until heated through. Remove the skillet from the heat. Line individual serving plates with lettuce leaves. Spoon the salad into the center of the leaves. Serve immediately.

4 SERVINGS
PREP TIME: 25 MINUTES
COOKING TIME: 10 MINUTES

EQUIPMENT LIST

Utility knife
Colander
Medium-size saucepan
Large skillet
Kitchen spoon
Plate
Paper towels

Turkey Pasta Salad
with Tarragon Dressing

6	ounces fresh or dried tri-colored rotini pasta (2½ cups)
1	pound roasted or smoked turkey, cut in 1½″ pieces
1	small yellow onion, chopped (½ cup)
1	stalk celery, chopped (½ cup)
2	tablespoons chopped fresh parsley
½	teaspoon dried tarragon leaves, crumbled

TARRAGON DRESSING (⅓ CUP)

1	tablespoon vegetable oil
2	tablespoons tarragon vinegar
1	tablespoon fresh lemon juice
2	tablespoons mayonnaise
1	teaspoon Dijon-style mustard
¼	teaspoon salt, or to taste
Freshly ground black pepper	

There is no doubt that this recipe is particularly useful around the holidays, but there is no need to wait for leftovers to try this pasta salad. Sliced roast turkey is widely available in supermarkets any time of year. Or, for a different flavor, use smoked ham.

The tri-colored rotini give this salad eye appeal, making it particularly suitable for a buffet. For a party, prepare the salad, without the dressing, up to two days ahead, cover with plastic wrap, and refrigerate. Add the dressing just before serving.

1 Bring a large saucepan of water to a boil over high heat. Cook the rotini in the boiling water for 1 to 2 minutes for fresh rotini and 8 to 10 minutes for dried, or until al dente. Drain the pasta well, rinse under cold running water, and drain again.

2 Meanwhile, make the Tarragon Dressing: In a small bowl, whisk together the oil, vinegar, lemon juice, mayonnaise, and mustard, or place the ingredients in a small jar with a tight-fitting lid and shake well to blend. Season to taste with the salt and pepper.

3 In a large bowl, combine the pasta, turkey, onion, celery, parsley, and tarragon and mix well. Pour the dressing over the salad, tossing gently to coat. Serve immediately.

4 SERVINGS
PREP TIME: 15 MINUTES
COOKING TIME: 10 MINUTES

EQUIPMENT LIST

Utility knife
Citrus juicer
Pepper mill
Large saucepan
Colander
Small bowl
Large bowl
Wire whisk
Kitchen spoon

Pacific Chicken and Tomato Salad

This artfully arranged salad is an interesting departure from the norm. The chicken is poached in a stock that is enhanced with fresh ginger, which adds a subtle, lightly pungent taste. If time is short, use cooked turkey breast meat from the deli.

2	whole chicken breasts, skinned and boned (1½ pounds), rinsed and patted dry
3	cups chicken stock or canned broth
1	1″ piece peeled, fresh ginger, cut in half
2	large ripe tomatoes, seeded and chopped (3 cups)
3	stalks celery, chopped (1½ cups)
1	ounce whole roasted cashews (¼ cup) (optional)
1	green onion (green part only) (optional)

PACIFIC DRESSING (⅔ CUP)

3	tablespoons rice wine vinegar or cider vinegar
2	teaspoons honey
2	teaspoons peeled, grated fresh ginger
1	large clove garlic, finely chopped
1	teaspoon sesame oil
1	teaspoon dry mustard
⅓	cup peanut oil or vegetable oil
⅛	teaspoon salt, or to taste
Freshly ground black pepper	

1 In a large skillet, combine the chicken, stock, and ginger pieces. Bring mixture to a simmer over moderately high heat. Reduce heat to low and cook, partially covered, for 15 minutes, or until chicken is tender. Remove from the heat and cool the chicken in the liquid.

2 To make the Pacific Dressing: In a small bowl, whisk together the vinegar, honey, 2 teaspoons of ginger, garlic, sesame oil, and mustard. Slowly add the peanut oil, whisking vigorously until well blended, or place the ingredients in a small jar with a tight-fitting lid and shake to blend. Season to taste with the salt and pepper.

3 In a large, shallow glass dish, combine the tomatoes and celery. Pour half the dressing over the vegetables and reserve the remaining half. Cover the dish with plastic wrap and marinate at room temperature for 30 minutes to allow the flavors to blend.

4 Using a slotted spoon, transfer the chicken to a cutting board. Discard liquid and ginger. Cut the chicken into thin slices.

5 Arrange the chicken slices in a fan shape on a serving plate. Drizzle some dressing over the chicken. Spoon the vegetables into the center of the plate. Garnish with cashews and green onion, if desired. Serve with any remaining dressing.

4 SERVINGS
PREP TIME: 15 MINUTES PLUS
30 MINUTES TO MARINATE
COOKING TIME: 15 MINUTES

EQUIPMENT LIST

Paper towels
Plastic wrap
Vegetable peeler
Utility knife
Grater
Pepper mill
Large skillet with lid
Kitchen spoon
Slotted spoon
Small bowl
Wire whisk
Large, shallow glass dish
Cutting board

Entertain with ease and style with this knock out chicken salad.

Turkey Steaks
with Caper Cream Sauce

Rubbing the dry herb mixture into the turkey has the same effect as marinating, and quickly imparts a wonderful flavor.

8 turkey steaks (3 ounces each)
2 tablespoons unsalted butter
¾ cup light cream
¼ cup chicken stock or canned broth
1 tablespoon capers, drained and rinsed
Sprigs of fresh rosemary and sage (optional)

HERB RUB

1½ teaspoons dried rosemary leaves, crumbled
1 teaspoon dried sage leaves, crumbled
½ teaspoon salt, or to taste
½ teaspoon coarsely ground black pepper
2 large cloves garlic, finely chopped

1 Rinse the turkey steaks under cold running water and pat dry with paper towels.

2 To make the Herb Rub: In a small bowl, combine the 1½ teaspoons of rosemary, the 1 teaspoon of sage, salt, pepper, and garlic. Rub the mixture into both sides of the turkey steaks, cover with plastic wrap, and let stand for 15 minutes.

3 In a large skillet over moderate heat, melt the butter. Add the turkey steaks and cook for 5 minutes on each side, or until the steaks are lightly golden and the juices run clear when the meat is pierced with a knife.

4 Transfer the turkey steaks to a serving platter and keep warm. Add the cream, stock, and capers to the skillet, and cook over moderate heat, stirring continuously, for 3 minutes, or until the sauce has thickened slightly.

5 Spoon the sauce over the turkey steaks. Garnish with sprigs of fresh rosemary and sage, if desired, and serve immediately.

4 SERVINGS
PREP TIME: 5 MINUTES PLUS
15 MINUTES TO STAND
COOKING TIME: 13 MINUTES

EQUIPMENT LIST

Strainer
Utility knife
Paper towels
Plastic wrap
Small bowl
Kitchen spoon
Large skillet
Large, metal spatula

Turkey Scaloppine
with Red Wine and Mushrooms

Here, turkey steaks are quickly sautéed, then finished with a red wine and mushroom sauce. Accompany them with a wild rice and steamed green beans.

4 turkey steaks (5 ounces each)
¼ cup all-purpose flour
¼ teaspoon salt, or to taste
¼ teaspoon coarsely ground black pepper
2 tablespoons vegetable oil
2 tablespoons unsalted butter
½ cup dry red wine or water
½ cup chicken stock or canned broth
2 ounces mushrooms, trimmed, cleaned, and sliced (¾ cup)

1 Rinse the turkey steaks under cold running water and pat dry with paper towels. On a sheet of wax paper, combine the flour, salt, and pepper. Dredge the turkey steaks in the flour mixture, coating them completely and shaking off the excess.

2 In a large skillet, heat the oil and 1 tablespoon of the butter over moderately high heat for 1 minute. Add the turkey steaks and cook for 5 minutes on each side, or until lightly golden and the juices run clear when the meat is pierced with a knife. Transfer the turkey steaks to a serving platter and keep warm.

3 Add the wine and stock to the skillet, stirring to scrape up the browned bits from the bottom of the pan. Add the mushrooms and cook, stirring frequently, for 3 to 4 minutes, or until the mushrooms are tender and the liquid is reduced to about ¼ cup. Remove the skillet from the heat. Stir the remaining tablespoon of butter into the sauce until melted and smooth.

4 Spoon the sauce and the mushrooms over the turkey steaks and serve immediately.

4 SERVINGS
PREP TIME: 15 MINUTES
COOKING TIME: 9 MINUTES

EQUIPMENT LIST

Utility knife
Paper towels
Wax paper
Large skillet
Large, metal spatula
Kitchen spoon

Quick Turkey and White Bean Chili

2	tablespoons olive oil
1	medium-size yellow onion, chopped (1 cup)
1	medium-size red or green bell pepper, cored, seeded, and cut in ¼″ pieces (¾ cup)
2	large cloves garlic, finely chopped
1½	pounds ground turkey
2	tablespoons chili powder, or to taste
¾	teaspoon ground cumin
½	teaspoon dried oregano leaves, crumbled
⅛	teaspoon ground cinnamon
¼	teaspoon salt, or to taste
2	tablespoons balsamic vinegar
1	16-ounce can whole tomatoes in purée
1	12-ounce bottle light or dark beer, or 1½ cups chicken stock or canned broth
1	16-ounce can cannellini or other white beans, drained and rinsed
4	green onions (including tops), chopped (½ cup)

Lime wedges (optional)

Traditional chili recipes made with beef and dried beans require long, slow cooking. This recipe, which uses ground turkey and canned cannellini, is quick to prepare, tastes great, and is lower in saturated fat than recipes made with red meat. Of course, it can be prepared ahead and reheated on the stove. Serve it with warm flour tortillas, tortilla chips, and a bowl of sour cream sprinkled with green onions.

1 In a large skillet, heat 1 tablespoon of the oil over moderate heat for 1 minute. Add the onion, bell pepper, and garlic and sauté for 5 minutes, or until the onion is translucent. Using a slotted spoon, transfer the vegetables to a plate.

2 Heat the remaining 1 tablespoon of oil over moderate heat for 1 minute. Add the ground turkey. Cook, stirring continuously, for 5 to 7 minutes, or until no pink color remains. Add the chili powder, cumin, oregano, cinnamon, and salt. Cook, stirring continuously, for 1 to 2 minutes more, or until fragrant.

3 Add the vinegar, tomatoes with the purée, and beer. Increase heat to high and bring the mixture to a boil, stirring to break up the tomatoes. Add the sautéed vegetables and reduce the heat to low. Simmer, covered, for 15 minutes. Stir in the beans and ¼ cup of the green onions. Cook, uncovered, stirring occasionally, for 3 minutes more, or until the mixture has thickened slightly and the beans are heated through.

4 Spoon chili into a serving dish and sprinkle with the remaining ¼ cup of green onions. Garnish with lime wedges, if desired, and serve immediately.

This dish is ideal for entertaining and can easily be doubled for crowds.

4 SERVINGS
PREP TIME: 10 MINUTES
COOKING TIME: 34 MINUTES

EQUIPMENT LIST

Utility knife
Colander
Large skillet with lid
Kitchen spoon
Slotted spoon
Plate

Thai-Style Turkey Stir-Fry

3	turkey steaks (5-6 ounces each)
3	teaspoons Chinese sesame oil
1	teaspoon granulated sugar
1	large clove garlic, finely chopped
¼	teaspoon peeled, grated fresh ginger, or ⅛ teaspoon ground ginger
8	ounces dried fettuccine
1	tablespoon vegetable oil
1	medium-size red bell pepper, cored, seeded, and cut in narrow strips (1 cup)
1	medium-size green bell pepper, cored, seeded, and cut in narrow strips (1 cup)
2	green onions (including tops), sliced diagonally in 1″ pieces (¼ cup)
4	teaspoons low-sodium soy sauce
3	tablespoons coarsely chopped unsalted roasted peanuts
1	tablespoon snipped fresh chives (optional)
	Sprigs of fresh cilantro (coriander leaves) or fresh parsley (optional)

Full of color and crunch, this recipe is a complete meal in itself. Chinese sesame oil, which is available in larger supermarkets and Asian food stores, gives the dish an authentic Asian flavor.

1 Rinse the turkey steaks under cold running water and pat dry with paper towels. Cut into ½″ strips.

2 In a medium-size bowl, combine 1 teaspoon of the sesame oil, sugar, garlic, and ginger. Add the turkey strips, turning to coat. Cover the dish with plastic wrap and marinate in the refrigerator for 1 hour, stirring the turkey occasionally.

3 Bring a large saucepan of water to a boil over high heat. Cook fettuccine in boiling water for 8 to 10 minutes, or until al dente.

4 Meanwhile, in a preheated wok or large, heavy skillet, heat the vegetable oil over high heat for 1 minute, or until very hot. Add the red and green bell peppers and green onions and stir-fry for 3 to 4 minutes, or until crisp-tender. Using a slotted spoon, transfer the vegetables to a plate.

5 Remove the turkey from the marinade. Discard the liquid. Add the turkey to the wok and stir-fry for 3 minutes, or until lightly browned and cooked through. Return the bell peppers and green onions to the wok and add the remaining 2 teaspoons of sesame oil, the soy sauce, and peanuts. Stir-fry for 1 minute, or until heated through.

6 Drain the fettuccine well and transfer to individual serving plates. Spoon the turkey mixture on top. Garnish with snipped fresh chives and sprigs of fresh cilantro, if desired, and serve immediately.

4 SERVINGS
PREP TIME: 10 MINUTES PLUS
1 HOUR TO MARINATE
COOKING TIME: 10 MINUTES

Equipment List

Utility knife
Vegetable peeler
Grater
Paper towels
Plastic wrap
Medium-size bowl
Kitchen spoon
Slotted spoon
Large saucepan
Wok or large, heavy skillet
Plate
Colander

Turkey adds a novel basis to this Thai-inspired stir-fry.

Orange-Soy Turkey Tenderloins

2   turkey tenderloins (10 ounces each)
Sprigs of fresh rosemary (optional)

ORANGE-SOY MARINADE (¾ CUP)

½   cup orange juice
3   tablespoons low-sodium soy sauce
4   teaspoons olive oil
2   large cloves garlic, finely chopped
3   sprigs of fresh parsley
3   sprigs of fresh rosemary, or ½ teaspoon dried rosemary leaves, crumbled
¼   teaspoon coarsely ground black pepper
⅛   teaspoon crushed red pepper flakes (optional)

The tenderloin is the thin strip of white meat that lies beneath each side of the turkey breast. It's very lean and tender and is among the cuts that are lowest in fat. Here, the pungent marinade glazes the tenderloin to a glorious golden color and helps the meat remain moist and succulent. Serve the tenderloins with steamed rice, peas, corn, and carrots.

1   Rinse the turkey tenderloins under cold running water and pat dry with paper towels.

2   To make the Orange-Soy Marinade: In a large, shallow glass dish, combine the orange juice, soy sauce, oil, garlic, parsley, 3 sprigs of fresh rosemary, pepper, and red pepper flakes, if desired. Add the tenderloins, turning to coat. Cover with plastic wrap and marinate in refrigerator for 2 hours, turning the tenderloins occasionally.

3   Preheat the broiler. Remove the tenderloins from the marinade and place the tenderloins under the broiler 4" from the heat source. Broil, brushing every 2 minutes with the marinade, for 7 to 8 minutes on each side, or until the juices run clear when the meat is pierced with a knife.

4   Remove the tenderloins from the broiler. Using a large metal spatula, transfer tenderloins to a carving board, cover with aluminum foil, and let stand for 5 minutes to allow juices to settle.

5   Cut the tenderloins diagonally into ⅜" slices and arrange on individual serving plates. Spoon any juices in the broiler pan over the tenderloins. Garnish with sprigs of fresh rosemary, if desired, and serve immediately.

4 SERVINGS
PREP TIME: 5 MINUTES PLUS
2 HOURS 5 MINUTES TO MARINATE
AND STAND
COOKING TIME: 16 MINUTES

EQUIPMENT LIST

Utility knife
Carving knife
Paper towels
Plastic wrap
Aluminum foil
Large shallow, glass dish
Kitchen spoon
Broiler pan
Pastry brush
Carving board

These turkey tenderloins are low in calories and fat but marinating makes them high in flavor.

Juniper Roast Squab

Squab are young, farm-raised pigeons. Cook squab just until the breast meat is medium-rare, with rosy juices.

4   squab (1 pound each), giblets removed
⅛   teaspoon salt, or to taste
Freshly ground black pepper
8   dried juniper berries, lightly crushed
1   small yellow onion, cut in 4 wedges
½   lemon, cut in 4 wedges
2   tablespoons olive oil
1   tablespoon unsalted butter

1 Preheat the oven to 450° F. Rinse the squab under cold running water and pat dry with paper towels. Season inside and out with the salt and pepper. Place 2 juniper berries, a wedge of onion, and a wedge of lemon in each cavity.

2 Truss squab by tucking the wing tips under the body and placing a length of kitchen twine under the tail and wing tips. Cross the twine between the squab legs, then loop each end around the knob of the nearest leg, then around the tail again. Pull the ends of the twine so that the legs are gathered to the body neatly and tied securely.

3 Combine oil and butter in a roasting pan and place in oven for 3 to 5 minutes, or until very hot but not browned. Arrange the squab, breast-sides down, in the pan and cook for 12 minutes.

4 Remove pan from oven and turn each squab breast-side up. Baste with pan juices. Cook for 15 minutes more, or until juices run pink (not red) when meat is pierced with a knife. Remove pan from oven, cover loosely with aluminum foil, and let stand for 5 minutes.

5 Place the squab on a carving board and, with a sharp knife, cut off the leg-thigh portions. Cut the breast, with wings attached, from the rib cage and arrange the sections on a serving platter. Repeat as directed with the remaining squab and serve immediately.

8 SERVINGS
PREP TIME: 15 MINUTES PLUS
5 MINUTES TO STAND
COOKING TIME: 30 MINUTES

EQUIPMENT LIST

Utility knife
Carving knife
Pepper mill
Paper towels
Aluminum foil
Kitchen twine
Strainer
Roasting pan
Poultry baster or kitchen spoon
Fork
Carving board

Raspberry-Orange Duck Breasts

Duck breasts are available at butchers and specialty food stores.

2   whole boneless duck breasts with skin, split (1¾ pounds)
8   ounces baby carrots, peeled (2 cups)
4   small yellow squash, cut in 1″ rounds and quartered (4 cups)
8   ounces fresh asparagus spears, trimmed or 8 ounces frozen asparagus, thawed and drained

RASPBERRY-ORANGE SAUCE
    (2 CUPS)

1½   cups fresh raspberries, or 1 12-ounce package frozen raspberries, thawed
¼   cup orange juice
2   teaspoons grated orange rind
1-2 tablespoons granulated sugar

1 Preheat the broiler. Rinse the duck breasts under cold running water and pat dry with paper towels. Using a sharp knife, cut the duck skin almost through to the meat, making a criss-cross pattern.

2 To make the sauce: In a small saucepan, combine the raspberries, orange juice and rind, and 1 tablespoon of sugar, or to taste. Cook over moderate heat, stirring occasionally, for 8 minutes, or until the raspberries are puréed. Strain the mixture through a fine sieve into a small bowl, discard solids, and return sauce to the pan. Keep warm.

3 Place the duck breasts, skin-sides up, under the broiler 4″ from the heat source. Broil for 5 to 6 minutes on each side.

4 Meanwhile, place carrots in a steamer set over boiling water in a large saucepan and cook, covered, for 3 minutes. Add squash, then place asparagus on top and cook, covered, for 3 to 4 minutes more, or until the vegetables are crisp-tender. Remove the pan from the heat.

5 Remove the duck breasts from the broiler and place on a carving board. Using a sharp knife, remove the skin from the breasts and discard. Slice the duck breasts diagonally ¼″ thick. Arrange the slices on individual serving plates. Spoon some of the sauce over the slices and serve with the vegetables.

4 SERVINGS
PREP TIME: 15 MINUTES
COOKING TIME: 27 MINUTES

EQUIPMENT LIST

Vegetable peeler
Utility knife
Carving knife
Grater
Broiler pan
Paper towels
Small saucepan
Large saucepan with lid
Kitchen spoon
Fine sieve
Small bowl
Vegetable steamer
Carving board

VEGETABLES

$\mathcal{V}$egetable dishes can add much to the success of a meal. Stuffed, sautéed, puréed, and baked—the variety of cooking methods rivals the wealth of vegetables now available. Cooks will be spoiled for choice by the recipes in this chapter, and amazed by how little time they take.

Glazed Vegetable Skillet.

Glazed Vegetable Skillet

Carrots and celery are given an imaginative twist in this subtly-flavored dish. Its colorful presentation makes it a perfect accompaniment to roast or grilled pork or chicken.

2	ounces slivered almonds (½ cup)
4	medium-size carrots, peeled and cut in ½″ thick pieces (3 cups)
4	stalks celery, cut in ½″ thick pieces (2 cups)
½	stick (¼ cup) unsalted butter
2	tablespoons honey
1	tablespoon orange juice
½	teaspoon ground allspice
¼	teaspoon salt, or to taste
	Freshly ground black pepper

1 To toast the almonds: Preheat the oven to 350° F. Spread the almonds in a thin layer on a baking sheet. Toast for 8 to 10 minutes, or until golden brown. Stir the almonds occasionally while toasting to prevent burning. Remove the baking sheet from the oven and set aside.

2 Bring a medium-size saucepan of water to a boil over high heat. Add the carrots and celery. Reduce the heat to moderate and cook, uncovered, for 5 minutes, or until the vegetables are crisp-tender. Drain well, rinse under running cold water, and drain again. Pat the vegetables dry with paper towels.

3 In a large skillet over moderate heat, melt the butter. Add the honey, orange juice, and allspice and cook, stirring occasionally, for 1 minute. Add the carrots and celery, tossing to coat. Cook, stirring frequently, for 8 to 10 minutes, or until the vegetables are glazed and sauce has thickened slightly. Season to taste with the salt and pepper.

4 Transfer the glazed vegetable mixture to a serving dish and serve immediately.

4 SERVINGS
PREP TIME: 15 MINUTES
COOKING TIME: 15 MINUTES

EQUIPMENT LIST

Vegetable peeler
Utility knife
Pepper mill
Baking sheet
Kitchen spoon
Medium-size saucepan
Colander
Paper towels
Large skillet

Marinated Tomato Wheels

Here is one of the easiest and most elegant ways to serve ripe tomatoes. They are wonderful with roast or grilled meats as well as fish or egg dishes and make a colorful decoration around a meat or vegetable platter.

To serve them baked: Prepare the tomatoes as directed but marinate for 45 minutes. Place them in a shallow baking dish and sprinkle each with 1 tablespoon of grated Parmesan cheese. Bake, uncovered, at 375° F. for 10 to 15 minutes, or until the tomatoes are tender but still hold their shape and the cheese is lightly browned.

2	large ripe tomatoes
1	large clove garlic, finely chopped
1	tablespoon Dijon-style mustard
¼	cup red wine vinegar
1	teaspoon dried oregano leaves, crumbled
1	teaspoon dried basil leaves, crumbled
½	teaspoon dried rosemary leaves, crumbled
½	cup olive oil
¼	teaspoon salt, or to taste
	Freshly ground black pepper
	Sprigs of fresh parsley (optional)

1 Using a small, sharp knife, halve the tomatoes crosswise making a zigzag cut. Place the tomatoes in a shallow glass or ceramic dish. In a small bowl, combine the garlic, mustard, vinegar, oregano, basil, and rosemary. Slowly add the oil, whisking vigorously until well blended, or place the ingredients in a small jar with a tight-fitting lid and shake to blend. Season to taste with the salt and pepper.

2 Pour the dressing over the tomatoes. Cover the dish with plastic wrap and marinate the tomatoes at room temperature for 30 minutes to allow the flavors to blend. Spoon the dressing over the tomatoes occasionally.

3 Using a slotted spoon, transfer the marinated tomatoes to a serving platter, garnish with sprigs of fresh parsley, if desired, and serve immediately.

4 SERVINGS
PREP TIME: 15 MINUTES PLUS
30 MINUTES TO MARINATE

EQUIPMENT LIST

Utility knife
Paring knife
Pepper mill
Shallow glass dish
Small bowl
Wire whisk
Plastic wrap
Kitchen spoon
Slotted spoon

Ginger Vegetable Kebabs

The vegetables in this do-ahead recipe make a stunning combination of colors, flavors, and textures. However, they require different cooking times. To remedy this, the potatoes, carrots, and artichokes are steamed ahead of time to ensure even cooking when grilling.

4   small red-skinned potatoes, scrubbed and halved (12 ounces)

8   baby artichokes, trimmed (1 pound)

1   small carrot, peeled and cut in 4 1¼″ slices (1 cup)

8   large mushrooms, cleaned

4   small plum tomatoes, cut in half crosswise (12 ounces)

1   medium-size yellow summer squash, trimmed and cut in 1″ pieces (2 cups)

1   medium-size red or green bell pepper, cored, seeded, and cut in 1″ pieces (¾ cup)

GINGER MARINADE (¾ CUP)

2   tablespoons red wine vinegar

1   teaspoon Dijon-style mustard

1   teaspoon low-sodium soy sauce

½   teaspoon ground ginger

1   large clove garlic, chopped

2   teaspoons fresh lemon juice

½   cup olive oil

Freshly ground black pepper

1   Place the potatoes in a steamer set over boiling water in a large saucepan. Cook, covered, for 10 minutes. Add the artichokes and carrot and cook, covered, for 10 minutes more. Remove the steamer from the water and cool the vegetables slightly.

2   Meanwhile, make the Ginger Marinade. In a small bowl, whisk together the vinegar, mustard, soy sauce, ginger, garlic, and lemon juice. Slowly add the oil, whisking vigorously until well blended, or place the ingredients in a small jar with a tight-fitting lid and shake to blend. Season to taste with the pepper.

3   Arrange the potatoes, artichokes, carrot, mushrooms, tomatoes, squash, and bell pepper alternately on four 10″ metal skewers. Place the kebabs in a large, shallow glass dish. Pour the marinade over the vegetables, turning to coat. Cover the dish loosely with plastic wrap and marinate the vegetables, turning occasionally, for 30 minutes at room temperature, or up to 2 hours in the refrigerator.

4   Prepare a charcoal grill until the coals form white ash, preheat a gas grill to high, or preheat the broiler.

5   Remove the kebabs from the marinade and reserve the liquid. Place kebabs on the grill or under the broiler 4″ from the heat source. Grill or broil, brushing occasionally with the marinade, for 5 minutes on each side, or until the vegetables are browned. Transfer the kebabs to a serving platter. Serve immediately.

4 SERVINGS
PREP TIME: 10 MINUTES PLUS 30 MINUTES TO MARINATE
COOKING TIME: 30 MINUTES

EQUIPMENT LIST

Vegetable brush
Utility knife
Vegetable peeler
Citrus juicer
Pepper mill
Vegetable steamer
Large saucepan with lid
Small bowl
Wire whisk
4 10″ metal skewers
Large, shallow glass dish
Plastic wrap
Charcoal or gas grill or broiler pan
Pastry brush

Basil Pea Purée

3 tablespoons salted butter or margarine

2 green onions (including tops), finely chopped (¼ cup)

1 16-ounce package frozen peas (3 cups)

2 cups shredded Boston lettuce

2 tablespoons finely chopped fresh basil, or 1 teaspoon dried basil leaves, crumbled

3 tablespoons sour cream

⅛ teaspoon salt, or to taste

Freshly ground black pepper

Fresh basil leaves (optional)

Orange rind (optional)

Sour cream (optional)

Purées add a different dimension to a meal when they are served with other vegetables. They also offer convenience because they can be prepared ahead of time, then heated gently before serving. Any leftovers can be used to liven up soups, dressings, or sauces. In this recipe there is no need to thaw and drain the frozen peas because their small amount of moisture helps to steam the other ingredients.

For a peppery version of this dish, substitute 1 bunch of watercress, stemmed and chopped, for the basil.

1 In a small saucepan over moderate heat, melt the butter. Add green onions and sauté for 5 minutes, or until softened. Add the peas and cover with the lettuce and chopped basil. Cook, covered, over low heat for 10 minutes, or until the peas are tender.

2 Pour the vegetable mixture into a blender or a food processor fitted with the metal blade. Blend or process for 1 minute, or until smooth, scraping down the side of the bowl whenever necessary.

3 Return the purée to the saucepan and stir in the 3 tablespoons of sour cream. Season to taste with the salt and pepper. Reheat over moderate heat for 1 to 2 minutes. Garnish the purée with fresh basil leaves, orange rind, and sour cream, if desired, and serve immediately.

4 Alternatively, prepare the purée ahead and then reheat it gently over low heat, stirring occasionally, for 5 to 7 minutes, or until heated through. Garnish as directed.

4 SERVINGS
PREP TIME: 10 MINUTES
COOKING TIME: 17 MINUTES

EQUIPMENT LIST

Utility knife
Pepper mill
Small saucepan with lid
Kitchen spoon
Blender or food processor with metal blade
Rubber spatula

Melting Onions

2 large Spanish onions, peeled (2 pounds)

2 cups chicken stock or canned broth

Here's a terrific lowfat and low-calorie alternative to fried onions. Use it as a topping for hamburgers, or as an accompaniment to steaks.

1 Cut the onions in half, then cut each half into 4 wedges. Separate the onion layers. In a large, heavy saucepan, combine the onions and 1 cup of the stock. Bring to a boil, covered, over high heat. Boil for 5 minutes, stirring twice.

2 Reduce the heat to low. Cook the onions, uncovered, stirring occasionally, for 5 minutes, or until the stock is absorbed and the onions begin to stick to the bottom of pan.

3 Add 2 tablespoons of the stock, stirring to scrape up the browned bits from the bottom of the pan. Cook for 10 to 12 minutes, adding the remaining stock, 2 tablespoons at a time, until the onions are very tender and the stock is absorbed. Transfer the onions to a serving dish and serve immediately.

4 SERVINGS
PREP TIME: 5 MINUTES
COOKING TIME: 25 MINUTES

EQUIPMENT LIST

Utility knife
Large, heavy saucepan with lid
Kitchen spoon

Golden Crusty Potatoes

1 tablespoon unsalted butter
1 tablespoon vegetable oil
2 pounds Idaho or other baking potatoes, peeled and cut in ½" pieces (4 cups)
1½ teaspoons whole mustard seeds
2 tablespoons sesame seeds
1 teaspoon ground turmeric
⅛ teaspoon salt, or to taste
Freshly ground black pepper

These spicy potatoes make a great accompaniment to an Indian-style meal.

1 In a large, nonstick skillet, heat the butter and oil over moderately high heat for 1 minute. Add the potatoes and cook, stirring occasionally, for 5 minutes.

2 Using a mortar and pestle or the end of a rolling pin, crush the mustard seeds. Add mustard seeds, sesame seeds, and turmeric to the potatoes, stirring to coat. Season to taste with the salt and pepper. Reduce the heat to low and cook, covered, stirring occasionally, for 15 minutes, or until potatoes are tender when tested with a fork. Remove skillet from the heat and serve immediately.

4 SERVINGS
PREP TIME: 10 MINUTES
COOKING TIME: 20 MINUTES

EQUIPMENT LIST

Vegetable peeler
Utility knife
Pepper mill
Large, nonstick skillet with lid
Kitchen spoon
Mortar and pestle or rolling pin
Fork

Sweet Potato Home-Fries

2 pounds sweet potatoes, peeled and cut in 1½" chunks (4 cups)
1 tablespoon unsalted butter
1 tablespoon vegetable oil
1 large yellow onion, finely chopped (1½ cups)
1 large clove garlic, finely chopped
½ teaspoon caraway seeds
½ teaspoon dill seeds
⅛ teaspoon salt, or to taste

Include these subtly flavored sweet potatoes on a brunch menu.

1 Bring a large saucepan of water to a boil over high heat. Cook the potatoes in the boiling water for 10 minutes, or until tender when tested with a fork. Drain well.

2 In a large skillet, heat the butter and oil over moderate heat for 1 minute. Add onion and garlic and sauté for 5 minutes, or until onion is translucent. Add potatoes, tossing to coat. Sprinkle with the caraway and dill seeds and cook, stirring frequently, for 8 to 10 minutes. Season to taste. Remove skillet from the heat. Serve immediately.

4 TO 6 SERVINGS
PREP TIME: 10 MINUTES
COOKING TIME: 25 MINUTES

EQUIPMENT LIST

Vegetable peeler
Utility knife
Large saucepan
Fork
Colander
Large skillet
Kitchen spoon

Home-fries using sweet potatoes make a welcome change from white potatoes.

Spaghetti Squash with Tomato Coulis

1 spaghetti squash
(3½ pounds)
¼ teaspoon salt, or to taste
Freshly ground black pepper
2 green onions (including
tops), chopped (¼ cup)
2 ounces shredded sharp
Cheddar cheese (½ cup)
½ cup half-and-half

TOMATO COULIS

3 tablespoons olive oil
2 large cloves garlic, finely
chopped
4 large ripe tomatoes, peeled,
seeded, and chopped, or 1
14-ounce can whole
tomatoes, drained, seeded,
and chopped

Spaghetti squash has a remarkable flesh that resembles strands of pasta when cooked. Serve it with a delicate sauce, such as a tomato coulis—a simple reduced purée that can be used hot or cold.

For an easy way to peel tomatoes: Bring a large saucepan of water to a boil over high heat. Fill a large bowl with ice water. Drop the tomatoes into the boiling water. Let stand for 30 seconds. Using a slotted spoon, transfer the tomatoes to the ice water for 5 seconds. Remove the tomatoes from the water, make a small cut in the surface, and peel off the skin.

1 Cut the spaghetti squash in half and scoop out the seeds with a spoon. Place the squash, cut-sides down, in a large saucepan, and add enough water to cover. Bring the water to a boil over high heat, reduce the heat to moderate, and cook, covered, for 20 minutes, or until the skin is tender when pierced with a knife.

2 Meanwhile, make the Tomato Coulis. In a medium-size skillet, heat the oil over moderate heat for 1 minute. Add the garlic and sauté for 2 minutes, or until golden. Add the tomatoes and cook, stirring continuously, for 1 minute. Remove the skillet from the heat and set aside.

3 Preheat the broiler. Lightly grease a large, flameproof baking dish. Drain the squash and, using a fork, loosen the spaghetti-like strands from the shell. Scoop them into the baking dish and season to taste with the salt and pepper. Spoon the tomato mixture over the squash and sprinkle with the green onions and the Cheddar cheese. Pour the half-and-half over the top.

4 Place the dish under the broiler 4″ from the heat source. Broil for 5 to 10 minutes, or until the cheese is melted and is beginning to bubble. Serve immediately.

4 SERVINGS
PREP TIME: 10 MINUTES
COOKING TIME: 30 MINUTES

EQUIPMENT LIST

Pepper mill
Utility knife
Paring knife
Grater
Kitchen spoons
Large saucepan with lid
Medium-size skillet
Large, flameproof baking dish
Colander
Fork

Sweet and Sour Marinated Brussels Sprouts

1	pound Brussels sprouts, trimmed and rinsed (4 cups) or 16-ounce package frozen Brussels sprouts, thawed and drained
¼	cup tarragon vinegar or white wine vinegar
¼	cup olive oil
1	teaspoon granulated sugar
⅛	teaspoon salt, or to taste
⅛	teaspoon hot pepper sauce
1	large clove garlic, finely chopped
1	small yellow onion, finely chopped (½ cup)
1	small tomato, peeled, seeded, and finely chopped (½ cup)
1	stalk celery, thinly sliced (½ cup)
2	teaspoons chopped fresh sage (optional)

Brussels sprouts are at their best when their delicate, slightly nutty flavor and compact shape are preserved. Choose small, compact Brussels sprouts that have a bright green color. For faster and more even cooking, cut an X in the stem ends with a sharp knife.

This make-ahead recipe is equally good when 2 cups of cauliflower florets are substituted for 2 cups of the Brussels sprouts. Simply proceed as directed with the recipe below. Either way this is a pretty, piquant side dish that goes well with roast poultry or pork.

1 Place the Brussels sprouts in a steamer set over boiling water in a medium-size saucepan and steam, covered, for 10 minutes, or until crisp-tender. Remove the steamer from the water and transfer the Brussels sprouts to a serving dish.

2 Meanwhile, in a small bowl, combine the vinegar, oil, sugar, salt, hot pepper sauce, and garlic until well blended. Pour the mixture over the Brussels sprouts, turning gently to coat. Stir in the onion, tomato, and celery. Cover the dish with plastic wrap and marinate in the refrigerator for 6 hours, or overnight. Stir the vegetable mixture occasionally.

3 Remove the serving dish from the refrigerator, discard the plastic wrap, and sprinkle with the chopped fresh sage, if desired. Serve the Brussels sprouts chilled or at room temperature.

4 SERVINGS
PREP TIME: 10 MINUTES PLUS 6 HOURS TO MARINATE
COOKING TIME: 10 MINUTES

EQUIPMENT LIST
Utility knife
Paring knife
Vegetable steamer
Medium-size saucepan with lid
Small bowl
Wire whisk
Kitchen spoon
Plastic wrap

Sprout lovers will adore this smashing side dish, and those who don't will be converted to this versatile vegetable.

Butter-Crumbed Cauliflower

1 head cauliflower, leaves trimmed (12 ounces)
2 tablespoons white wine vinegar or cider vinegar
3 tablespoons salted butter or margarine
2 tablespoons coarse dry bread crumbs
¼ teaspoon salt, or to taste
Freshly ground black pepper
1 tablespoon chopped fresh parsley
Grated Parmesan cheese (optional)

Plain boiled cauliflower is given a new lease with the addition of a bread crumb and Parmesan cheese topping. The vinegar that is added to the cooking liquid provides an unexpected piquancy. Serve this dish as an accompaniment to roast beef or lamb dishes.

When purchasing cauliflower, choose a firm, compact head with a crisp, creamy white curd (the white portion of the vegetable). Avoid cauliflower with brown curd as this indicates it is not fresh. Old cauliflower will also have a stronger flavor and smell when cooked.

1 Place the cauliflower, head down, in a large saucepan and cover with cold water and the vinegar. Bring to a boil over high heat. Reduce the heat to low and cook, partially covered, for 20 minutes, or until the cauliflower is crisp-tender. Drain well, rinse under cold running water, and drain again. Cool the cauliflower slightly and then break into florets.

2 In a medium-size skillet over moderate heat, melt the butter. Add the cauliflower and sauté for 6 to 8 minutes, or until lightly golden. Add the bread crumbs, tossing to coat. Season to taste with the salt and pepper. Cook over moderately low heat, stirring frequently, for 3 minutes, or until the bread crumbs are crisp and golden.

3 Stir in the parsley and cook for 1 minute more. Transfer the cauliflower to a serving dish. Sprinkle with Parmesan cheese, if desired, and serve immediately.

4 SERVINGS
PREP TIME: 10 MINUTES
COOKING TIME: 31 MINUTES

EQUIPMENT LIST

Utility knife
Pepper mill
Large saucepan with lid
Colander
Medium-size skillet
Kitchen spoon

Grape and Winter Squash Sauté

3 tablespoons salted butter
⅛ teaspoon curry powder
⅛ teaspoon ground cinnamon
1 medium-size butternut squash, peeled, seeded, and cut in 1″ pieces (4 cups), or 4 cups frozen butternut squash, thawed
¼ cup finely chopped celery
2 green onions (including tops), finely chopped (¼ cup)
3 tablespoons water
¼ teaspoon salt
1½ cups red or green seedless grapes, cut in half
3 tablespoons finely chopped fresh parsley
Freshly ground black pepper
1 ounce chopped cashews (¼ cup)

This unusual combination of grapes and butternut squash is spiced with curry powder and cinnamon. It will add a cheerful grace note to the holiday table, yet it is simple enough to prepare for everyday meals. The sauté goes particularly well with the complete range of poultry entrées, from chicken to squab.

1 In a large skillet over low heat, melt the butter. Add the curry powder and cinnamon and cook, stirring occasionally, for 1 minute. Add the squash, celery, and green onions and sauté for 2 minutes. Add the water and salt. Cook, covered, over low heat for 10 minutes, stirring frequently.

2 Stir in the grapes and cook, covered, for 8 to 10 minutes, or until the squash is just tender and the liquid is absorbed. Stir in the parsley and season to taste with the pepper. Transfer the sauté to a serving dish. Garnish with the cashews and serve immediately.

4 SERVINGS
PREP TIME: 15 MINUTES
COOKING TIME: 25 MINUTES

EQUIPMENT LIST

Vegetable peeler
Kitchen spoon
Utility knife
Pepper mill
Large skillet with lid
Kitchen spoon

Vegetable Tempura

A Japanese specialty, tempura are batter coated foods, in this case vegetables, that are quickly deep-fried and served with a dipping sauce. Serve them as an appetizer, a first course, or as a meatless entrée.

Vegetable oil
1   medium-size yam or sweet potato, peeled and cut in very thin slices (1½ cups)
1   small yellow squash, trimmed and cut in ¼″ thick slices (1 cup)
1   medium-size yellow onion, cut in ¼″ thick slices (1½ cups)
1   small eggplant, trimmed and cut in ¼″ thick slices (1½ cups)
1   medium-size red or green bell pepper, cored, seeded, and cut in ¼″ thick strips (1 cup)
12 snow peas, strings removed
6   medium-size mushrooms, trimmed and cleaned

Dipping Sauce (¾ cup)

½   cup low-sodium soy sauce
2   tablespoons rice wine vinegar or cider vinegar
1   teaspoon Chinese sesame oil
2   teaspoons granulated sugar
½   teaspoon peeled, grated fresh ginger, or ¼ teaspoon ground ginger
2   green onions (white parts only), thinly sliced (2 tablespoons)

Tempura Batter

1⅔ cups all-purpose flour
1   teaspoon baking soda
2   cups cold water
1   egg yolk

Serve guests this Japanese favorite —it will disappear fast!

1 Preheat the oven to 200° F. To make the Dipping Sauce: In a small bowl, combine the soy sauce, vinegar, sesame oil, sugar, and ginger. Stir in the green onions. Set aside.

2 To make the Tempura Batter: In a medium-size bowl, combine the flour, baking soda, water, and egg yolk.

3 In a wok, large, heavy skillet, or deep-fat fryer, heat 3″ of the vegetable oil over moderately high heat to 375° F. Dip a small batch of vegetables into the batter to coat evenly. Carefully add some of vegetables to the oil (avoid overcrowding). Cook, turning occasionally with a fork, for 1 to 2 minutes, or until batter is crisp and golden and the vegetables are crisp-tender. Using a slotted spoon, transfer the vegetables to a plate lined with paper towels to drain, then to a baking pan, and keep them warm in the oven. Working in small batches, dip, cook, drain, and keep warm the remaining vegetables as directed.

4 Transfer the vegetables to a serving platter. Serve immediately with the Dipping Sauce.

6 SERVINGS
PREP TIME: 25 MINUTES
COOKING TIME: 18 MINUTES

Equipment List

Vegetable peeler
Utility knife
Grater
Small bowl
Medium-size bowl
Kitchen spoons
Slotted spoon
Wok, large, heavy skillet, or deep-fat fryer
Fork
Plate
Paper towels
Baking pan

Zucchini-Potato Pancakes

Take advantage of a glut of zucchini in the garden or farmer's market and try this easy and flavorful gloss on standard potato pancakes. Serve them on their own for a light lunch or as dinner fare, or offer them as an accompaniment to roast lamb. Either way they're delicious!

For a colorful variation, substitute a large sweet potato, peeled and grated, for the Idaho potato and proceed as directed.

2	small zucchini, trimmed and shredded (2 cups)
1	large Idaho or other baking potato, peeled and shredded (2 cups)
1	small yellow onion, finely chopped (½ cup)
¼	cup all-purpose flour
2	large eggs, lightly beaten
2	teaspoons curry powder
⅛	teaspoon salt, or to taste
	Ground white pepper
	Vegetable oil
	Plain lowfat yogurt or sour cream (optional)

1 Preheat the oven to 200° F. Squeeze as much liquid as possible from the shredded zucchini and potato, then place the vegetables in a large bowl. Add the onion, flour, eggs, and curry powder and stir until well blended. Season with the salt and pepper.

2 In a large, heavy skillet, heat ½″ of oil over moderately high heat for 2 minutes, or until very hot. Cook the pancakes in 3 batches, using 3 tablespoons of the batter for each. With a large, metal spatula, flatten each pancake to ¼″ thick. Cook for 3 to 4 minutes on each side, or until crisp and golden.

3 Using the spatula, transfer the pancakes to a plate lined with paper towels to drain, then to a baking pan. Keep the pancakes warm in the oven. Cook the remaining batter as directed. Stir the batter occasionally and add more oil to the skillet, if needed.

4 Transfer the pancakes to a serving platter. Garnish with the yogurt, if desired, and serve immediately.

4 SERVINGS OR 12 PANCAKES
PREP TIME: 15 MINUTES
COOKING TIME: 26 MINUTES

EQUIPMENT LIST

Utility knife
Grater
Vegetable peeler
Paper towels
Small bowl
Large bowl
Wire whisk
Kitchen spoons
Large, heavy skillet
Large, metal spatula
Plate
Baking pan

Caramelized New England Vegetables

This flavorsome medley is a variation of caramelized onions, which are often served at Thanksgiving. It makes an excellent accompaniment to roasts, particularly during the winter months, when parsnips, carrots, and turnips are at their peaks of perfection.

3	small parsnips, peeled and cut in 1½″ lengths (1 cup)
3	small carrots, peeled and cut in 1½″ lengths (¾ cup)
1	medium-size turnip, peeled and cut in 8 wedges (1½ cups)
⅛	teaspoon salt, or to taste
2	tablespoons granulated sugar
¼	cup (½ stick) unsalted butter
8	red radishes, trimmed
8	green onions (including tops), cut in 1″ lengths (1 cup)
	Freshly ground black pepper
	Sprigs of fresh parsley (optional)

1 In a large skillet, place the parsnips, carrots, and turnip. Add the salt, sugar, butter, and enough water to cover. Cook, uncovered, stirring occasionally, over high heat, for 10 minutes, or until the vegetables are slightly tender on the outside but still firm in the center.

2 Add the radishes and cook, uncovered, stirring occasionally, for 15 minutes more, or until the vegetables are almost tender and the water has nearly evaporated.

3 Add the green onions. Cook, uncovered, stirring occasionally, for 2 minutes more, or until the vegetables are caramelized and golden. Season to taste with the pepper.

4 Transfer the vegetables to a serving bowl. Garnish with sprigs of fresh parsley, if desired, and serve immediately.

4 SERVINGS
PREP TIME: 10 MINUTES
COOKING TIME: 25 MINUTES

EQUIPMENT LIST

Vegetable peeler
Utility knife
Pepper mill
Large skillet
Kitchen spoon

Summer-Fresh Succotash

5   medium-size ears corn, shucked, or 2 cups frozen corn kernels, thawed
2   medium-size ripe tomatoes, peeled, seeded, and chopped (2 cups)
¼   teaspoon salt
1½   cups water
1   10-ounce package baby lima beans, partially thawed
1   teaspoon chopped fresh thyme, or ¼ teaspoon dried thyme leaves, crumbled
2   teaspoons unsalted butter
⅓   cup heavy cream (optional)
Freshly ground black pepper
2   tablespoons chopped fresh parsley

When made with fresh corn, this vegetable standby takes on a surprisingly lively flavor. This recipe is based on "misickquatash," a dish of corn and beans that early American settlers learned to make from the Narraganset Indians. Though not part of the original recipe, the tomatoes add color and flavor to this old favorite.

1   If using fresh corn, hold 1 ear of corn vertically over a shallow dish and, using a sharp knife, cut the kernels from the cob. Repeat cutting the kernels from the remaining ears of corn as directed.

2   Place the tomatoes in a colander set in a large bowl. Sprinkle the tomatoes with the salt and let drain for 15 to 20 minutes.

3   Meanwhile, in a medium-size saucepan, bring the water to a boil over high heat. Add the lima beans and half of the thyme to the boiling water. Reduce the heat to low and cook, partially covered, for 15 minutes, or until the beans are tender but not mushy. Holding a lid over the pan, pour off some of the cooking liquid, leaving the beans quite moist.

4   Gently stir in the corn kernels, 1 teaspoon of the butter, and the cream, if desired. Season to taste with the pepper. Cook, covered, over moderately low heat, stirring occasionally, for 3 minutes, or until the corn is crisp-tender.

5   Uncover the pan and stir in the tomatoes and the remaining thyme. Cook, uncovered, stirring continuously, over low heat for 1 minute, or until the cream has thickened slightly and the tomatoes are heated through. Remove the pan from the heat. Stir in the parsley and the remaining 1 teaspoon of the butter.

6   Transfer the succotash to a serving dish and serve immediately.

Succotash is a delicious update on a Native American recipe.

4 SERVINGS
PREP TIME: 20 MINUTES
COOKING TIME: 25 MINUTES

EQUIPMENT LIST

Paring knife
Utility knife
Pepper mill
Shallow dish
Colander
Large bowl
Medium-size saucepan with lid
Kitchen spoon

Kale Gratinée

Kale is a winter green that is in season from late November until early March. It is an excellent source of vitamin A and calcium. Look for dark green kale with slightly curly stalks and avoid any yellowed or wilted leaves.

Here, kale acquires a tasty twist when it is baked with bacon, garlic, and cheese. Serve this hearty dish with roast chicken or broiled salmon.

2 pounds kale, stemmed and chopped (8 cups)
1 6-ounce piece slab bacon, rind removed and cut in ½" pieces
2 large cloves garlic, finely chopped
Freshly ground black pepper
4 ounces shredded Jarlsberg cheese (1 cup)
3 tablespoons fresh white bread crumbs

1 Rinse the kale thoroughly under cold running water and drain well. Bring a large stockpot of water to a boil over high heat. Add the kale and stir well. Cook, uncovered, for 15 minutes, or until the kale is crisp-tender.

2 Meanwhile, preheat the oven to 400° F. In a large skillet, cook the bacon over moderate heat for 8 to 10 minutes, or until crisp. Add the garlic and cook for 30 seconds, or until fragrant. Remove the skillet from the heat.

3 Drain the kale thoroughly and add to the skillet with the bacon and garlic, stirring gently to combine. Season to taste with the pepper.

4 Transfer the kale mixture to a 2-quart casserole. Sprinkle with the cheese and bread crumbs. Bake, uncovered, for 20 minutes, or until the cheese is melted and the crumbs are golden. Serve immediately.

6 SERVINGS
PREP TIME: 25 MINUTES
COOKING TIME: 20 MINUTES

EQUIPMENT LIST

Utility knife
Pepper mill
Grater
Colander
Stockpot
Kitchen spoon
Large skillet
2-quart casserole

Get the goodness of greens with this satisfying baked kale dish.

*S*alads feature largely in home cooked meals because they're healthful, versatile, and easy to prepare. There are salads for every season of the year. Experiment with serving them as main courses as well as side dishes—some are even interchangeable.

Fruited Pork Salad with Endive.

Fruited Pork Salad with Endive

1   pound pork tenderloin, cut in
     ¼″ slices
½   teaspoon salt, or to taste
Freshly ground black pepper
1   tablespoon vegetable oil
2   heads Belgian endive
1   small head chicory (curly
     endive) or leafy lettuce
2   small pink grapefruit, peeled
     and segmented
1½   cups green seedless grapes
1   cup strawberries, hulled and
     halved

POPPY SEED DRESSING (½ CUP)

1   teaspoon poppy seeds
¼   cup fresh grapefruit juice
2   teaspoons honey
2   tablespoons red wine vinegar
1   teaspoon Dijon-style mustard
1   tablespoon vegetable oil

This salad has a zesty poppy seed and grapefruit juice dressing that teams perfectly with the pork and fruit. Serve it with whole grain crackers and an assortment of cheeses for a light lunch or supper.

To make slicing the pork tenderloin easier, wrap the meat in aluminum foil or plastic wrap and freeze it for 30 minutes before using.

1   To make the Poppy Seed Dressing: In a small bowl, whisk together the poppy seeds, grapefruit juice, honey, vinegar, and mustard. Slowly add the oil, whisking vigorously until well blended, or place the ingredients in a small jar with a tight-fitting lid and shake to blend. Let stand for 15 minutes to allow the flavors to blend.

2   Meanwhile, make the salad. Sprinkle the pork slices with the salt and pepper. In a medium-size skillet, heat the oil over moderately high heat for 1 minute. Add the pork and cook, turning frequently, for 3 minutes, or until no pink color remains. Remove the skillet from the heat and keep warm.

3   Arrange the endive and the chicory leaves on individual serving plates. Place the pork slices in the center of each plate. Arrange the grapefruit segments, grapes, and strawberries around the pork. Whisk the dressing, drizzle over the salad, and serve immediately.

4 SERVINGS
PREP TIME: 10 MINUTES PLUS
15 MINUTES TO STAND
COOKING TIME: 5 MINUTES

EQUIPMENT LIST

Chef's knife
Paring knife
Pepper mill
Citrus juicer
Small bowl
Wire whisk
Medium-size skillet
Large, metal spatula

Gingery Green Bean and Red Pepper Salad

1   pound green beans, trimmed
2   medium-size red bell peppers,
     cored, seeded, and cut in thin
     strips (2 cups)

GINGER VINAIGRETTE (½ CUP)

1   teaspoon peeled, grated fresh
     ginger
½   teaspoon dry mustard, or 1
     teaspoon Dijon-style mustard
1   tablespoon cider vinegar
3   tablespoons vegetable oil
1   tablespoon olive oil
½   teaspoon salt, or to taste
Freshly ground black pepper
2   teaspoons finely chopped
     fresh cilantro (coriander
     leaves) or fresh parsley
     (optional)

This tasty and attractive green bean salad is a wonderful dish for casual entertaining because it can be prepared several hours in advance and tossed with the fresh herbs at the last minute.

When buying fresh ginger remember that there are two types—young and mature. Young ginger has a pale, thin skin that need not be peeled, while mature ginger has a tougher skin that must be peeled before grating the flesh. Refrigerate fresh ginger, tightly wrapped, for up to a week.

1   Bring a large saucepan of water to a boil over high heat. Cook the green beans in the boiling water for 5 minutes, or until the beans are crisp-tender. Drain well, rinse under cold running water, and drain again. Pat the green beans dry with paper towels. In a large bowl, combine the green beans and bell pepper strips.

2   To make Ginger Vinaigrette: In a small bowl, whisk together the ginger, mustard, and vinegar. Slowly add the vegetable and olive oils, whisking vigorously until well blended, or place the ingredients in a small jar with a tight-fitting lid and shake to blend. Season to taste with the salt and pepper.

3   Pour the vinaigrette over the green beans and bell peppers, tossing gently to coat. Cover the bowl with plastic wrap and let the salad stand at room temperature for 30 minutes to allow the flavors to blend. Just before serving, toss the salad with the fresh cilantro, if desired.

4 SERVINGS
PREP TIME: 10 MINUTES PLUS
30 MINUTES TO MARINATE
COOKING TIME: 5 MINUTES

EQUIPMENT LIST

Utility knife
Vegetable peeler
Grater
Pepper mill
Large saucepan
Colander
Paper towels
Plastic wrap
Large bowl
Small bowl
Kitchen spoon
Wire whisk
Salad servers

Alsace Potato Salad

4	large red-skinned potatoes, scrubbed and cut in ½″ cubes (6 cups)
4	strips lean bacon, chopped
1	small yellow onion, finely chopped (½ cup)
1	stalk celery, finely chopped (½ cup)
¼	cup white wine vinegar
¼	cup water
1	small dill pickle, finely chopped (2 tablespoons)
1	teaspoon granulated sugar
¼	teaspoon dry mustard
¼	teaspoon paprika
⅛	teaspoon salt, or to taste
2	tablespoons chopped fresh parsley (optional)
1	tablespoon snipped fresh chives or chopped green onion tops (optional)

This potato salad is wonderful with veal chops, German-style sausages, or baked ham and a mixed green salad and dark rye bread. For a hearty main dish, add 2 cups of cubed baked ham to the salad.

1 In a large saucepan, combine the potatoes with enough cold water to cover. Bring to a boil over high heat. Reduce the heat to moderately low and cook, partially covered, for 10 minutes, or until the potatoes are tender when tested with a fork. Drain the potatoes well and pat dry with paper towels.

2 Meanwhile, cook the bacon in a large skillet over moderate heat for 8 to 10 minutes, or until crisp. Using a slotted spoon, transfer the bacon to a plate lined with paper towels to drain. Pour off all but 2 tablespoons of the bacon fat from the skillet. Return the skillet to moderate heat.

3 Add the onion and celery to the skillet and sauté for 5 minutes, or until the onion is translucent. Add the vinegar, water, and pickle and bring the mixture to a boil over high heat. Reduce the heat to low and stir in the sugar, mustard, paprika, and salt. Add the potatoes and bacon to the skillet, tossing gently to coat with the dressing.

4 Transfer the potato salad to a serving dish. Garnish with the parsley and chives, if desired, and serve warm.

4 SERVINGS
PREP TIME: 10 MINUTES
COOKING TIME: 15 MINUTES

EQUIPMENT LIST

Vegetable brush
Utility knife
Large saucepan with lid
Fork
Paper towels
Large skillet
Slotted spoon
Kitchen spoon
Plate

Vary traditional potato salad recipes with the addition of bacon and pickle for a taste of the cuisine of Alsace.

Arugula and Roquefort Salad

This elegant salad combines toasted pine nuts and Roquefort, a famous blue-veined French cheese made from ewe's milk. It is aged in caves, under controlled conditions, where a constant natural breeze encourages mold to grow in the cheese, which gives it its characteristic appearance and flavor.

1   ounce pine nuts (pignoli) (¼ cup)
1   small ripe avocado
2   tablespoons fresh lemon juice
2   cups iceberg lettuce, rinsed and torn in pieces
2   cups chicory, rinsed and torn in pieces
1   bunch arugula, coarse stems removed, rinsed
2   ounces Roquefort cheese, crumbled (½ cup)

CHIVE DRESSING (½ CUP)

1   large clove garlic, chopped
2   teaspoons Dijon-style mustard
1   tablespoon snipped fresh chives or chopped green onion tops
1   tablespoon fresh lemon juice
2   tablespoons white wine vinegar
¼   cup olive oil
⅛   teaspoon salt, or to taste
Freshly ground black pepper

1   To toast the pine nuts: In a small skillet over moderate heat, toast the pine nuts, stirring continuously, for 2 minutes, or until fragrant and golden. Remove the skillet from the heat and cool slightly.

2   Peel, pit, and slice the avocado. Place the slices in a medium-size bowl. Sprinkle them with the 2 tablespoons of lemon juice, tossing gently to coat. (Coating the avocado with the lemon juice as soon as it is peeled and/or sliced prevents discoloration.)

3   In a large bowl, combine the iceberg lettuce, chicory, and arugula. Sprinkle with the pine nuts and the Roquefort cheese, tossing gently to combine.

4   To make the Chive Dressing: In a small bowl, whisk together the garlic, mustard, chives, the 1 tablespoon of lemon juice, and vinegar. Slowly add the oil, whisking vigorously until well blended, or place the ingredients in a small jar with a tight-fitting lid and shake to blend. Season to taste with the salt and pepper.

5   Pour the dressing over the salad, tossing gently to coat. Drain the avocado slices, if necessary, and arrange them on top of the salad. Serve immediately.

4 SERVINGS
PREP TIME: 15 MINUTES
COOKING TIME: 2 MINUTES

EQUIPMENT LIST

Citrus juicer
Colander
Paring knife
Kitchen scissors
Pepper mill
Small skillet
Kitchen spoon
Medium-size bowl
Large bowl
Small bowl
Salad servers
Wire whisk

Athens Egg Salad

This zesty egg salad can be served on a bed of lettuce or as a filling for pita pockets for an easy, Greek-inspired lunch dish. For a summer supper, omit the tomatoes from the recipe and use the egg salad as a stuffing for large, home grown tomatoes. Complete the meal with crusty peasant bread.

6   large eggs
½   cup plain lowfat yogurt
2   ounces crumbled feta cheese (½ cup)
¼   cup sliced, pitted black olives
2   green onions (including tops), finely chopped (¼ cup)
¼   teaspoon dried oregano leaves, crumbled
8   ounces ripe plum tomatoes, seeded and chopped (1½ cups)
⅛   teaspoon salt, or to taste
Freshly ground black pepper
6   medium-size pita pockets, split (optional)
2   anchovy fillets, drained, rinsed, and finely chopped (optional)

1   In a large saucepan, combine the eggs with enough cold water to cover. Bring to a boil over high heat. Reduce the heat to low and cook, uncovered, for 15 minutes. Drain well. Place the eggs in a medium-size bowl with enough cold water to cover. Let stand for 15 minutes. Peel and finely chop the eggs.

2   In a medium-size bowl, combine the chopped eggs, yogurt, feta cheese, olives, green onions, and oregano until well blended. Stir in the tomatoes. Season to taste with the salt and pepper.

3   Spoon some egg salad into the pita pockets and top with the chopped anchovies, if desired. Serve immediately.

6 SERVINGS
PREP TIME: 10 MINUTES PLUS
15 MINUTES TO STAND
COOKING 15 MINUTES

EQUIPMENT LIST

Utility knife
Pepper mill
Large saucepan
Colander
Medium-size bowl
Kitchen spoon

Tri-Colored Coleslaw with Dill Dressing

4 cups shredded green cabbage
1 medium-size red bell pepper, cored, seeded, and cut in narrow strips (1 cup)
1 medium-size green bell pepper, cored, seeded, and cut in narrow strips (1 cup)
2 tablespoons chopped red onion
2 tablespoons chopped green onion tops
Sprigs of fresh dill (optional)

DILL DRESSING (⅔ CUP)

¼ cup cider vinegar
¼ cup chopped fresh dill, or 4 teaspoons dried dillweed
⅓ cup olive oil
¼ teaspoon salt, or to taste
⅛ teaspoon coarsely ground black pepper

Coleslaw is always a crowd pleaser. It teams well with grilled poultry and sausages besides being the traditional accompaniment to fried fish. This version is a truly delicious and light alternative to the traditional carrot and cabbage mixture. What's more it's quick to make and can be prepared the night before and kept, covered, in the refrigerator until ready to serve.

1 In a large bowl, mix together the cabbage, red and green bell peppers, and the red and green onions.

2 To make the Dill Dressing: In a small bowl, combine the vinegar and chopped dill. Slowly add the oil, whisking vigorously until well blended, or place the ingredients in a small jar with a tight-fitting lid and shake to blend. Season to taste with the salt and pepper.

3 Pour the dressing over the salad, tossing gently to coat. Cover the bowl with plastic wrap and chill in the refrigerator for at least 1 hour, or until ready to serve. Garnish the coleslaw with sprigs of fresh dill, if desired, and serve chilled or at room temperature.

4 SERVINGS
PREP TIME: 15 MINUTES PLUS
1 HOUR TO CHILL

EQUIPMENT LIST

Chef's knife
Utility knife
Large bowl
Small bowl
Kitchen spoon
Wire whisk
Salad servers
Plastic wrap

Vibrant and refreshing, this salad raises coleslaw to new and tasteful heights.

Tex-Mex Style Black Bean and Rice Salad

This easy and economical salad, with its vibrant colors, makes an excellent side dish. It can also be prepared a day ahead, kept covered, in the refrigerator, and served chilled.

Serve it with roast or grilled poultry or beef, or for a hearty lunch with corn tortillas or oven-baked tortilla chips topped with melted Monterey Jack cheese.

1½ cups water
¾ cup long-grain white rice
1 15-ounce can black beans, drained and rinsed
1 medium-size ripe tomato, seeded and chopped (1 cup)
1 tablespoon chopped flat-leaf parsley
1 tablespoon chopped fresh cilantro (coriander leaves) or fresh parsley
Sprigs of flat-leaf parsley (optional)

TEX-MEX DRESSING (½ CUP)

¼ cup red wine vinegar
1 tablespoon fresh lime juice
¼ teaspoon ground cumin
¼ teaspoon hot pepper sauce
¼ cup olive oil
¼ teaspoon salt, or to taste
Freshly ground black pepper

4 SERVINGS
PREP TIME: 10 MINUTES
COOKING TIME: 20 MINUTES

EQUIPMENT LIST

Strainer
Utility knife
Citrus juicer
Pepper mill
Medium-size saucepan with lid
Kitchen spoon
Fork
Small bowl
Wire whisk

1 In a medium-size saucepan, bring the water to a boil over high heat. Stir in the rice. Reduce the heat to low and cook, covered, for 20 minutes, or until the rice is tender and the liquid is absorbed. Fluff the rice with a fork and transfer to a serving dish.

2 Add the black beans, tomato, the chopped flat-leaf parsley, and the cilantro to the rice. Mix well and set aside.

3 To make the Tex-Mex Dressing: In a small bowl, whisk together the vinegar, lime juice, cumin, and hot pepper sauce. Slowly add the oil, whisking vigorously until well blended, or place the ingredients in a small jar with a tight-fitting lid and shake to blend. Season to taste with the salt and pepper.

4 Pour the dressing over the salad, tossing gently to coat. Garnish with sprigs of flat-leaf parsley, if desired. Serve at room temperature.

This visually appealing salad is characterized by Southwestern flavors that are sure to please.

Cobb Salad

4   strips lean bacon, chopped
Vegetable oil
2   whole chicken breasts
     (4 halves), skinned, boned,
     rinsed, and patted dry
     (1½ pounds)
8   ounces fresh spinach,
     stemmed, rinsed, and cut in
     narrow strips (2 cups)
2   cups shredded red cabbage
2   cups shredded Napa
     (Chinese) cabbage
1   medium-size cucumber,
     peeled, seeded, and chopped
     (1 cup)
4   green onions (including
     tops), thinly sliced (½ cup)
1   medium-size ripe avocado

BLUE CHEESE DRESSING
     (1¼ CUPS)

¼   cup red wine vinegar or
     balsamic vinegar
1   shallot, finely chopped
     (1 tablespoon), or 1
     tablespoon finely chopped
     white onion
1   small clove garlic, finely
     chopped
¼   cup vegetable oil
¼   cup extra virgin olive oil
4   ounces blue cheese, finely
     crumbled (1 cup)
⅛   teaspoon salt, or to taste
Freshly ground black pepper

Cobb Salad was created in 1936 at Hollywood's famous Brown Derby Restaurant. This variation includes some additions to the original recipe.

1 Prepare a charcoal grill until the coals form white ash, preheat a gas grill to high, or preheat the broiler.

2 Meanwhile, in a medium-size skillet, cook the bacon over moderate heat for 8 to 10 minutes, or until crisp. Using a slotted spoon, transfer the bacon to a plate lined with paper towels to drain.

3 Brush the grill rack or broiler pan with oil. Place the chicken breasts on the grill or under the broiler 4″ from the heat source. Grill or broil for 5 to 6 minutes on each side, or until the juices run clear when the meat is pierced with a knife. Set aside to cool slightly.

4 Meanwhile, make the Blue Cheese Dressing. In a small bowl, whisk together the vinegar, shallot, and garlic. Slowly add the vegetable and olive oils, whisking vigorously until well blended, or place the ingredients in a small jar with a tight-fitting lid and shake to blend. Whisk in the cheese and season to taste with the salt and pepper.

5 In a large bowl, combine the spinach, red and Napa cabbages, cucumber, and green onions. Pour half the dressing over the salad greens, tossing gently to coat.

6 Cut chicken into narrow strips. Pit, peel, and cut the avocado into thin slices. Arrange the salad greens on individual serving plates. Top each with some chicken and avocado. Drizzle the remaining dressing over the salad and sprinkle with the bacon. Serve immediately.

4 SERVINGS
PREP TIME: 20 MINUTES
COOKING TIME: 15 MINUTES

EQUIPMENT LIST

Utility knife
Chef's knife
Paper towels
Colander
Vegetable peeler
Pepper mill
Charcoal or gas grill or broiler pan
Medium-size skillet
Slotted spoon
Kitchen spoon
Plate
Pastry brush
Small bowl
Large bowl
Wire whisk
Salad servers

This entrée salad is a great variation on the classic.

Bulgur Salad with Kiwi and Lemon-Mint Dressing

1 whole chicken breast
  (2 halves), skinned and boned
  (8 ounces)
2 tablespoons salted butter or
  margarine
1 cup medium or coarse bulgur
½ cup mushrooms, trimmed,
  cleaned, and sliced
1 small clove garlic, finely
  chopped
2 cups chicken stock or canned
  chicken broth
2 green onions (including
  tops), finely chopped (¼ cup)
1 cup shredded red cabbage
2 ripe kiwi, peeled and sliced
Sprigs of fresh mint (optional)

LEMON-MINT DRESSING (½ CUP)

6 tablespoons fresh lemon juice
1 tablespoon honey
2 teaspoons grated lemon rind
1 tablespoon chopped fresh
  mint, or 1 teaspoon dried
  mint leaves, crumbled
1 tablespoon chopped fresh
  parsley
2 tablespoons vegetable oil
Ground white pepper

Red cabbage and kiwi add pizzazz to this traditional combination of bulgur, lemon, and mint. It is a hearty and healthful salad that makes a refreshing lunch or supper dish.

Bulgur is most familiar as a staple of Middle Eastern cuisines. Its popularity is spreading though, and with good reason. Since bulgur undergoes only minimal processing, it is nutrient-rich and an excellent source of protein, calcium, phosphorous, and potassium. And, because bulgur is steamed before it is dried, ground, and packaged, it requires little in the way of presoaking or cooking.

Although they are derived from the same source—the whole wheat berry—bulgur and cracked wheat are not interchangeable. Cracked wheat is not steamed before it is milled and packaged, and therefore it requires an extended cooking period.

Bulgur is available in three different grinds: coarse, medium, and fine. Medium and coarse are preferred for salads but try all of them and let personal preference be the guide. For maximum shelf life, store bulgur in an airtight container in the refrigerator or freezer. If bulgur is not available in the supermarket, try health food stores.

1 Bring a medium-size saucepan of water to a boil over high heat. Reduce the heat to low. Add the chicken breast and cook, covered, for 10 to 12 minutes, or until no pink color remains. Remove the pan from heat and cool the chicken breast in the liquid.

2 In a large skillet over moderate heat, melt the butter. Add the bulgur and mushrooms and sauté for 5 minutes, or until bulgur is golden brown. Add the garlic and sauté for 30 seconds, or until fragrant. Add the stock and bring to a boil over high heat. Reduce the heat to low and cook, covered, for 15 minutes, or until the bulgur is tender and the liquid is absorbed.

3 Meanwhile, prepare the Lemon-Mint Dressing. In a small bowl, whisk together the lemon juice, honey, lemon rind, the chopped mint, and parsley. Slowly add the oil, whisking vigorously until well blended, or place the ingredients in a small jar with a tight-fitting lid and shake to blend. Season to taste with the pepper.

4 Transfer the bulgur to a medium-size bowl and cool to room temperature. Using a slotted spoon, transfer the chicken breast to a cutting board and discard the liquid. Cut the chicken breast into thin strips and add to the bulgur with the green onions and red cabbage. Pour the dressing over the salad, tossing gently to coat.

5 Cut the kiwi slices into quarters and arrange over the top of the salad. Garnish with sprigs of fresh mint, if desired, and serve the salad chilled or at room temperature. To serve chilled: Cover the bowl with plastic wrap and chill in the refrigerator for 1 hour, or overnight.

4 SERVINGS
PREP TIME: 10 MINUTES
COOKING TIME: 20 MINUTES

EQUIPMENT LIST

Utility knife
Paring knife
Chef's knife
Citrus juicer
Grater
Medium-size saucepan with lid
Large skillet with lid
Kitchen spoon
Slotted spoon
Small bowl
Medium-size bowl
Wire whisk
Cutting board

Asparagus, Carrot, and Pasta Salad

1   pound fresh asparagus
8   ounces medium-size pasta
     shells (2 cups)
2   medium-size carrots, peeled
     and sliced (1½ cups)
1   small yellow onion, finely
     chopped (½ cup)
1   small red or green bell
     pepper, cored, seeded, and
     finely chopped (½ cup)

CELERY SEED DRESSING (½ CUP)

½   teaspoon celery seeds
½   teaspoon dried oregano
     leaves, crumbled
½   teaspoon Dijon-style mustard
2   tablespoons red wine vinegar
     or white wine vinegar
6   tablespoons olive oil
¼   teaspoon salt, or to taste
¼   teaspoon coarsely ground
     black pepper

The arrival of the first asparagus in the stores used to announce that spring was here at last. With agricultural advances, this vegetable is now available from January to July, although the quality and taste vary considerably. Usually, the most flavorful asparagus are those available from April to late June. Serve this asparagus-based salad with assorted cheeses for a smashing lunch dish.

1 To make the Celery Seed Dressing: In a small bowl, mix together the celery seeds, oregano, mustard, and vinegar. Slowly add the oil, whisking vigorously until well blended, or place the ingredients in a small jar with a tight-fitting lid and shake to blend. Season to taste with the salt and pepper.

2 To make the salad: Snap off the woody ends of the asparagus and rinse the spears under cold running water. If the skins seem tough, peel the stalks with a vegetable peeler or sharp knife. Cut the asparagus spears into 2″ pieces and set aside.

3 Bring a large saucepan of water to a boil over high heat. Cook the pasta in the boiling water for 8 to 10 minutes, or until al dente.

4 Meanwhile, bring a medium-size saucepan of water to a boil over high heat. Add the asparagus and carrots and cook for 2 minutes, or until crisp-tender. Drain well, rinse under cold running water, and drain again. Transfer vegetables to a large bowl.

5 Drain the pasta well, rinse under cold running water, and drain again. Add the pasta to asparagus and carrots. Stir in the onion and the bell pepper. Pour the dressing over the vegetables and pasta, tossing gently to coat. Cover the bowl with plastic wrap and chill in the refrigerator for 2 hours to allow the flavors to blend. Serve chilled or at room temperature.

4 SERVINGS
PREP TIME: 10 MINUTES PLUS
2 HOURS TO CHILL
COOKING TIME: 15 MINUTES

EQUIPMENT LIST

Vegetable peeler
Utility knife
Small bowl
Large bowl
Wire whisk
Large saucepan
Medium-size saucepan
Colander
Kitchen spoon
Plastic wrap

Tomato and Red Onion Salad
with Basil Vinaigrette

3 large ripe tomatoes, each cut in 8 slices
2 large red onions, each cut in 12 thin slices
36 yellow or red ripe cherry tomatoes (1 pound), stems removed
⅛ teaspoon salt, or to taste
Ground white pepper
Sprigs of fresh basil (optional)

BASIL VINAIGRETTE (½ CUP)

2 tablespoons red wine vinegar
2 tablespoons finely chopped fresh basil
1 large clove garlic, finely chopped
⅓ cup olive oil
⅛ teaspoon salt, or to taste
Ground white pepper

What better way to enjoy the bounty of summer vegetables and herbs than with a salad that features fresh ripe tomatoes, red onion, and fresh basil. Make sure that the tomatoes are very ripe and juicy and that the salad is served at room temperature to bring out the flavors. Serve the salad as an accompaniment to grilled poultry or beef.

For a light lunch dish, substitute 8 ounces of thinly sliced fresh mozzarella for the red onions and proceed as directed. Offer the tomato and mozzarella salad with crusty Italian bread .

1 To make the Basil Vinaigrette: In a small bowl, combine the vinegar, chopped basil, and garlic. Slowly add the oil, whisking vigorously until well blended, or place the ingredients in a small jar with a tight-fitting lid and shake to blend. Season to taste with the ⅛ teaspoon of salt and the pepper.

2 Arrange 4 tomato slices and 4 onion slices alternately on 6 individual serving plates. Arrange 6 cherry tomatoes in the center of each plate. Season to taste with the ⅛ of teaspoon salt and the pepper. Drizzle the vinaigrette over the salads. Garnish each salad with a sprig of fresh basil, if desired, and serve at room temperature.

Enjoy the lazy days of summer with this terrific, tomato-rich summer salad bathed in a fresh basil vinaigrette.

6 SERVINGS
PREP TIME: 10 MINUTES

EQUIPMENT LIST

Utility knife
Small bowl
Wire whisk

*H*ealthy and wholesome, pasta and grain dishes have come into their own. The recipes that follow are colorful, unusual, and flavorful, and can be served for lunch and dinner, as an entrée or side dish. Plus they only take minutes to make.

Spaghetti Puttanesca.

Spaghetti Puttanesca

12	ounces fresh or dried spaghetti

Grated Parmesan cheese (optional)
Sprigs of fresh basil (optional)

PUTTANESCA SAUCE

3	tablespoons olive oil
3	large cloves garlic, finely chopped
12	ripe plum tomatoes, chopped (6 cups)
1	tablespoon balsamic vinegar or red wine vinegar
6	anchovies, drained, rinsed, and finely chopped
2	tablespoons capers, drained and rinsed
1	tablespoon dried oregano leaves, crumbled
⅛	teaspoon salt, or to taste

Freshly ground black pepper

¼	cup chopped fresh basil
½	cup whole pitted black olives
2	tablespoons grated Parmesan cheese

For a quick and satisfying meal, it's really hard to beat pasta with Puttanesca Sauce. A Sicilian favorite, this pungent sauce is made with garlic, anchovies, capers, and basil, which add character and depth to the tomato base. Serve it with a crisp green salad, herbed garlic bread, and slices of mozzarella cheese sprinkled with coarsely ground black pepper.

1 To make the Puttanesca Sauce: In a large skillet, heat the oil over moderate heat for 1 minute. Add the garlic and sauté for 30 seconds, or until fragrant. Add the tomatoes, vinegar, anchovies, capers, and oregano. Season to taste with the salt and pepper. Cook, uncovered, over moderately low heat, stirring occasionally, for 25 minutes, or until the juices thicken. Stir the chopped basil, olives, and the 2 tablespoons of Parmesan cheese into the sauce and simmer for 5 minutes more, or until heated through.

2 Meanwhile, bring a large stockpot of water to a boil over high heat. Cook the spaghetti in the boiling water for 3 to 4 minutes for fresh pasta and 8 to 10 minutes for dried, or until al dente.

3 Drain the spaghetti well and transfer to a large, shallow serving dish. Spoon some of the Puttanesca Sauce over the spaghetti, tossing gently to coat.

4 Transfer the spaghetti to individual serving plates and top with the remaining sauce. Garnish with Parmesan cheese and sprigs of fresh basil, if desired, and serve immediately.

4 SERVINGS
PREP TIME: 10 MINUTES
COOKING TIME: 32 MINUTES

EQUIPMENT LIST

Paring knife
Utility knife
Strainer
Colander
Pepper mill
Large skillet
Kitchen spoon
Large stockpot
Large, shallow dish
Spaghetti fork

Pasta Carbonara

12	ounces dried small pasta shells (3 cups)
6	strips lean bacon, chopped
4	egg yolks, at room temperature
½	cup light cream or half-and-half
1	tablespoon unsalted butter
2	ounces grated Parmesan cheese (½ cup)
⅛	teaspoon salt, or to taste

Freshly ground black pepper

This rich pasta dish is simplicity itself and can be assembled quickly for unexpected guests. A fresh spinach salad makes a colorful accompaniment.

1 Bring a large stockpot of water to a boil over high heat. Cook the pasta shells in the boiling water for 8 to 10 minutes, or until al dente. Drain well.

2 Meanwhile, cook the bacon in a large skillet over moderate heat for 8 to 10 minutes, or until crisp. Drain off the bacon fat.

3 In a small bowl, combine the egg yolks, cream, and Parmesan cheese. Add the butter and pasta shells to the skillet with the bacon. Stir in the egg yolk mixture and cook, stirring continuously, over low heat for 30 seconds. (Be careful not to overcook the pasta after the egg yolk mixture has been added.) Remove the skillet from the heat. Season to taste with the salt and pepper.

4 Transfer the pasta mixture to individual serving plates and serve immediately.

4 SERVINGS
PREP TIME: 10 MINUTES
COOKING TIME: 11 MINUTES

EQUIPMENT LIST

Utility knife
Small bowl
Pepper mill
Large stockpot
Large skillet
Colander
Wire whisk
Kitchen spoon

Straw and Hay Fettuccine

6 ounces dried egg fettuccine
6 ounces dried spinach fettuccine
2 tablespoons unsalted butter
2 large cloves garlic, finely chopped
12 ounces mushrooms, trimmed, cleaned, and sliced (3½ cups)
1 cup frozen peas, thawed and drained
½ cup light cream or half-and-half
2 ounces grated Parmesan cheese (½ cup)
⅓ cup part-skim ricotta cheese

This colorful pasta dish is easy to prepare and is a good choice for a weekday meal. Add crunch by sprinkling it with cooked, crumbled bacon just before serving. Serve the pasta with steamed vegetables, such as snow peas and asparagus.

1 Bring a large stockpot of water to a boil over high heat. Cook the egg and spinach fettuccine in the boiling water for 8 to 10 minutes, or until al dente. Drain the fettuccine well and return it to the pan.

2 Meanwhile, in a large skillet over moderate heat, melt the butter. Add the garlic and sauté for 30 seconds, or until fragrant. Add mushrooms and sauté for 3 minutes more, or until softened. Stir in the peas. Reduce the heat to moderately low and cook, covered, for 3 to 5 minutes, or until the peas are tender.

3 Add the cream and the Parmesan and ricotta cheeses to the skillet. Cook over moderate heat, stirring frequently, for 2 to 3 minutes, or until heated through.

4 Pour the cream sauce over the pasta, tossing gently to coat. Transfer pasta to individual serving plates and serve immediately.

4 SERVINGS
PREP TIME: 15 MINUTES
COOKING TIME: 12 MINUTES

EQUIPMENT LIST

Utility knife
Colander
Large stockpot
Large skillet with lid
Kitchen spoon
Spaghetti fork

Here's a dish that doubles the pleasure for fettuccine lovers.

Spaghetti with Vegetable Cream Sauce

12 ounces dried spaghetti
Sprigs of fresh basil (optional)
Red leaf lettuce (optional)

VEGETABLE CREAM SAUCE
(4 CUPS)

6 tablespoons unsalted butter
3 tablespoons all-purpose flour
3 cups chicken stock or canned broth
½ cup half-and-half
1 small yellow onion, finely chopped (½ cup)
4 ounces mushrooms, trimmed, cleaned, and sliced (1¼ cups)
1 small zucchini, trimmed and cut in narrow strips (1 cup)
1 15-ounce can artichoke hearts, drained and quartered
2 ounces prosciutto or smoked ham, cut in narrow strips
1 ounce grated Parmesan cheese (¼ cup)
¼ cup chopped fresh basil
⅛ teaspoon coarsely ground black pepper

For casual but stylish entertaining, this dish is the answer. Serve the spaghetti with a tomato and onion salad in a vinaigrette dressing and crusty Italian bread for a festive meal.

1 Bring a large stockpot of water to boil over high heat. Cook the spaghetti in the boiling water for 8 to 10 minutes, or until al dente. Drain the spaghetti well and return it to the pan.

2 Meanwhile, make Vegetable Cream Sauce. In a large saucepan over moderate heat, melt 3 tablespoons of the butter. Slowly add the flour and cook, stirring continuously, for 2 minutes, or until a pale straw color. Stir in the stock, a little at a time, until smooth. Bring the sauce to a boil over high heat. Reduce the heat to low and simmer, uncovered, for 5 minutes. Stir in the half-and-half. Remove the pan from the heat and keep warm.

3 In a large skillet over moderate heat, melt the remaining 3 tablespoons of butter. Add onion and sauté for 2 minutes, or until softened. Add the mushrooms and zucchini and sauté for 2 minutes more. Add artichokes and prosciutto and sauté for 2 minutes more.

4 Stir the vegetable mixture, Parmesan cheese, and chopped basil into the sauce. Season to taste with the pepper. Pour the vegetable sauce over the spaghetti, tossing gently to coat.

5 Transfer the spaghetti to individual serving plates and garnish with sprigs of fresh basil and red leaf lettuce, if desired. Serve immediately.

A vegetable sauce made with artichokes, mushrooms, and zucchini adds a sophisticated touch to spaghetti.

6 SERVINGS
PREP TIME: 15 MINUTES
COOKING TIME: 13 MINUTES

EQUIPMENT LIST

Utility knife
Colander
Large stockpot
Large saucepan
Kitchen spoon
Large skillet
Spaghetti fork

Quick Sesame Noodles

1   pound dried egg noodles
3   tablespoons sesame seeds
4   green onions (green parts only), cut in ½″ pieces (¼ cup)
2   tablespoons Chinese sesame oil
1   tablespoon peanut oil
1   teaspoon Chinese 5-spice powder
⅛   teaspoon salt, or to taste
Ground white pepper
Chopped roasted peanuts (optional)

This simplified version of the classic dish is very easy to make and has a distinct Asian flavor. Serve the noodles hot or chilled as an accompaniment to a spicy chicken, pork, or beef dish.

For chilled sesame noodles: Prepare the recipe as directed. Transfer the noodles to a medium-size bowl and cool to room temperature. Cover the bowl with plastic wrap and chill in the refrigerator for 2 hours. Garnish the chilled noodles with sliced cucumber.

1 Bring a large stockpot of water to a boil over high heat. Cook the noodles in the boiling water for 6 to 8 minutes, or until al dente. Drain well, rinse under cold running water, and drain again.

2 Meanwhile, toast the sesame seeds. In a small skillet over moderate heat, toast the sesame seeds, stirring continuously, for 2 minutes, or until fragrant and golden. Remove the skillet from the heat.

3 Place the green onions in a steamer set over boiling water in a medium-size saucepan and cook, covered, over moderately high heat for 3 to 4 minutes, or until softened. Remove the pan from the heat.

4 In a preheated wok or large, heavy skillet, heat 1 tablespoon of the sesame oil and the peanut oil over high heat for 1 minute, or until very hot. Add the green onions and stir-fry for 1 minute. Add the 5-spice powder and noodles and stir-fry for 1 minute, or until heated through. Add the remaining 1 tablespoon of sesame oil and the sesame seeds, tossing to coat with the oil. Season to taste with the salt and pepper.

5 Transfer the sesame noodles to a serving dish. Garnish with the chopped peanuts, if desired, and serve immediately.

These noodles go beautifully with a selection of Chinese dishes.

6 SERVINGS
PREP TIME: 10 MINUTES
COOKING TIME: 15 MINUTES

EQUIPMENT LIST

Utility knife
Large stockpot
Medium-size saucepan with lid
Colander
Small skillet
Wok or large, heavy skillet
Kitchen spoons
Vegetable steamer

Herbed Orzo and Lamb Pilaf

This delicious main-dish pilaf offers a balanced combination of orzo, bulgur, ground lamb, and fresh herbs. Steamed broccoli or green beans will round out the meal nicely. For an unusual and flavorful side dish omit the lamb and serve the pilaf with roasted meats or poultry.

¼   cup (½ stick) unsalted butter
2   green onions (including tops), finely chopped (¼ cup)
4   ounces orzo (1 cup)
2½ cups chicken stock or canned broth
½   cup coarse bulgur
1   teaspoon vegetable oil
1   large clove garlic, finely chopped
12 ounces ground lamb
1   tablespoon chopped fresh rosemary, or 1 teaspoon dried rosemary leaves, crumbled
1   tablespoon chopped fresh basil, or 1 teaspoon dried basil leaves, crumbled
1   tablespoon chopped fresh parsley
⅛   teaspoon salt, or to taste
⅛   teaspoon coarsely ground black pepper
Sprigs of fresh rosemary (optional)
Sprigs of fresh basil (optional)

1 In a medium-size saucepan over moderate heat, melt the butter. Add the green onions and sauté for 1 minute. Add the orzo and cook, stirring continuously, for 4 minutes. Add the stock and bring the mixture to a boil over moderately high heat. Stir in the bulgur. Reduce the heat to low and simmer, covered, for 20 minutes, or until the orzo and bulgur are tender and the liquid is absorbed. Remove the pan from the heat and let stand, covered, for 10 minutes.

2 Meanwhile, in a medium-size skillet, heat the oil over moderate heat for 1 minute. Add the garlic and sauté for 30 seconds, or until fragrant. Add the lamb and cook, stirring frequently, for 5 minutes, or until no pink color remains. Remove the skillet from the heat and drain off excess fat.

3 Fluff the orzo and bulgur with a fork. Stir the chopped rosemary, basil, parsley, and lamb into the orzo mixture until well blended. Season to taste with the salt and pepper. Garnish with sprigs of fresh rosemary and basil, if desired. Serve immediately.

4 SERVINGS
PREP TIME: 15 MINUTES PLUS
10 MINUTES TO STAND
COOKING TIME: 20 MINUTES

EQUIPMENT LIST

Utility knife
Medium-size saucepan with lid
Kitchen spoon
Medium-size skillet
Fork

For a winter warm-up with a difference, try this wonderful pilaf.

Broccoli-Bowtie Salad
with Warm Walnut Dressing

12 ounces dried bowtie pasta
    (3 cups)
1   small head broccoli, cut in
    florets (4 cups)
1   medium-size red or green bell
    pepper, cored, seeded, and
    cut in narrow strips (1 cup)
2   ounces grated Parmesan or
    Romano cheese (½ cup)
    (optional)

WARM WALNUT DRESSING
    (½ CUP)

4   tablespoons olive oil
1   ounce chopped walnuts
    (¼ cup)
1   large clove garlic, finely
    chopped
3   tablespoons red wine vinegar
1   teaspoon Dijon-style mustard
¼   teaspoon salt, or to taste
Ground white pepper

This warm salad of pasta and vegetables served with an aromatic dressing flavored with toasted walnuts is a snap to prepare. Serve it as a colorful supper dish, or offer it as part of a holiday buffet. It will also make a tasty accompaniment to broiled chicken or steak.

1 Bring a large stockpot of water to a boil over high heat. Cook the pasta in the boiling water for 6 minutes.

2 Add the broccoli to the pasta water (do not drain) and cook for 2 minutes more. Add the bell pepper to the pasta water and cook for 2 minutes more.

3 Meanwhile, make the Warm Walnut Dressing. In a small skillet, heat 2 tablespoons of the oil over moderate heat for 1 minute. Add the walnuts and cook, stirring occasionally, for 3 minutes. Add the garlic and sauté for 30 seconds, or until fragrant. Add the remaining 2 tablespoons of oil, vinegar, and mustard to the skillet. Stir until well combined and heated through. Remove the pan from the heat and season to taste with salt and pepper.

4 Drain the pasta and the vegetables well and transfer to a serving dish. Pour the dressing over the pasta and vegetables, tossing gently to coat. Garnish with the Parmesan cheese, if desired, and serve immediately.

Bowtie pasta, broccoli, and bell pepper tossed in a nutty dressing make this an incomparable dish.

4 SERVINGS
PREP TIME: 10 MINUTES
COOKING TIME: 10 MINUTES

EQUIPMENT LIST

Utility knife
Large stockpot
Small skillet
Kitchen spoon
Colander

Pasta al Forno

This rustic baked pasta dish is sure to be well received by the whole family. If ground veal is not available, substitute ground turkey and proceed as directed. Try making two casseroles and freezing the extra one for later.

12	ounces dried penne or ziti
3	tablespoons olive oil
2	large cloves garlic, finely chopped
8	ounces ground veal
1	28-ounce can whole tomatoes in purée, chopped
¼	cup chopped fresh basil, or 4 teaspoons dried basil leaves, crumbled
½	teaspoon dried oregano leaves, crumbled
⅛	teaspoon salt, or to taste
¼	teaspoon coarsely ground black pepper
2	tablespoons capers, drained and rinsed
8	ounces shredded mozzarella (2 cups)
2	ounces grated Parmesan cheese (½ cup)
¼	cup dry unseasoned bread crumbs

1 Preheat the oven to 400° F. Grease a large baking dish or shallow casserole. Bring a large stockpot of water to a boil over high heat. Cook the penne in the boiling water for 10 to 12 minutes, or until al dente. Drain well.

2 Meanwhile, in a large skillet, heat the oil over moderate heat for 1 minute. Add the garlic and sauté for 30 seconds, or until fragrant. Add the ground veal and cook, stirring frequently, for 5 minutes, or until no pink color remains.

3 Add the tomatoes with the purée, basil, and oregano to the veal mixture. Season to taste. Cook, stirring frequently, for 10 minutes, or until the sauce has thickened slightly. Stir in the capers.

4 In a large bowl, combine the penne, veal mixture, 1½ cups of the mozzarella cheese, and the Parmesan cheese. Transfer the mixture to the prepared baking dish. Sprinkle the remaining ½ cup of mozzarella cheese and the bread crumbs over the top.

5 Bake for 15 minutes, or until the top is golden. Remove the baking dish from the oven. Let stand for 5 minutes before serving.

6 SERVINGS
PREP TIME: 5 MINUTES PLUS
5 MINUTES TO STAND
COOKING TIME: 32 MINUTES

EQUIPMENT LIST

Utility knife
Strainer
Grater
Large baking dish
Large stockpot
Colander
Large skillet
Kitchen spoon
Large bowl

Egg Noodles and Cabbage

This delicious combination of noodles and cabbage is simple to prepare and can save the day in the winter when fresh vegetables are in short supply. It makes a great accompaniment to pork chops, or turn the dish into a savory one-pot meal by adding 2 cups of thinly sliced cooked ham when incorporating the noodles and basil. Proceed as directed.

Choose cabbage with leaves that are brightly colored and crisp-looking. The head of cabbage should feel heavy for its size. Firm, compact cabbage can be stored in the refrigerator, unwashed and tightly wrapped, for up to 2 weeks. The looser leaf varieties will keep for up to a week.

3	tablespoons salted butter or margarine
4	cups shredded green cabbage
1	medium-size green or red bell pepper, cored, seeded, and cut in thin strips (1 cup)
¼	cup water
12	ounces dried medium-width egg noodles (3 cups)
1	tablespoon chopped fresh basil, or 1 teaspoon dried basil leaves, crumbled
¼	teaspoon salt, or to taste
	Freshly ground black pepper

1 In a large skillet over moderately low heat, melt the butter. Stir in the cabbage and bell pepper, tossing to coat with the butter. Add the water and cook, covered, stirring occasionally, for 15 minutes, or until the vegetables are crisp-tender.

2 Meanwhile, bring a large stockpot of water to a boil over high heat. Cook the noodles in the boiling water for 6 to 8 minutes, or until al dente. Drain well, rinse under cold running water, and drain again.

3 Stir the noodles and basil into the cabbage mixture. Cook, covered, over low heat for 10 minutes, or until the noodles are just heated through. Season to taste with the salt and pepper. Transfer the noodle mixture to individual serving plates. Serve immediately.

4 SERVINGS
PREP TIME: 15 MINUTES
COOKING TIME: 25 MINUTES

EQUIPMENT LIST

Chef's knife
Utility knife
Pepper mill
Large skillet with lid
Kitchen spoon
Large stockpot
Colander

Ratatouille-Rice Primavera

This springtime version of ratatouille, the classic Mediterranean vegetable stew, is combined here with boiled white rice. Serve it as a side dish with roasted meats or chicken, or on its own as a light entrée.

2 cups water
1 cup long-grain white rice
1 tablespoon olive oil
3 small cloves garlic, finely chopped
1 small yellow onion, sliced (1 cup)
1 small green bell pepper, cored, seeded, and cut in narrow strips (¾ cup)
1 small red bell pepper, cored, seeded, and cut in narrow strips (¾ cup)
1 medium-size zucchini, trimmed and cut in narrow strips (2 cups)
1 medium-size yellow summer squash, trimmed and cut in narrow strips (1½ cups)
1 28-ounce can whole tomatoes, drained and chopped
1 tablespoon chopped fresh basil, or 1 teaspoon dried basil leaves, crumbled
1 tablespoon chopped fresh thyme, or 1 teaspoon dried thyme leaves, crumbled
1 bay leaf
½ cup frozen peas, thawed and drained
2 tablespoons chopped fresh parsley (optional)

1 In a medium-size saucepan, bring the water to a boil over high heat. Stir in the rice. Reduce the heat to low and cook, covered, for 20 minutes, or until the rice is tender and the liquid is absorbed. Fluff the rice with a fork and keep warm.

2 Meanwhile, in a 4-quart Dutch oven, heat the oil over moderate heat for 1 minute. Add the garlic and sauté for 30 seconds, or until fragrant. Add the onion and green and red bell peppers and stir well. Reduce the heat to low and cook, covered, for 10 minutes, or until the vegetables are softened.

3 Add the zucchini, yellow squash, tomatoes, basil, thyme, and bay leaf. Increase the heat to moderately high and cook, covered, for 10 to 12 minutes, or until the zucchini and yellow squash are crisp-tender. Add the peas and cook for 3 minutes more.

4 Remove the pan from the heat and transfer the mixture to a colander to drain off the excess liquid. Remove and discard the bay leaf.

5 Return the vegetables to the pan. Cook, covered, over low heat for 1 to 2 minutes, or until heated through. Transfer the rice to individual serving plates. Spoon the vegetable mixture over the rice, sprinkle with the chopped fresh parsley, if desired, and serve immediately.

6 SERVINGS
PREP TIME: 15 MINUTES
COOKING TIME: 30 MINUTES

EQUIPMENT LIST

Utility knife
Colander
Medium-size saucepan with lid
Kitchen spoon
Fork
4-quart Dutch oven

When the weather turns warmer, serve this delicious duo—ratatouille and rice.

Watercress and Parsley Rice

2 cups water
1 cup long-grain white rice
1 pound fresh spinach, stemmed and chopped (4 cups)
1 bunch watercress, coarse stems removed
1 bunch fresh parsley
2 tablespoons unsalted butter
3 tablespoons grated Parmesan cheese
1½ teaspoons fresh lemon juice
½ teaspoon salt, or to taste
Freshly ground black pepper

To prepare this dish in advance: Cook the rice, cool to room temperature, then chill, covered, in the refrigerator. Before serving, combine the rice and purée, cheese, lemon juice, salt, and pepper. Heat over moderate heat, stirring continuously, for 10 minutes, or until heated through.

1 In a medium-size saucepan, bring the water to a boil over high heat. Stir in the rice. Reduce the heat to low and cook, covered, for 20 minutes, or until the rice is tender and the liquid is absorbed.

2 Meanwhile, rinse the spinach, watercress, and parsley under cold running water. Drain well.

3 In a large saucepan, cook the spinach, watercress, and parsley with the water clinging to the leaves over moderately high heat, stirring continuously, for 30 seconds, or until wilted. Remove the pan from the heat and drain the greens well.

4 Transfer the greens to a blender or food processor fitted with the metal blade. Blend or process for 30 seconds, or until greens are coarsely puréed, scraping down the side of the bowl whenever necessary.

5 Fluff the rice with a fork. Add the butter and stir until melted. Stir in the purée, Parmesan cheese, lemon juice, salt, and pepper until well blended. Cook over low heat for 1 minute, or until heated through. Serve immediately.

4 SERVINGS
PREP TIME: 15 MINUTES
COOKING TIME: 20 MINUTES

EQUIPMENT LIST

Utility knife
Citrus juicer
Pepper mill
Medium-size saucepan with lid
Large saucepan
Kitchen spoon
Colander
Blender or food processor with metal blade
Rubber spatula
Fork

Indian Kedgeree with Mixed Vegetables

3 tablespoons vegetable oil
1 tablespoon cumin seeds
4 whole cloves
1" stick cinnamon
½ teaspoon ground turmeric
¼ teaspoon ground cardamom
1½ teaspoons ground ginger
4 medium-size yellow onions, finely chopped (4 cups)
3½ cups water
½ cup basmati rice
4 ounces green lentils (½ cup)
1 cup cauliflower florets
1 small zucchini, trimmed, halved lengthwise, and thickly sliced (1 cup)
2 small red-skinned potatoes, scrubbed and quartered (½ cup)
4 ounces snow peas, trimmed and strings removed (2 cups)
⅛ teaspoon salt, or to taste

Kedgeree is a distinguished English breakfast dish traditionally made with rice, smoked fish, hard-cooked eggs, and curry powder. This lighter version features an interesting blend of spices and vegetables. Serve it as part of a brunch buffet, as a light main course, or as an accompaniment to grilled fish or chicken.

1 In a 5-quart Dutch oven, heat the oil over moderate heat for 1 minute. Add the cumin seeds, cloves, and cinnamon stick and cook, stirring continuously, for 1 minute, or until fragrant. Add the turmeric, cardamom, ginger, and onions and sauté for 2 minutes, or until the onions are slightly softened.

2 Add the water and bring the mixture to a boil over high heat. Stir in the rice, lentils, cauliflower, zucchini, and potatoes. Reduce the heat to low and cook, covered, for 17 minutes. Add the snow peas and cook for 3 minutes more, or until the rice and lentils are tender and the liquid is absorbed. Remove the pan from the heat and let stand, covered, for 10 minutes.

3 Remove and discard the cloves and the cinnamon stick. Season to taste with the salt. Transfer the kedgeree to a large serving bowl and serve immediately.

4 SERVINGS
PREP TIME: 15 MINUTES PLUS
10 MINUTES TO STAND
COOKING TIME: 25 MINUTES

EQUIPMENT LIST

Utility knife
Vegetable brush
5-quart Dutch oven
Kitchen spoon

Mediterranean Rice Pilaf

2 tablespoons unsalted butter
¼ cup chopped green bell pepper
¼ cup chopped red bell pepper
4 green onions (green parts only), cut in ½" pieces (¼ cup)
1 cup long-grain white rice
½ teaspoon dried oregano leaves, crumbled
¼ teaspoon ground coriander
2 cups chicken stock or canned broth
3 tablespoons pine nuts (pignoli)
¼ cup small, pitted, oil-cured black olives
Ground white pepper
Chopped fresh parsley (optional)

Pilaf is a Mediterranean specialty in which rice is sautéed in butter or oil and then simmered in stock until tender. This pilaf dish contains long-grain white rice cooked in the traditional manner, but its particularly Mediterranean character is derived from oil-cured olives and toasted pine nuts. Serve it with grilled fish or lamb.

1 In a large skillet over moderate heat, melt the butter. Add the green and red bell peppers and green onions and sauté for 5 minutes, or until the vegetables are softened. Add rice and cook, stirring frequently, for 2 to 3 minutes, or until opaque and coated with butter. Stir in the oregano, coriander, and stock.

2 Bring the mixture to a boil over moderately high heat. Reduce the heat to low and cook, covered, for 20 minutes, or until the rice is tender and the liquid is absorbed.

3 Meanwhile, toast the pine nuts. In a small skillet over moderate heat, toast the pine nuts, stirring continuously, for 2 minutes, or until fragrant and golden. Remove the skillet from the heat.

4 Stir pine nuts and olives into the rice mixture and cook, stirring frequently, for 2 to 3 minutes more. Season to taste with the pepper. Remove the skillet from the heat.

5 Fluff the rice with a fork and transfer the pilaf to a serving bowl. Garnish with chopped fresh parsley, if desired, and serve immediately.

4 SERVINGS
PREP TIME: 10 MINUTES
COOKING TIME: 33 MINUTES

EQUIPMENT LIST

Utility knife
Large skillet with lid
Small skillet
Kitchen spoons
Fork

This pilaf exemplifies Mediterranean cuisine in both the cooking method and the choice of ingredients.

Saffron Rice and Tuna Timbale

½ teaspoon saffron threads
2 cups hot water
2 tablespoons salted butter or margarine
1 small clove garlic, finely chopped
1 small red or green bell pepper, cored, seeded, and chopped (½ cup)
5 whole cloves
1 cup long-grain white rice
1 6½-ounce can solid white tuna in water, drained
Cherry tomatoes (optional)
Cucumber slices (optional)

Saffron is the dried stigma of a type of crocus that grows predominantly in Spain. It is available in many large supermarkets and specialty food stores and only sold in small quantities. Alternatively, obtain a saffron color by using a teaspoon of turmeric, a mild Indian spice.

1 Grease a 1-quart mold or bowl and set aside. In a small bowl, combine the saffron and the hot water and let stand for 5 minutes.

2 In a medium-size skillet over moderate heat, melt the butter. Add the garlic, bell pepper, and cloves and sauté for 3 minutes, or until bell pepper is slightly softened. Add the rice, stirring to coat with the butter. Stir in the saffron water and bring the mixture to a boil over high heat. Reduce heat to low and cook, covered, for 20 minutes, or until the rice is tender and the liquid is absorbed.

3 Meanwhile, remove the tuna from the can and place it in a small bowl. Using a fork, separate the tuna into small pieces. Set aside.

4 Remove the pan from the heat. Remove and discard the cloves. Stir in the tuna. Spoon the rice mixture into the prepared mold. Using the back of the spoon, gently press mixture into the mold and let stand for 5 minutes. Invert the timbale onto a serving platter and garnish with the cherry tomatoes and cucumber slices, if desired. Serve warm or at room temperature.

4 SERVINGS
PREP TIME: 10 MINUTES PLUS
5 MINUTES TO STAND
COOKING TIME: 25 MINUTES

Equipment List

Utility knife
1-quart mold or bowl
2 small bowls
Medium-size skillet with lid
Kitchen spoon
Fork

Red Bean and Rice Cakes

1 cup water
½ cup long-grain white rice
2 large eggs, separated
1 cup canned small red beans, drained and rinsed
1 green onion (white part only), finely chopped (1 tablespoon)
1 tablespoon chopped fresh cilantro (coriander leaves) or fresh parsley
¼ teaspoon ground cumin
⅛ teaspoon ground red pepper (cayenne)
⅛ teaspoon salt, or to taste
Vegetable oil
Sour cream (optional)
Sprigs of fresh cilantro (coriander leaves) or fresh parsley (optional)

These protein-rich rice cakes will add a flavorful accent to grilled flank steak or chicken.

1 In a medium-size saucepan, bring the water to a boil over high heat. Stir in the rice. Reduce the heat to low and cook, covered, for 20 minutes, or until the rice is tender and the liquid is absorbed. Remove the pan from the heat. Fluff the rice with a fork. Transfer the rice to a large bowl, stirring to cool slightly.

2 Meanwhile, in a medium-size bowl, using an electric mixer set on high speed, beat the egg whites to stiff peaks.

3 Stir the red beans, green onion, chopped cilantro, cumin, and ground red pepper into the rice. Season to taste with the salt. Stir in the egg yolks just until blended. Fold in the egg whites.

4 In a large, heavy skillet, heat ½″ of oil over moderately high heat for 2 minutes, or until very hot. Cook rice cakes in 2 batches, using ¼ cup of the mixture for each. With the back of a large, metal spatula, flatten each cake to ½″ thick. Cook for 2 minutes on each side, or until lightly golden. Using the metal spatula, transfer the cakes to a plate lined with paper towels to drain. Keep warm. Repeat cooking the remaining mixture as directed, adding more oil, if needed.

5 Transfer the cakes to a serving platter. Garnish with sour cream and sprigs of fresh cilantro, if desired, and serve immediately.

4 SERVINGS OR 8 RICE CAKES
PREP TIME: 10 MINUTES
COOKING TIME: 30 MINUTES

Equipment List

2 small bowls
Large bowl
Medium-size bowl
Strainer
Utility knife
Medium-size saucepan with lid
Fork
Large, heavy skillet
Electric mixer
Kitchen spoon
Rubber spatula
Large, metal spatula
Plate
Paper towels

BISCUITS, MUFFINS, AND MORE

*B*akers will love the recipes in this chapter. Wafers, biscuits, scones, and muffins will make welcome additions to everyday meals and will dazzle family and guests alike with a minimum of effort. In very little time tempting aromas will waft from the oven.

Blue Cheese-Walnut Wafers.

Blue Cheese-Walnut Wafers

4	ounces blue cheese, crumbled (1 cup)
¼	cup (½ stick) unsalted butter, softened
1	cup all-purpose flour
4	ounces finely chopped walnuts (1 cup)

These wafers make a wonderful accompaniment to fruit and cheese. Because they can be made ahead, they are great for entertaining.

1 In a small bowl, cream the blue cheese and butter with a wooden spoon until fluffy. Add flour and walnuts and mix to form a soft dough. Place the dough on a sheet of wax paper and shape into a roll about 2″ in diameter and 12″ long. Wrap the roll in wax paper or plastic wrap and chill in the refrigerator for 1 hour.

2 Preheat the oven to 375° F. Slice the dough ½″ thick. Place the slices ½″ apart on a baking sheet and bake for 12 to 14 minutes, or until the wafers are lightly browned on the edges. Remove the baking sheet from the oven and set on a wire rack to cool slightly. Using a thin, metal spatula, transfer the wafers to the wire rack and cool completely. Store the wafers in an airtight container for up to 1 week.

2 DOZEN WAFERS
PREP TIME: 15 MINUTES PLUS
1 HOUR TO CHILL
COOKING TIME: 14 MINUTES

EQUIPMENT LIST

Small bowl
Wooden spoon
Wax paper
Utility knife
Baking sheet
Wire rack
Thin, metal spatula

Creole Cheese Straws

1	10″ x 8″ sheet frozen puff pastry, thawed
4	ounces shredded sharp Cheddar cheese (1 cup)
¼	cup sesame seeds
¼	teaspoon ground red pepper (cayenne)
¼	teaspoon ground white pepper

Serve these cheese straws as a snack, for picnics, or for parties.

1 Preheat the oven to 375° F. Lightly flour a work surface and a rolling pin. Roll the puff pastry evenly, from the center outward, into a 10″ x 12″ rectangle. Sprinkle the Cheddar cheese, sesame seeds, and ground red pepper over it. Gently press the topping into the dough with the rolling pin. Cut the dough into ½″ x 10″ strips.

2 Twist the strips and place on a baking sheet, spacing them 1″ apart. Bake for 13 to 15 minutes, or until golden brown and puffed. Remove the baking sheet from the oven and set on a wire rack to cool slightly. Using a thin, metal spatula, carefully transfer the straws to the rack and cool completely. Store the straws in an airtight container for up to 1 week.

2 DOZEN CHEESE STRAWS
PREP TIME: 20 MINUTES
COOKING TIME: 15 MINUTES

EQUIPMENT LIST

Grater
Rolling pin
Utility knife
Baking sheet
Wire rack
Thin, metal spatula

Gruyère Cheese Balls

1	cup all-purpose flour
¼	teaspoon salt
¼	teaspoon ground nutmeg
½	cup (1 stick) unsalted butter, softened
6	ounces shredded Gruyère cheese (1½ cups)

Because they take so little time to prepare, these cheese balls are just the answer for unexpected guests.

1 Preheat the oven to 350° F. Lightly grease 2 baking sheets. In a small bowl, combine the flour, salt, and nutmeg.

2 In a medium-size bowl, using an electric mixer set on medium-high speed, beat the butter until light and fluffy. Beat in the cheese. Reduce the mixer speed to low and beat in the flour mixture until well blended.

3 Shape the mixture into 1″ balls and place on the prepared baking sheets, spacing them 1″ apart. Bake for 15 to 18 minutes, or until lightly golden. Remove the baking sheets from the oven. Using a thin, metal spatula, transfer the cheese balls to a serving platter. Serve warm.

3 DOZEN CHEESE BALLS
PREP TIME: 15 MINUTES
COOKING TIME: 18 MINUTES

EQUIPMENT LIST

Grater
2 baking sheets
Small bowl
Medium-size bowl
Kitchen spoon
Electric mixer

Apricot Scones

1½ cups all-purpose flour
1 cup oat bran
1 tablespoon baking powder
¼ cup granulated sugar
½ teaspoon salt
¼ cup (½ stick) unsalted butter, chilled and cut in small pieces
1 large egg
3 tablespoons buttermilk or milk
1 pound ripe apricots, pitted and chopped, or 1 17-ounce can apricot halves, drained and chopped
Sliced fresh apricots (optional)
Sprigs of fresh mint (optional)

These scones make a marvelous addition to an elegant afternoon tea.

Scones have a texture that is similar to biscuits and should be served warm, split open, and buttered. For a special treat (but extra calories), serve these scones with whipped cream and jam or marmalade, or, just before baking, sprinkle them with a mixture of 1 teaspoon each of ground cinnamon and granulated sugar.

1 Preheat the oven to 400° F. In a large bowl, combine the flour, oat bran, baking powder, sugar, and salt. Using a pastry blender or 2 knives, cut the butter into flour mixture until the mixture resembles coarse crumbs.

2 In a small bowl, beat the egg with the buttermilk. Add the egg mixture to the flour mixture and stir until just mixed. Stir in the chopped apricots until well blended.

3 Lightly flour a work surface and a rolling pin. Roll dough evenly, from the center outward, into a 10″ circle ¾″ thick. Using a lightly floured, sharp knife, cut the dough into 12 wedges. Place the wedges on a baking sheet, spacing them 1″ apart.

4 Bake the scones for 15 minutes, or until golden brown. Remove the baking sheet from the oven and set on a wire rack to cool for 5 minutes. Using a thin, metal spatula, transfer the scones to the rack and cool for 10 minutes more. Garnish with sliced apricots and sprigs of fresh mint, if desired, and serve warm.

12 SCONES
PREP TIME: 15 MINUTES PLUS
15 MINUTES TO COOL
COOKING TIME: 15 MINUTES

EQUIPMENT LIST

Paring knife
Utility knife
Large bowl
Small bowl
Kitchen spoon
Pastry blender or 2 knives
Fork
Rolling pin
Baking sheet
Wire rack
Thin, metal spatula

Herb Butter Pan Biscuits

The secret to flaky biscuits is to knead the dough quickly to distribute the leavening and develop the gluten in the flour (gluten supports the biscuits as they rise). However, try not to overwork the dough or the biscuits will be tough. These biscuits will perk up a mid-week meal, but they are also delicious stuffed with ham and served for Sunday brunch.

2 cups all-purpose flour
1 ounce grated Parmesan cheese (¼ cup)
1 tablespoon baking powder
½ teaspoon salt
¼ teaspoon coarsely ground black pepper
5 tablespoons unsalted butter
¾ cup milk
1 tablespoon chopped fresh parsley
1 tablespoon snipped fresh chives or finely chopped green onion tops

1 Preheat the oven to 450° F. Lightly grease a baking sheet. In a medium-size bowl, mix together the flour, cheese, baking powder, salt, and pepper.

2 Using a pastry blender or 2 knives, cut 4 tablespoons of the butter into the flour mixture until the mixture resembles coarse crumbs. Add the milk, parsley, and chives, stirring until just mixed.

3 Lightly flour a work surface and a rolling pin. Turn the dough out onto the work surface and knead for 10 seconds. Roll the dough evenly, from the center outward, into a circle ½″ thick.

4 Using a 2″ round cookie cutter, cut out the biscuits and place them ½″ apart on the prepared baking sheet.

5 In a small saucepan over moderately low heat, melt the remaining 1 tablespoon of butter. Lightly brush the biscuits with the butter. Bake for 20 to 25 minutes, or until golden.

6 Remove the baking sheet from the oven. Using a thin, metal spatula, transfer biscuits to a wire rack and cool slightly. Serve warm.

12 BISCUITS
PREP TIME: 15 MINUTES
COOKING TIME: 25 MINUTES

EQUIPMENT LIST

Utility knife
Kitchen scissors
Baking sheet
Medium-size bowl
Kitchen spoon
Pastry blender or 2 knives
Rolling pin
2″ round cookie cutter
Small saucepan
Pastry brush
Thin, metal spatula
Wire rack

Vegetable Oat Biscuits

A wholesome alternative to rolls, these colorful biscuits complement soups, salads, or casseroles. They are easy to make because they are not rolled and cut out. To make the biscuits ahead: Cool them completely and wrap in aluminum foil. They can be stored for up to two weeks in the freezer. To reheat: Preheat the oven to 350° F., place the wrapped biscuits in the oven, and warm them for 12 to 15 minutes.

1 cup quick-cooking or old-fashioned rolled oats
1 cup all-purpose flour
1 tablespoon baking powder
¼ teaspoon dried oregano leaves, crumbled
¼ teaspoon dried basil leaves, crumbled
¼ teaspoon salt
⅛ teaspoon coarsely ground black pepper
3 tablespoons salted butter or margarine
1 cup fresh or frozen corn kernels, thawed and drained
1 small tomato, seeded and chopped (½ cup)
2 green onions (including tops), finely chopped (¼ cup)
1 8-ounce container plain lowfat yogurt (1 cup)
1 egg white

1 Preheat the oven to 400° F. Lightly grease a baking sheet. In a medium-size bowl, combine the oats, flour, baking powder, oregano, basil, salt, and pepper.

2 Using a pastry blender or 2 knives, cut the butter into the oat mixture until the mixture resembles coarse crumbs. Stir in the corn, tomato, and green onions. Add the yogurt and egg white, stirring until just mixed.

3 Drop the dough, using ⅓ cup for each biscuit, onto the prepared baking sheet. Bake for 25 to 30 minutes, or until golden brown.

4 Remove the baking sheet from the oven. Using a thin, metal spatula, transfer biscuits to a wire rack and cool slightly. Serve warm.

12 BISCUITS
PREP TIME: 15 MINUTES
COOKING TIME: 30 MINUTES

EQUIPMENT LIST

Strainer
Utility knife
Small bowl
Medium-size bowl
Baking sheet
Kitchen spoon
Pastry blender or 2 knives
Thin, metal spatula
Wire rack

Peppery Green Onion Muffins

Include these savory muffins on a brunch menu, or serve them with grilled meat and poultry. They also make a great accompaniment to hearty soups. Serve them warm with only a thin spread of butter for a snack.

1¼ cups milk
1 large egg
¼ cup vegetable oil
3 green onions (including tops), finely chopped (⅓ cup)
2 cups all-purpose flour
1 tablespoon granulated sugar
1 tablespoon baking powder
1 teaspoon salt
½ teaspoon ground white pepper
¼ teaspoon dried thyme leaves, crumbled
¼ teaspoon garlic powder
¼ teaspoon ground red pepper (cayenne)

1 Preheat the oven to 400° F. Grease 12 standard-size muffin pan cups or line with paper liners. In a small bowl, combine the milk, egg, and oil. Stir in the green onions.

2 In a large bowl, combine the flour, sugar, baking powder, salt, white pepper, thyme, garlic powder, and ground red pepper.

3 Add the green onion mixture to the flour mixture, stirring until just mixed. Spoon the batter into the prepared muffin pan cups, filling them two-thirds full. Bake the muffins for 15 to 20 minutes, or until golden and springy to the touch and a toothpick inserted in the center comes out clean.

4 Remove the pan from the oven, set on a wire rack, and cool for 10 minutes. Using a thin, metal spatula, loosen the sides of the muffins, turn out onto the rack, and cool for 5 minutes. Serve warm.

12 STANDARD-SIZE MUFFINS
PREP TIME: 10 MINUTES PLUS
15 MINUTES TO COOL
COOKING TIME: 20 MINUTES

EQUIPMENT LIST

Utility knife
12-cup muffin pan
Small bowl
Large bowl
Kitchen spoon
Rubber spatula
Thin, metal spatula
Toothpick
Wire rack

Versatile and tasty, these muffins are sure to be a hit.

Strawberry Muffins

1¾ cups all-purpose flour
1   tablespoon baking powder
¼   cup granulated sugar
½   teaspoon salt
2   large eggs
1   cup sour cream
2   teaspoons grated orange rind
2   tablespoons water
1½ cups fresh strawberries,
     hulled and cut in ½″ pieces

ORANGE BUTTER

½   cup unsalted butter, softened
2   tablespoons orange juice
1½ teaspoons grated orange rind
1½ teaspoons confectioners'
     sugar

The taste of fresh strawberries really comes through in these muffins. They would look wonderful on a Mother's Day breakfast tray, served in a napkin-lined basket with a crock of Orange Butter.

1 Preheat the oven to 400° F. Grease 12 standard-size muffin pan cups or line with paper liners. In a large bowl, combine the flour, baking powder, granulated sugar, and salt.

2 In a medium-size bowl, lightly beat together the eggs, sour cream, the 2 teaspoons of orange rind, and water.

3 Add the egg mixture to the flour mixture, stirring lightly until just mixed. Gently fold the strawberries into the batter. Spoon the batter into the prepared muffin pan cups, filling them two-thirds full.

4 Bake for 20 to 25 minutes, or until springy to the touch and a toothpick inserted in the center comes out clean.

5 Meanwhile, make the Orange Butter. In a blender or food processor fitted with the metal blade, combine the butter, orange juice, 1½ teaspoons of orange rind, and confectioners' sugar. Blend or process for 30 seconds, or until smooth, scraping down the side of the bowl whenever necessary. Transfer the mixture to a small bowl.

6 Remove the muffin pan from the oven and set on a wire rack to cool for 10 minutes. Using a thin, metal spatula, loosen the sides of the muffins, turn out onto the rack, and cool for 5 minutes. Serve the muffins warm with the Orange Butter.

12 STANDARD-SIZE MUFFINS
PREP TIME: 15 MINUTES PLUS
15 MINUTES TO COOL
COOKING TIME: 25 MINUTES

EQUIPMENT LIST

Grater
Paring knife
12-cup muffin pan
Large bowl
Medium-size bowl
Small bowl
Kitchen spoon
Rubber spatula
Thin, metal spatula
Toothpick
Blender or food processor with
     metal blade
Wire rack

Spiced Date-Nut Muffins

2   ounces chopped pitted dates
     (½ cup)
1   cup boiling water
1¼ cups all-purpose flour
¾   cup granulated sugar
1½ teaspoons baking soda
½   teaspoon ground cinnamon
¾   teaspoon baking powder
¼   teaspoon ground nutmeg
⅛   teaspoon salt
½   cup quick-cooking rolled oats
¼   cup (½ stick) unsalted butter
2   large eggs
¼   cup orange juice
2   teaspoons grated orange rind
2   ounces chopped walnuts
     (½ cup)

Serve these moist, dense muffins with fresh fruit and plain lowfat yogurt for a well-rounded breakfast.

1 Preheat the oven to 350° F. Grease 12 standard-size muffin pan cups or line with paper liners. In a medium-size bowl, soak the dates in the boiling water for 15 minutes. Drain well.

2 Meanwhile, in a large bowl, combine flour, sugar, baking soda, cinnamon, baking powder, nutmeg, salt, and oats. In a small saucepan over moderate heat, melt the butter. Remove pan from heat.

3 Stir the butter into the dates and let cool to room temperature. Add the eggs and orange juice and rind to the date mixture, stirring until well blended. Add date mixture to flour mixture, stirring gently until just mixed. Stir in the walnuts. Spoon the batter into the prepared muffin pan cups, filling them two-thirds full.

4 Bake for 20 to 25 minutes, or until springy to the touch and a toothpick inserted in the center comes out clean.

5 Remove the muffin pan from the oven and set on a wire rack to cool for 10 minutes. Using a thin, metal spatula, loosen the sides of the muffins, turn out onto the rack, and cool for 5 minutes. Serve the muffins warm.

12 STANDARD-SIZE MUFFINS
PREP TIME: 15 MINUTES PLUS
30 MINUTES TO COOL
COOKING TIME: 25 MINUTES

EQUIPMENT LIST

Grater
12-cup muffin pan
Medium-size bowl
Large bowl
Colander
Kitchen spoons
Small saucepan
Rubber spatula
Thin, metal spatula
Toothpick
Wire rack

DESSERTS

*C*hoose a dessert from the recipes in this chapter and be surprised at how little time it takes to produce spectacular results. Featured are an eye-catching fruit platter, a homey crumble, crisp banana fritters, a trendy raspberry tiramisu, and, without a doubt, the best brownies ever.

Exotic Fruit Platter with Honey-Yogurt Dressing.

Exotic Fruit Platter
with Honey-Yogurt Dressing

3 cups strawberries, hulled and sliced

2 ripe kiwi, peeled and sliced (1 cup)

1 cup fresh raspberries

2 medium-size ripe starfruit, sliced crosswise (1 cup)

1 small ripe papaya, peeled, seeded, and thinly sliced lengthwise (¾ cup)

Sprigs of fresh mint (optional)

HONEY-YOGURT DRESSING (1½ CUPS)

1 8-ounce container plain lowfat yogurt (1 cup)

1 3-ounce package cream cheese, softened

1 tablespoon honey

¼ teaspoon ground cinnamon

2 tablespoons fresh lemon juice

½ teaspoon grated lemon rind

Simple yet elegant, this rainbow of exotic fruit served with a Honey-Yogurt Dressing makes a truly spectacular finale to a luncheon or dinner party. Tropical fruits add a taste of paradise to desserts and they're healthful, too! Starfruit provides vitamin C and fiber. Kiwi, also an excellent source of vitamin C and fiber, contains minerals. High in vitamin C, papaya is also a good source of vitamin A and potassium. Kiwi, starfruit (also called carambola), and papaya are available at many larger supermarkets and specialty produce stores.

1 In a large bowl, combine the strawberries, kiwi, raspberries, starfruit, and papaya.

2 To make the Honey-Yogurt Dressing: In a blender or food processor fitted with the metal blade, blend or process the yogurt, cream cheese, honey, cinnamon, and lemon juice and rind for 1 minute, or until smooth, scraping down the side of the bowl whenever necessary.

3 Transfer the dressing to 4 small bowls. Spoon the fruit onto individual serving plates. Garnish with sprigs of fresh mint, if desired, and serve chilled or at room temperature with the dressing.

4 SERVINGS
PREP TIME: 20 MINUTES

EQUIPMENT LIST

Paring knife
Utility knife
Citrus juicer
Grater
Large bowl
Kitchen spoon
Blender or food processor with metal blade
Rubber spatula

Three Berry Crumble

⅓ cup firmly packed light brown sugar

¼ cup all-purpose flour

½ teaspoon ground cinnamon

¼ teaspoon ground nutmeg

2 cups fresh blueberries, stemmed

2 cups strawberries, hulled and sliced

2 cups fresh raspberries

1 tablespoon fresh lemon juice

CRUMBLE TOPPING (2¾ CUPS)

½ cup all-purpose flour

½ cup firmly packed light brown sugar

¼ cup granulated sugar

½ teaspoon ground cinnamon

½ cup (1 stick) unsalted butter, chilled and cut in small pieces

½ cup quick-cooking rolled oats

Who can resist this homey crumble, bursting with fresh fruit? This recipe lends itself to fruit variations. Try substituting 6 cups of sweet, pitted fresh cherries for the berries. For a special treat, serve the crumble with whipped cream or vanilla ice cream.

1 Preheat the oven to 400° F. Grease a 9″ x 13″ baking dish. In a large bowl, combine the ⅓ cup of brown sugar, ¼ cup of flour, ½ teaspoon of cinnamon, and the nutmeg. Add the berries and lemon juice, stirring gently to combine. Spoon the fruit mixture into the prepared dish.

2 To make the Crumble Topping: In a medium-size bowl, combine the ½ cup of flour, ½ cup brown sugar, the granulated sugar, and ½ teaspoon of cinnamon. Using a pastry blender or 2 knives, cut the butter into the flour mixture until the mixture resembles coarse crumbs. Stir in the oats. Sprinkle the topping evenly over the fruit mixture.

3 Bake for 20 to 25 minutes, or until the berries are bubbling around the edges and the topping is lightly golden. Remove the baking dish from the oven. Serve the berry crumble hot, warm, or at room temperature.

6 TO 8 SERVINGS
PREP TIME: 15 MINUTES
COOKING TIME: 25 MINUTES

EQUIPMENT LIST

Paring knife
Citrus juicer
9″ x 13″ baking dish
Large bowl
Medium-size bowl
Kitchen spoon
Pastry blender or 2 knives

Grapefruit-Mint Granita

Cool, refreshing, and low in calories, granitas make wonderful prepare-ahead desserts and are surprisingly quick and easy. A fruit purée or juice is added to a sugar syrup, then frozen. The mixture is then stirred occasionally (or chopped in a food processor) to break up the ice crystals and give it a crunchy, slushy texture.

The secret of a successful fruit granita is to use fresh fruit at its peak to ensure that the essence will shine through. A little lemon juice added to the base will also help to intensify the fruit flavor.

7 medium-size seedless pink or white grapefruit
1 teaspoon fresh lemon juice
1 cup granulated sugar
2 cups water
4-5 fresh mint leaves
Sprigs of fresh mint (optional)

1 QUART
PREP TIME: 15 MINUTES PLUS
6 HOURS TO FREEZE
COOKING TIME: 5 MINUTES

EQUIPMENT LIST

Citrus juicer
Utility knife
Paring knife
Teaspoon
Kitchen spoon
Slotted spoon
Blender or food processor with metal blade
Medium-size saucepan
9" x 13" baking pan
Medium-size metal bowl
Plastic wrap

1 Cut 6 of the grapefruits in half crosswise. Using a small, sharp knife, cut around the perimeter of each grapefruit half, then cut around each section to loosen it from the interior membrane. Using a small spoon, scoop out the pulp and place it in a blender or food processor fitted with the metal blade.

2 Add the lemon juice to the grapefruit pulp and blend or process for 1 minute, or until smooth. (There should be about 3 cups of grapefruit purée.)

3 In a medium-size saucepan, combine the sugar, water, and mint leaves. Cook, uncovered, over moderate heat, stirring frequently, for 5 minutes, or until the sugar dissolves. Using a slotted spoon, remove the mint leaves. Stir in the grapefruit purée.

4 Pour the grapefruit mixture into a 9" x 13" baking pan, and freeze, uncovered, for 5 hours, or until firm.

5 Cut the ice into 1" pieces and place in a blender or food processor fitted with the metal blade. Blend or process for 2 minutes, or until smooth. Pour the grapefruit mixture into a medium-size metal bowl, cover with plastic wrap, and freeze for 1 hour, or until firm.

6 Meanwhile, peel remaining grapefruit and cut away the membrane and white pith. Divide the grapefruit into sections and set aside.

7 Before serving, let the granita soften slightly at room temperature. Place scoops in stemmed glasses and garnish with the reserved grapefruit sections and sprigs of fresh mint, if desired.

Banana Fritters
with Warm Custard Sauce

1	cup all-purpose flour
1	tablespoon granulated sugar
1	teaspoon baking powder
¼	teaspoon ground cinnamon
½	teaspoon salt
2	large eggs
½	cup milk
2	tablespoons vegetable oil plus oil for frying
6	medium-size firm, ripe bananas

WARM CUSTARD SAUCE
(1¼ CUPS)

2	egg yolks
1	cup heavy cream
2	tablespoons granulated sugar
⅛	teaspoon salt
1	teaspoon vanilla extract
	Ground cinnamon (optional)

These easy-to-prepare fritters make great use of that all-time favorite—bananas. Here they are showcased by a crisp batter coating and served with a wonderful custard sauce.

Be sure to use firm bananas for this recipe, not ones that are over-ripe. To ripen green bananas, leave them uncovered at room temperature for a few days. For quick ripening, place them in a perforated brown paper bag. After ripening, store bananas in the refrigerator for up to a week. The skin will turn black but the pulp will remain edible.

Experiment with other types of fruit for the fritters. Apples, pears, apricots, pineapples, peaches, and nectarines make good substitutes for the bananas. To make apple fitters: Prepare the sauce and batter as directed. Peel, core, and cut 4 medium-size Granny Smith apples into ¼" rings or wedges and transfer them to a medium-size bowl. Pat the apple slices dry, if necessary, with paper towels. Dip them into the batter, fry, and drain as directed. Serve the fritters with the sauce.

For a breakfast treat, omit the custard sauce and sprinkle the warm fritters with confectioners' sugar.

1 To make the Warm Custard Sauce: In a medium-size saucepan, combine the egg yolks, cream, the 2 tablespoons of sugar, and the ⅛ teaspoon of salt. Cook, stirring continuously, over moderately low heat, for 5 minutes, or until the mixture thickens slightly and coats the back of a spoon.

2 Remove the pan from the heat. Strain the sauce through a fine sieve into a medium-size bowl. Stir in the vanilla and set aside.

3 To make the fritters: In a medium-size bowl, combine the flour, the 1 tablespoon of sugar, baking powder, cinnamon, and the ½ teaspoon of salt.

4 In a small bowl, mix together the eggs, milk, and 2 tablespoons of oil until well blended. Pour egg mixture into the dry ingredients, stirring until the batter is just mixed.

5 In a large, deep skillet, heat 2" of oil over moderately high heat for 5 minutes, or until it reaches 375° F.

6 Peel and cut the bananas into 2" pieces. Using a fork, dip the bottom half of each banana into the batter, draining any excess.

7 Carefully lower the bananas into the hot oil so they do not splatter, and fry for 3 to 4 minutes, turning once with tongs, or until golden brown. Using a slotted spoon, transfer the fritters to a plate lined with paper towels to drain and keep warm. Repeat cooking and draining the remaining bananas as directed.

8 Transfer the fritters to individual serving dishes. Return the sauce to the saucepan and warm over very low heat. Pour the sauce into a pitcher and sprinkle with cinnamon, if desired. Serve immediately.

6 SERVINGS
PREP TIME: 15 MINUTES
COOKING TIME: 15 MINUTES

EQUIPMENT LIST

2 small bowls
2 medium-size bowls
Medium-size saucepan
Kitchen spoons
Slotted spoon
Fine sieve
Wire whisk
Large, deep skillet
Paring knife
Fork
Kitchen tongs
Plate
Paper towels

Zesty Lemon Squares

½ cup (1 stick) unsalted butter, softened
¼ cup granulated sugar
1¼ cups all-purpose flour
2 teaspoons grated lemon rind
Lemon slices (optional)

LEMON TOPPING

6 tablespoons fresh lemon juice
⅔ cup granulated sugar
2 large eggs plus 1 egg yolk
6 tablespoons unsalted butter, cut in small pieces

Simple to make, these lemon squares are great with coffee or tea, or serve them with berries for a refreshing dessert.

1 Preheat the oven to 350° F. Line an 8″ square baking pan with a double layer of aluminum foil.

2 To make the pastry crust: In a large bowl, using an electric mixer set on medium speed, cream the ½ cup of butter with the ¼ cup of sugar for 1 minute, or until light and fluffy. Reduce the mixer speed to low and beat in the flour and lemon rind until the mixture resembles coarse crumbs.

3 Transfer the pastry crust mixture to the baking pan and, using the back of a spoon, press it in an even layer into the bottom of the pan. Prick the surface with a fork and bake for 25 minutes, or until golden and firm to the touch.

4 Meanwhile, make the Lemon Topping. In a double boiler set over simmering (not boiling) water, combine the lemon juice and the ⅔ cup of sugar. In a small bowl, lightly beat the eggs and the egg yolk. Add the eggs and the 6 tablespoons of butter to the lemon juice mixture. Cook over low heat, stirring continuously with a wooden spoon, for 6 minutes, or until the mixture is opaque and thick and coats the back of the spoon. (Do not cook the mixture over too high a flame or it will curdle.)

5 Remove pastry crust from the oven. Reduce the oven temperature to 325° F. Strain the topping through a fine sieve over the pastry crust and spread evenly. Bake for 10 minutes, or until the topping is just set.

6 Remove the lemon squares from the oven and set on a wire rack to cool for 15 minutes. Chill, uncovered, in the refrigerator for 45 minutes.

7 Remove the lemon squares from the pan by lifting the foil. Transfer to a cutting board and carefully pull away the foil from the sides. Cut into sixteen 2″ squares and, using a large, metal spatula, transfer them to a serving platter. Garnish with lemon slices, if desired, and serve immediately.

These lovely lemon squares will make taste buds tingle.

16 SQUARES
PREP TIME: 15 MINUTES PLUS
1 HOUR TO COOL AND CHILL
COOKING TIME: 35 MINUTES

EQUIPMENT LIST

Grater
Citrus juicer
2 small bowls
Large bowl
Utility knife
8″ square baking pan
Aluminum foil
Electric mixer
Wooden spoons
Fork
Double boiler
Fine sieve
Thin, metal spatula
Wire rack
Cutting board

Key Lime Pie

The limes grown in the Florida Keys lend their name to this dessert. If key limes are not available, use ordinary limes; however, the flavor will not be as tart. To save time, use a ready-made 9" graham cracker crust.

1½ cups graham cracker crumbs
2 tablespoons granulated sugar
6 tablespoons unsalted butter

KEY LIME FILLING

4 egg yolks
½ cup fresh lime juice
1 14-ounce can sweetened condensed milk (not evaporated)
¼ teaspoon grated lime peel
1 cup heavy cream
Grated lime peel (optional)

1 Preheat the oven to 325° F. To make the crumb crust: In a medium-size bowl, mix the graham cracker crumbs and the sugar. In a small saucepan over moderately low heat, melt the butter. Add to the crumb mixture, stirring until well combined.

2 Spread the crumb mixture evenly over the base and side of a 9" pie pan and press gently with the back of a spoon. Bake the crust in the oven for 7 minutes, or until the edges are lightly browned. Remove the pan from the oven and set on a wire rack to cool.

3 Meanwhile, make the Key Lime Filling. In a double boiler set over simmering (not boiling) water, whisk the egg yolks and lime juice for 2 to 3 minutes, or until mixture thickens and coats the back of a spoon. Remove pan from heat and strain the egg yolk mixture into a medium-size bowl. Add condensed milk and lime peel and mix well.

4 Pour the filling into the pie shell and smooth over with a thin, metal spatula. Cover the pie with plastic wrap and freeze for 3 hours. Remove the pie from the freezer 5 minutes before serving.

5 In a medium-size bowl, using an electric mixer set on high speed, beat the cream to soft peaks. Spoon the cream on top of the pie. Garnish with grated lime peel, if desired, and serve immediately.

8 SERVINGS
PREP TIME: 20 MINUTES PLUS
3 HOURS TO FREEZE
COOKING TIME: 7 MINUTES

EQUIPMENT LIST

Small bowl
2 medium-size bowls
Citrus juicer
Grater
Kitchen spoons
Small saucepan
Double boiler
9" pie pan
Wire rack
Strainer
Wire whisk
Thin, metal spatula
Plastic wrap
Electric mixer

Raspberry Tiramisu

⅓ cup granulated sugar
⅓ cup water
¼ cup dark rum (optional)
1 15-ounce container part-skim ricotta cheese
1 3-ounce package cream cheese, softened
16 ladyfingers
3 cups fresh or frozen unsweetened raspberries, thawed and drained

1 In a small saucepan, combine the sugar, water, and rum, if desired. Cook over moderate heat, stirring frequently, for 2 to 3 minutes, or until the sugar is dissolved. Remove pan from heat and cool slightly.

2 In a blender or food processor fitted with the metal blade, combine ricotta and cream cheeses. Blend or process for 1 minute, or until smooth, scraping down side of the bowl whenever necessary.

3 Separate and split the ladyfingers in half. Place, curved-side down, on a sheet of wax paper. Lightly brush with the sugar syrup. Stand 16 ladyfinger halves, curved-sides out, around sides of a 9" x 5" loaf pan. Spoon half the ricotta mixture into the pan. Press 1 cup of the raspberries into the cheese. Cover with 8 of the remaining ladyfinger halves. Repeat the layers as directed, using the remaining cheese mixture, 1 cup of the raspberries, and the 8 remaining ladyfinger halves. Cover the pan with plastic wrap, place another loaf pan on top, then place two 16-ounce cans in the loaf pan to weigh it down. Chill in the refrigerator for 3 hours or overnight, or until firm.

4 Remove the pan from the refrigerator. Remove weights and plastic wrap. Using a thin, metal spatula, loosen the sides of the Tiramisu and spoon onto individual serving plates. Garnish with some of the remaining 1 cup of raspberries, if desired. Serve chilled.

8 SERVINGS
PREP TIME: 30 MINUTES PLUS
3 HOURS TO CHILL
COOKING TIME: 3 MINUTES

EQUIPMENT LIST

Strainer
Small saucepan
Kitchen spoons
Blender or food processor with metal blade
Rubber spatula
Thin, metal spatula
Wax paper
Plastic wrap
Pastry brush
2 9" x 5" loaf pans
2 16-ounce cans or weights

Chocolate-Raspberry Trifle

1 cup heavy cream
1 tablespoon granulated sugar
1 10¾-ounce frozen pound cake, thawed, or sponge cake or angel food cake
2 tablespoons crème de cacao (optional)
¼ cup seedless raspberry jam
Fresh raspberries (optional)

CHOCOLATE CUSTARD

1 tablespoon granulated sugar
1 tablespoon cornstarch
⅛ teaspoon salt, or to taste
3 egg yolks
2 cups milk
6 ounces milk chocolate chips (1 cup)

Trifle is an easy and elegant dessert that originated in England. It is often made with sponge cake doused with sherry, covered with jam and custard, and topped with whipped cream. This version calls for a chocolate custard, a sprinkling of crème de cacao, and a garnish of fresh raspberries.

The trifle can be assembled up to four hours ahead. Cover it with plastic wrap and chill in the refrigerator until ready to serve. Garnish with the whipped cream and raspberries just before serving.

1 To make the Chocolate Custard: In a medium-size saucepan, combine the 1 tablespoon of sugar, cornstarch, and salt. Whisk in egg yolks until smooth. Slowly stir in the milk and bring to a boil over moderate heat, stirring continuously. Cook for 1 minute and remove pan from the heat. Stir in chocolate chips until melted and smooth.

2 Transfer the custard to a medium-size bowl, press a piece of plastic wrap directly onto the surface, and set aside to cool. Chill in the refrigerator for 1 hour.

3 To make the trifle: In a medium-size bowl, using an electric mixer set on high speed, beat the cream with the 1 tablespoon of sugar to stiff peaks.

4 Cut cake into ½" thick slices. Reserve 2 slices for the top. Arrange half of the cake slices in the bottom of a 2-quart dessert bowl and sprinkle with 1 tablespoon of the crème de cacao, if desired. Spread 2 tablespoons of the raspberry jam over the cake. Spoon half of the custard over the jam and top with half of the whipped cream. Repeat layers of cake, liqueur, if desired, jam, and custard once. Slice reserved cake slices into thin strips. Arrange cake slices on top of the custard.

5 Just before serving, garnish the trifle with the remaining whipped cream and the fresh raspberries, if desired.

10 SERVINGS
PREP TIME: 20 MINUTES PLUS 1 HOUR TO CHILL
COOKING TIME: 5 MINUTES

EQUIPMENT LIST

Small bowl
2 medium-size bowls
2-quart bowl
Medium-size saucepan
Kitchen spoon
Wire whisk
Plastic wrap
Electric mixer
Serrated knife
Thin, metal spatula

Decadent Chocolate Truffles

24 ounces semisweet chocolate chips (4 cups)
¼ cup (½ stick) unsalted butter, softened
¼ cup heavy cream
1 teaspoon grated orange rind
1 teaspoon almond extract
Confectioners' sugar
½ cup sifted cocoa powder
4 ounces finely chopped pecans (1 cup)

One simple recipe, two great tastes. When it comes to truffles, what more could one want? A great gift idea, these truffles are a breeze to make.

1 Line 2 baking sheets with wax paper and set aside. In a double boiler set over simmering (not boiling) water, heat chocolate chips, butter, and cream, stirring occasionally, until chocolate is melted and mixture is smooth. Remove pan from the simmering water.

2 Divide the mixture evenly between 2 small bowls. Stir 1 of the flavorings (orange rind or almond extract) into each bowl. Drop level tablespoonfuls of each of the mixtures onto the baking sheets. Chill for 20 minutes, or until almost firm. Dust your hands with confectioners' sugar and shape the chilled chocolate mixture into balls. Freeze for 30 minutes, or until hard.

3 Place the cocoa and pecans on separate plates. Roll the orange rind truffles in the cocoa and the almond extract truffles in the pecans. Store in the refrigerator in an airtight container for up to 6 weeks.

4 DOZEN TRUFFLES
PREP TIME: 30 MINUTES PLUS 50 MINUTES TO CHILL

EQUIPMENT LIST

Grater
Sifter
2 baking sheets
Wax paper
Double boiler
Kitchen spoon
Tablespoon
2 small bowls
2 plates

Black Bottom Cupcakes

1 cup granulated sugar
1½ cups all-purpose flour
¼ cup unsweetened cocoa powder
1 teaspoon baking soda
½ teaspoon salt
2 large extra-ripe bananas, mashed (1 cup)
⅓ cup vegetable oil
1 teaspoon vanilla extract
1 large firm banana, cut in 12 ½" slices

CREAM CHEESE LAYER

1 8-ounce package cream cheese, softened
⅓ cup granulated sugar
1 large egg
6 ounces semisweet chocolate chips (1 cup)

Here's a moist, melt-in-your-mouth cupcake that will be popular with children and adults alike. When berries are plentiful, replace the sliced bananas with sliced strawberries or some raspberries.

Make up a second batch of cupcakes and freeze it for snacks and packed lunches. Wrap the cooled cupcakes tightly in aluminum foil and freeze for up to 3 months. Defrost at room temperature for 1 hour, or wrap in a paper towel and microwave on High (100 percent power) for 15 seconds for each cupcake until warm.

1 Preheat the oven to 350° F. Grease 12 standard-size muffin pan cups or line with foil liners.

2 To make the Cream Cheese Layer: In a medium-size bowl, using an electric mixer set on medium speed, beat the cream cheese until light and fluffy. Add the ⅓ cup of sugar and the egg and beat until well blended. Stir in the chocolate chips and set aside.

3 To make the cake layer: In a large bowl, mix the 1 cup of sugar, flour, cocoa powder, baking soda, salt, mashed bananas, oil, and vanilla until well blended.

4 Spoon the batter evenly into the prepared muffin pan cups. Place 1 slice of banana on top of the batter in each cup. Divide the cream cheese mixture evenly over the slices.

5 Bake for 30 minutes, or until a cake tester inserted in the center of a cupcake comes out clean. Remove the pan from the oven and set on a wire rack to cool for 5 minutes. Turn cupcakes out onto rack and cool completely.

12 CUPCAKES
PREP TIME: 20 MINUTES PLUS
30 MINUTES TO COOL
COOKING TIME: 30 MINUTES

EQUIPMENT LIST

Potato masher
Utility knife
12-cup muffin pan
Medium-size bowl
Large bowl
Electric mixer
Kitchen spoons
Cake tester or toothpick
Wire rack

Bananas and chocolate—a fantastic flavor combination!

Lemon-Blueberry Cupcakes

1⅔ cups cake flour
1 teaspoon baking powder
¼ teaspoon salt
½ teaspoon baking soda
¼ cup (½ stick) unsalted butter, softened
⅔ cup granulated sugar
2 large eggs
1 cup sour cream
1 tablespoon grated lemon rind
1½ cups blueberries, stemmed
1 tablespoon confectioners' sugar

Serve these elegant and fruity cupcakes as part of a cake selection for afternoon tea. They also make a splendid addition to a summer brunch.

1 Preheat the oven to 350° F. Grease 12 standard-size muffin pan cups or line with paper liners. In a small bowl, combine the flour, baking powder, salt, and baking soda.

2 In a medium-size bowl, using an electric mixer set on medium speed, cream the butter and granulated sugar until light and fluffy. Add the eggs, one at a time, beating well after each addition. Beat in the sour cream until well blended. Stir in the flour until just moistened. Gently fold in the lemon rind and blueberries.

3 Spoon the batter evenly into prepared muffin pan cups, filling them three-fourths full. Bake for 30 to 35 minutes, or until a cake tester inserted in the center comes out clean. Remove the pan from the oven and set on a wire rack to cool for 15 minutes. Turn the cupcakes out onto the rack and cool completely. Sprinkle the cupcakes with confectioners' sugar, if desired.

12 CUPCAKES
PREP TIME: 10 MINUTES PLUS
30 MINUTES TO COOL
COOKING TIME: 35 MINUTES

EQUIPMENT LIST

Grater
12-cup muffin pan
Small bowl
Medium-size bowl
Kitchen spoon
Electric mixer
Rubber spatula
Cake tester or toothpick
Wire rack

Heavenly Brownies

1 cup cake flour
1 teaspoon baking powder
¼ teaspoon salt
½ cup (1 stick) unsalted butter, softened
2 ounces unsweetened chocolate (2 squares), coarsely chopped
2 ounces semisweet chocolate (2 squares), coarsely chopped
1 cup granulated sugar
2 large eggs
1 teaspoon vanilla extract
3 ounces chopped walnuts (¾ cup)

CHOCOLATE FROSTING

1 ounce semisweet chocolate (1 square), coarsely chopped
3 tablespoons unsalted butter, softened
½ teaspoon vanilla extract
1 cup confectioners' sugar, sifted
1 tablespoon milk

For true chocolate lovers these frosted brownies will be the ultimate.

1 Preheat the oven to 350° F. Grease an 8" square baking pan. In a small bowl, combine the flour, baking powder, and salt.

2 In a small saucepan, combine the ½ cup of butter, the unsweetened chocolate, the 2 ounces of semisweet chocolate, and the granulated sugar. Cook, stirring frequently, over moderately low heat for 5 minutes, or until the butter and chocolate are melted and the mixture is smooth. Remove the pan from the heat.

3 Transfer the chocolate mixture to a medium-size bowl and let cool slightly. Add the eggs, one at a time, beating well after each addition. Stir in the 1 teaspoon of vanilla. Add flour mixture and stir until just mixed. Stir in the walnuts. Scrape the batter into the prepared pan. Bake for 25 to 30 minutes, or until the brownies are set.

4 Meanwhile, make the Chocolate Frosting. Place the 1 ounce of semisweet chocolate in a double boiler set over simmering (not boiling) water and stir until melted and smooth. Remove the pan from the water and cool slightly. In a medium-size bowl, combine the 3 tablespoons of butter, ½ teaspoon of vanilla, and the confectioners' sugar. Add the milk, stirring until well blended. Stir in the melted chocolate and set aside

5 Remove the pan from the oven and set on a wire rack to cool for 15 minutes. Using a thin, metal spatula, spread the frosting over the top of the cooled brownie. Cut the brownies into 2" squares.

16 BROWNIES
PREP TIME: 15 MINUTES PLUS
15 MINUTES TO COOL
COOKING TIME: 30 MINUTES

EQUIPMENT LIST

Utility knife
Sifter
8" square baking pan
Small bowl
2 medium-size bowls
Kitchen spoons
Small saucepan
Double boiler
Rubber spatula
Thin, metal spatula
Wire rack

Chocolate Chip Cookies

1 cup plus 2 tablespoons all-purpose flour
½ teaspoon baking soda
½ teaspoon salt
½ cup (1 stick) unsalted butter, softened
6 tablespoons granulated sugar
6 tablespoons firmly packed light brown sugar
½ teaspoon vanilla extract
1 large egg
6 ounces semisweet chocolate chips (1 cup)
2 ounces chopped walnuts (½ cup)

Ever since Ruth Wakefield of the Toll House Inn added pieces of chocolate bar to her butter cookie dough in 1930, these rich-tasting cookies have remained high on the taste charts and are still one of America's favorites. If time is really short, try Chocolate Chip Pan Squares (recipe below). Either way, this recipe can easily be doubled or tripled for a larger yield and stored in an airtight container for up to a week.

1 Preheat the oven to 375° F. In a small bowl, combine the flour, baking soda, and salt.

2 In a large bowl, using an electric mixer set on medium speed, cream the butter with the granulated and brown sugars and the vanilla until light and fluffy. Beat in the egg. Reduce the mixer speed to low and slowly beat in the flour mixture until well blended. Stir in the chocolate chips and the walnuts.

3 Drop 12 rounded teaspoonfuls of dough onto a baking sheet, spacing them 2″ apart. Bake for 9 to 11 minutes, or until lightly golden. Remove the baking sheet from the oven and set on a wire rack to cool for 5 minutes. Using a thin, metal spatula, transfer the cookies to the rack and cool slightly. Repeat as directed with the remaining dough.

4 Alternatively, to make Chocolate Chip Pan Squares: Preheat the oven and prepare the dough as directed. Spread the dough into a 9″ square baking pan. Bake for 12 to 15 minutes, or until the top is lightly golden. Remove the pan from the oven and set on a wire rack to cool completely. Cut into sixteen 2¼″ squares.

2 DOZEN COOKIES
PREP TIME: 10 MINUTES
COOKING TIME: 22 MINUTES

EQUIPMENT LIST

Small bowl
Large bowl
Kitchen spoon
Teaspoon
Electric mixer
Baking sheet
Wire rack
Thin, metal spatula

Pineapple-Macadamia Nut Cookies

1	8-ounce can crushed pineapple
2	cups all-purpose flour
1	teaspoon baking powder
¼	teaspoon salt
½	teaspoon baking soda
½	cup (1 stick) unsalted butter, softened
½	cup granulated sugar
½	cup firmly packed light brown sugar
1	large egg
4	ounces chopped macadamia nuts (1 cup)

Macadamia nuts are grown in Hawaii and California, but are actually native to Australia. Their rich, buttery taste is well suited to a variety of desserts. These cookies go particularly well with iced tea, but they can be served at anytime of the year.

1 Preheat oven to 375° F. Line 2 baking sheets with aluminum foil. Drain the pineapple well and reserve 1 tablespoon of juice.

2 In a small bowl, combine the flour, baking powder, salt, and baking soda. In a large bowl, using an electric mixer set on medium speed, cream the butter with the granulated and brown sugars until light and fluffy. Add the egg and beat until well blended. Beat in the pineapple and reserved juice. Reduce the mixer speed to low and beat until well blended. Stir in the nuts.

3 Drop rounded tablespoonfuls of dough onto 1 of the prepared baking sheets, spacing them 2″ apart. Bake for 15 minutes, or until lightly golden. Remove baking sheet from oven and set on a wire rack to cool for 5 minutes. Using a thin, metal spatula, transfer the cookies to the rack and cool completely. Repeat with remaining dough. Store the cookies in an airtight container for up to 3 days, or freeze them for up to 1 month. Thaw at room temperature for 30 minutes before serving.

2 DOZEN COOKIES
PREP TIME: 10 MINUTES PLUS
30 MINUTES TO COOL
COOKING TIME: 30 MINUTES

EQUIPMENT LIST

Utility knife
2 baking sheets
Aluminum foil
Strainer
2 small bowls
Large bowl
Kitchen spoon
Tablespoon
Electric mixer
Wire rack
Thin, metal spatula

Sesame Praline Wafers

⅓	cup sesame seeds
¼	cup (½ stick) salted butter or margarine
¼	cup light corn syrup
¼	cup firmly packed light brown sugar
½	cup plus 2 tablespoons all-purpose flour
¼	teaspoon baking powder
¼	teaspoon ground cinnamon
⅛	teaspoon ground nutmeg
24	pecan halves

These wafers are similar to Benne Seed Wafers, a famous cookie from South Carolina. The benne seeds, or sesame seeds, were once thought to bring good luck to those who ate them. The plant was originally brought by slaves from West Africa to the coastal region of the state, particularly around the city of Charleston.

1 Preheat the oven to 350° F. Grease 2 baking sheets. Spread sesame seeds in a thin layer in a baking pan. Toast in the oven, shaking pan occasionally, for 10 minutes, or until golden. Remove the pan from the oven and set aside. Reduce oven temperature to 325° F.

2 Meanwhile, place butter, corn syrup, and sugar in a medium-size saucepan. Cook over moderate heat stirring occasionally, for 3 minutes, or until butter is melted. Remove pan from heat. Set aside.

3 In a medium-size bowl, sift together the flour, baking powder, cinnamon, and nutmeg. Add the butter mixture and the toasted sesame seeds and mix until well blended.

4 Drop rounded teaspoonfuls of the dough onto 1 of the prepared baking sheets, spacing them 2″ apart, and top each with a pecan half. Bake for 8 to 10 minutes, or until lightly browned.

5 Remove the baking sheet from the oven and set on a wire rack to cool for 2 minutes. Using a thin, metal spatula, transfer cookies to the wire rack and cool completely. Repeat with the remaining dough. Store the cookies in an airtight container for up to 3 days, or freeze them for up to 1 month. Thaw at room temperature for 30 minutes before serving.

2 DOZEN COOKIES
PREP TIME: 15 MINUTES PLUS
30 MINUTES TO COOL
COOKING TIME: 20 MINUTES

EQUIPMENT LIST

2 baking sheets
Baking pan
Medium-size saucepan
Kitchen spoon
Teaspoon
Medium-size bowl
Sifter
Wire rack
Thin, metal spatula

N Autumn Dinner Party

Salute the change of seasons with this lovely autumn menu. It features lemon sole lightly poached in a white wine sauce, with leeks, potatoes, and a flavorful filled squash as accompaniments. Round out the meal with banana fritters in a creamy custard sauce.

Lemon Sole with White Wine and Leeks

Boiled Red Potatoes

Marinated Tomato Wheels
(page 79)

Sausage-Filled Acorn Squash

Banana Fritters with Warm Custard Sauce
(page 121)

PREPARATION TIME-SAVERS

• *The night before,* prepare and marinate the tomatoes, cover with plastic wrap, and refrigerate. Remove the tomatoes from the refrigerator about 15 minutes before serving.

• Prepare the vegetables. Rinse and slice the leeks and wrap in wet paper towels. Scrub the potatoes and place in a bowl of water. Prepare the squash and wrap in plastic wrap. Refrigerate until ready to use.

• Prepare the sauce and batter for the fritters, cover with plastic wrap, and refrigerate until ready to use.

Lemon Sole
with White Wine and Leeks

Here, sole is poached in a savory mixture of white wine, fish stock, and leeks. After poaching the fish, boil the poaching liquid to reduce it to a flavorful sauce. While preparing the sole, boil red potatoes for an accompaniment.

1	cup dry white wine
½	cup fish stock or bottled clam juice
1	medium-size lemon, sliced
2	medium-size leeks (green parts only), rinsed and sliced ½″ thick (1 cup)
2	tablespoons olive oil
⅛	teaspoon dried thyme leaves, crumbled
⅛	teaspoon salt, or to taste
	Freshly ground black pepper
4	lemon sole fillets (6 ounces each), rinsed and patted dry
	Sprigs of fresh dill (optional)

1 In a large skillet, combine the wine, stock, and lemon slices. Bring to a boil over high heat. Reduce the heat to moderately low. Add the leeks, oil, and thyme. Season to taste with the salt and pepper. Cook, uncovered, for 5 minutes, or until the leeks are softened.

2 Fold each fillet in half lengthwise, making sure that the inside, where the bones were, is on the outside. (If in doubt, fold fillets both ways: the one that lays the flattest is correct.) Place fillets in the skillet in a single layer. Cook, covered, for 8 minutes, or until fish flakes easily when tested with a fork. Using a slotted spoon, transfer the fillets to a serving platter, cover with aluminum foil, and keep warm.

3 Strain the broth into a medium-size bowl and discard lemon slices. Transfer the leeks to a plate. Return broth to the skillet and bring to a boil over high heat. Boil, stirring occasionally, for 5 to 6 minutes, or until the sauce has thickened slightly and is reduced by one-half. Scatter the leeks over fillets. Spoon the sauce over the fillets, garnish with sprigs of fresh dill, if desired, and serve immediately.

4 SERVINGS
PREP TIME: 20 MINUTES
COOKING TIME: 20 MINUTES

EQUIPMENT LIST

Utility knife
Pepper mill
Paper towels
Aluminum foil
Large skillet with lid
Fork
Slotted spoon
Kitchen spoon
Strainer
Medium-size bowl
Plate

Sausage-Filled Acorn Squash

2	medium-size acorn squash (4 pounds)

SAUSAGE STUFFING (3½ CUPS)

8	ounces mild sausage meat or sausage links
1	tablespoon vegetable oil
1	small yellow onion, finely chopped (½ cup)
1	stalk celery, finely chopped (½ cup)
1½	cups cubed cornbread stuffing mix
⅓	cup chicken stock or canned broth
¼	teaspoon dried thyme leaves, crumbled
¼	teaspoon ground cumin (optional)
⅛	teaspoon ground red pepper (cayenne) (optional)

1 Preheat the oven to 350° F. Cut the squash in half lengthwise. Using a spoon, scoop out the seeds and discard. Place the squash halves, cut-side down, in a large, shallow baking dish. Bake the squash, uncovered, for 25 minutes, or until they begin to soften.

2 Meanwhile, make the Sausage Stuffing. If using sausage links, remove the casings from the sausages and discard. In a large skillet over moderate heat, cook the sausage, stirring to break up the pieces with a wooden spoon, for 6 minutes, or until browned. Using a slotted spoon, transfer the sausage to a plate lined with paper towels to drain.

3 Wipe the skillet clean with a paper towel. Heat the oil in the skillet over moderate heat for 1 minute. Add the onion and celery and sauté for 5 minutes, or until the onion is translucent. Remove the skillet from the heat. Return the sausage to the skillet, add the stuffing mix, stock, thyme, and cumin and ground red pepper, if desired, and stir until well blended.

4 Remove the squash from the oven. Turn the squash halves cut-side up and return them to the baking dish. Divide the stuffing equally among the squash cavities, mounding it slightly.

5 Bake, uncovered, for 10 minutes, or until the stuffing is heated through and the squash is very tender. Transfer the stuffed squash to a serving dish and serve immediately.

4 SERVINGS
PREP TIME: 10 MINUTES
COOKING TIME: 35 MINUTES

EQUIPMENT LIST

Utility knife
Kitchen spoon
Wooden spoon
Slotted spoon
Large, shallow baking dish
Large skillet
Plate
Paper towels

 PARTY ON THE PATIO

Make the highlight of summer a party on the patio, terrace, or in the garden. Serve a buffet of cheese and nut balls, spicy drumsticks, cooling melon slices, and a colorful Southwestern-style salad.

Mixed Cheese and Nut Balls

Cantaloupe Slices

Drumsticks Diablo

Tex-Mex Style Black Bean and Rice Salad
(page 95)

PREPARATION TIME-SAVERS

• *The night before*, prepare the cheese and nut balls (halve the recipe), cover with plastic wrap, and refrigerate until ready to serve.

• Prepare the Diablo Mixture, cover with plastic wrap, and refrigerate. To really cut down on the time (and produce spicier drumsticks), brush the chicken with the Diablo Mixture, place the drumsticks in a large, shallow bowl, cover with plastic wrap, and refrigerate until ready to bake.

• Cut the melon in half and scoop out and discard seeds. Cut into slices, arrange on a serving platter, cover with plastic wrap, and refrigerate until ready to serve.

• Prepare the black bean and rice salad and toss with the dressing. Cover the bowl with plastic wrap and refrigerate until ready to serve.

Mixed Cheese and Nut Balls

1 pound lean bacon, chopped
1 pound sharp yellow Cheddar cheese, at room temperature, cubed
2 8-ounce packages lowfat cream cheese, softened
1 pound gorgonzola cheese, at room temperature, cubed
¼ cup chopped red onion
½ teaspoon ground red pepper (cayenne)
¼ teaspoon salt, or to taste
3 ounces finely chopped pistachio nuts (¾ cup)
3 ounces finely chopped pecans (¾ cup)
¾ cup snipped fresh chives or chopped green onion tops
Crackers (optional)

These colorful cheese balls are an attractive way to serve cheese as an appetizer, and they are also an ideal accompaniment to fruit. Create an eye-catching buffet arrangement by varying the nut coatings and by serving the cheese balls with assorted shaped crackers.

1 In a large skillet over moderately high heat, cook the bacon for 8 to 10 minutes, or until crisp. Remove the pan from the heat. Using a slotted spoon, transfer the bacon to a plate lined with paper towels to drain.

2 Place the Cheddar, cream, and gorgonzola cheeses, onion, and ground red pepper in a blender or food processor fitted with the metal blade. Blend or process for 1 minute, or until smooth, scraping down the side of the bowl whenever necessary. Scrape the cheese mixture into a large bowl. Stir in the bacon. Cover the bowl with plastic wrap and chill in the refrigerator for 1 hour.

3 Place the pistachios, pecans, and chives on separate plates. Line a baking sheet with wax paper. Shape a rounded tablespoon of the cheese mixture into a ball. Lightly roll the ball in one of the coatings and place on the baking sheet. Shape and roll the remaining cheese balls as directed. Cover the cheese balls loosely with plastic wrap and chill in the refrigerator for 1 hour, or until ready to serve.

4 Arrange the cheese balls and the crackers, if desired, on a serving platter and serve immediately.

40 CHEESE BALLS
PREP TIME: 30 MINUTES PLUS
2 HOURS TO CHILL
COOKING TIME: 10 MINUTES

Equipment List

Utility knife
Kitchen scissors
Large skillet
Slotted spoon
Kitchen spoon
Tablespoon
Paper towels
Plastic wrap
Wax paper
4 plates
Blender or food processor with metal blade
Rubber spatula
Large bowl
Baking sheet

Drumsticks Diablo

12 chicken drumsticks (3-3½ pounds)

Diablo Mixture
1 small yellow onion, finely chopped (½ cup)
1 tablespoon Dijon-style mustard
1 tablespoon Worcestershire sauce
1 teaspoon ground red pepper (cayenne)

Diablo, the Spanish word for the devil, describes any dish that is hot and fiery. Here, mustard, Worcestershire sauce, and ground red pepper are combined to create a potent mixture that transforms roast chicken.

1 Preheat the oven to 350° F. Rinse the drumsticks under cold running water and pat dry with paper towels. Place the drumsticks in a large baking dish.

2 To make the Diablo Mixture: In a small bowl, mix together the onion, mustard, Worcestershire sauce, and ground red pepper. Brush the mixture liberally over the chicken.

3 Bake the drumsticks for 45 minutes, or until the juices run clear when the meat is pierced with a knife. Transfer the drumsticks to a serving platter and serve immediately.

4 SERVINGS
PREP TIME: 15 MINUTES
COOKING TIME: 45 MINUTES

Equipment List

Utility knife
Paper towels
Large baking dish
Small bowl
Kitchen spoon
Pastry brush

# A FAMILY SUNDAY DINNER

Roasts make a great dinner party centerpiece, and here eye of round roast is teamed with a wonderful red wine and vegetable sauce. Offer crisp Brussels sprouts and baby carrots as accompaniments. And, for the finale, present an artfully arranged platter of exotic fruit accompanied by a delightful honey and yogurt dressing.

Eye of Round Roast with Red Wine Sauce

Buttered Brussels Sprouts and Baby Carrots

Arugula and Roquefort Salad
(page 93)

Exotic Fruit Platter with Honey-Yogurt Dressing
(page 119)

PREPARATION TIME-SAVERS

• *The night before,* prepare the salad but do not slice and add the avocados as they will turn brown. Cover the bowl with plastic wrap and refrigerate until ready to serve.

• Prepare the fruit platter and the dressing, cover separately with plastic wrap, and refrigerate until ready to serve.

• Prepare the vegetables. Trim and rinse the Brussels sprouts and trim and peel the carrots. Wrap in wet paper towels and refrigerate until ready to use.

Eye of Round Roast
with Red Wine Sauce

Eye of round roast is a favorite cut of meat for a dinner party because it's both economical—there is virtually no waste—and easy. Here it is accompanied by a wonderfully flavorful Red Wine Sauce.

1 2½-pound eye of round roast
1 large clove garlic, cut in half
1 teaspoon olive oil
¼ teaspoon salt, or to taste
Ground white pepper

RED WINE SAUCE (1¾ CUPS)

3 tablespoons unsalted butter
2 tablespoons all-purpose flour
1½ cups beef stock or canned broth
½ cup dry red wine
1 small yellow onion, coarsely chopped (½ cup)
1 small carrot, coarsely chopped (½ cup)
1 sprig fresh thyme, or ½ teaspoon dried thyme leaves, crumbled
5 stems fresh parsley
1 tablespoon tomato paste
⅛ teaspoon salt, or to taste
Freshly ground black pepper
Chopped fresh parsley (optional)

1 Preheat the oven to 425° F. Place the roast on a rack in a roasting pan. Rub the roast with the garlic halves, then brush the roast with the oil. Season with the salt and white pepper. Roast, uncovered, for 40 minutes, turning once.

2 Meanwhile, make the Red Wine Sauce. In a medium-size saucepan over moderate heat, melt 2 tablespoons of the butter. Stir in the flour and cook, stirring continuously, for 30 seconds. Stir in the stock and wine until well blended. Add the onion, carrot, thyme, and parsley stems. Bring the mixture to a boil over high heat. Reduce heat to low and cook, uncovered, stirring frequently, for 30 minutes, or until the sauce has thickened slightly. Stir in the tomato paste and cook, stirring continuously, for 1 minute.

3 Remove the pan from the heat. Strain the sauce through a fine sieve into a small bowl and discard the vegetables and herbs. Return the sauce to the pan. Stir the remaining 1 tablespoon of butter into sauce until well blended. Season to taste with the salt and black pepper.

4 Remove the roast from the oven. Transfer the roast to a carving board and let stand, loosely covered, for 5 minutes. Slice the roast thinly and transfer to a serving platter. Transfer the sauce to a sauceboat, garnish with chopped fresh parsley, if desired, and serve immediately with the roast.

6 SERVINGS
PREP TIME: 10 MINUTES PLUS
5 MINUTES TO STAND
COOKING TIME: 40 MINUTES

EQUIPMENT LIST

Utility knife
Pepper mill
Roasting pan with rack
Pastry brush
Medium-size saucepan
Kitchen spoon
Fine sieve
Small bowl
Carving board

Buttered Brussels Sprouts
and Baby Carrots

This colorful and simply prepared vegetable combination will complement the eye of round roast beautifully.

1 pound Brussels sprouts, trimmed and rinsed (4 cups)
12 baby carrots, trimmed and peeled
3 tablespoons unsalted butter
¼ teaspoon salt, or to taste
Ground white pepper

1 Place the Brussels sprouts and the carrots in a steamer set over boiling water in a medium-size saucepan and steam, covered, for 10 minutes, or until crisp-tender. Remove the steamer from the water and transfer the vegetables to a large bowl.

2 Meanwhile, in a small saucepan over moderate heat, melt the butter. Set aside.

3 Pour the butter over the vegetables, tossing gently to coat. Season to taste with the salt and pepper. Transfer the buttered vegetables to the serving platter with the eye of round roast. Serve immediately.

6 SERVINGS
PREP TIME: 10 MINUTES
COOKING TIME: 10 MINUTES

EQUIPMENT LIST

Paring knife
Vegetable peeler
Vegetable steamer
Medium-size saucepan with lid
Small saucepan
Large bowl
Kitchen spoon

Nutritional Information

Unless otherwise noted, the analyses are based on a single serving.

page 13 **Herb-Stuffed Shrimp** *Calories 319; Cholesterol 177 mg; Sodium 394 mg; Protein 22 g; Total Fat 16 g; Saturated Fat 9 g*

page 13 **Garlic-Stuffed Mussels** *Calories 115; Cholesterol 34 mg; Sodium 332 mg; Protein 8 g; Total Fat 7 g; Saturated Fat 4 g*

page 14 **Broiled Oysters with Cilantro Pesto** (per oyster) *Calories 98; Cholesterol 18 mg; Sodium 151 mg; Protein 3 g; Total Fat 9 g; Saturated Fat 1 g*

page 15 **Sicilian Mini Pizzas** (per pizza) *Calories 71; Cholesterol 1 mg; Sodium 131 mg; Protein 2 g; Total Fat 3 g; Saturated Fat 0 g*

page 15 **Prosciutto-Mozzarella Balls** (per piece) *Calories 60; Cholesterol 14 mg; Sodium 178 mg; Protein 4 g; Total Fat 5 g; Saturated Fat 0 g*

page 16 **Goat Cheese and Herb Spread** (per tablespoon) *Calories 48; Cholesterol 10 mg; Sodium 41 mg; Protein 2 g; Total Fat 4 g; Saturated Fat 2 g*

page 17 **Smoked Herbed Salmon and Cream Cheese Roll** *Calories 147; Cholesterol 40 mg; Sodium 341 mg; Protein 8 g; Total Fat 12 g; Saturated Fat 7 g*

page 18 **Festive Brie in Phyllo Pastry** *Calories 232; Cholesterol 62 mg; Sodium 302 mg; Protein 11 g; Total Fat 18 g; Saturated Fat 4 g*

page 19 **Cheese and Crabmeat Quesadillas** (per wedge) *Calories 141; Cholesterol 19 mg; Sodium 218 mg; Protein 5 g; Total Fat 8 g; Saturated Fat 3 g*

page 19 **Fresh from the Garden Guacamole** (per tablespoon) *Calories 13; Cholesterol 0 mg; Sodium 2 mg; Protein 0 g; Total Fat 1 g; Saturated Fat 0 g*

page 21 **Chilled Tomato and Avocado Soup** *Calories 138; Cholesterol 0 mg; Sodium 685 mg; Protein 4 g; Total Fat 8 g; Saturated Fat 1 g*

page 21 **Pasta e Fagioli** *Calories 261; Cholesterol 0 mg; Sodium 250 mg; Protein 10 g; Total Fat 6 g; Saturated Fat 1 g*

page 22 **Harvest Festival Pumpkin-Cheese Soup** *Calories 293; Cholesterol 65 mg; Sodium 590 mg; Protein 11 g; Total Fat 23 g; Saturated Fat 14 g*

page 23 **Southwestern Corn Chowder** *Calories 226; Cholesterol 0 mg; Sodium 546 mg; Protein 8 g; Total Fat 6 g; Saturated Fat 1 g*

page 24 **Chinese Asparagus and Noodle Soup** *Calories 117; Cholesterol 0 mg; Sodium 470 mg; Protein 4 g; Total Fat 4 g; Saturated Fat 1 g*

page 25 **Gingered Cream of Carrot Soup** *Calories 170; Cholesterol 0 mg; Sodium 583 mg; Protein 5 g; Total Fat 6 g; Saturated Fat 1 g*

page 25 **Hot or Not Vegetable Soup** *Calories 228; Cholesterol 16 mg; Sodium 194 mg; Protein 7 g; Total Fat 5 g; Saturated Fat 3 g*

page 26 **White Gazpacho** *Calories 136; Cholesterol 16 mg; Sodium 218 mg; Protein 6 g; Total Fat 7 g; Saturated Fat 4 g*

page 27 **Curried Avocado Soup** *Calories 432; Cholesterol 44 mg; Sodium 346 mg; Protein 8 g; Total Fat 30 g; Saturated Fat 11 g*

page 27 **Artichoke Vichyssoise** *Calories 229; Cholesterol 38 mg; Sodium 578 mg; Protein 5 g; Total Fat 13 g; Saturated Fat 7 g*

page 29 **Waffles with Blueberry-Spice Sauce** (with 3 tablespoons sauce) *Calories 434; Cholesterol 203 mg; Sodium 583 mg; Protein 13 g; Total Fat 19 g; Saturated Fat 10 g*

page 29 **Corn Pancakes with Cherry Sauce** (with 2 tablespoons sauce) *Calories 342; Cholesterol 130 mg; Sodium 413 mg; Protein 10 g; Total Fat 13 g; Saturated Fat 6 g*

page 30 **Fruit and Nut Granola Parfait** *Calories 365; Cholesterol 5 mg; Sodium 104 mg; Protein 10 g; Total Fat 11 g; Saturated Fat 2 g*

page 31 **Rise and Shine Muesli** *Calories 287; Cholesterol 26 mg; Sodium 37 mg; Protein 12 g; Total Fat 13 g; Saturated Fat 5 g*

page 31 **Spiced Oatmeal with Honeyed Orange Sections and Raisins** *Calories 189; Cholesterol 0 mg; Sodium 104 mg; Protein 12 g; Total Fat 15 g; Saturated Fat 3 g*

page 33 **Swiss Cheese Gougère** *Calories 287; Cholesterol 154 mg; Sodium 202 mg; Protein 10 g; Total Fat 19 g; Saturated Fat 11 g*

page 33 **Three-Pepper Filling** *Calories 67; Cholesterol 0 mg; Sodium 72 mg; Protein 1 g; Total Fat 4 g; Saturated Fat 0 g*

page 33 **Spinach-Tomato Filling** *Calories 97; Cholesterol 0 mg; Sodium 140 mg; Protein 3 g; Total Fat 7 g; Saturated Fat 1 g*

page 34 **Peach Blintzes** *Calories 430; Cholesterol 192 mg; Sodium 454 mg; Protein 18 g; Total Fat 17 g; Saturated Fat 8 g*

page 35 **Molded Spanish Salad** *Calories 52; Cholesterol 0 mg; Sodium 686 mg; Protein 4 g; Total Fat 0 g; Saturated Fat 0 g*

page 35 **Broccoli-Ham Rolls with Cheese Sauce** *Calories 283; Cholesterol 71 mg; Sodium 693 mg; Protein 17 g; Total Fat 20 g; Saturated Fat 9 g*

page 36 **Pasta Frittata with Fontina Cheese** *Calories 284; Cholesterol 294 mg; Sodium 358 mg; Protein 16 g; Total Fat 16 g; Saturated Fat 7 g*

page 37 **Chilled Picnic Baguette** *Calories 434; Cholesterol 15 mg; Sodium 661 mg; Protein 13 g; Total Fat 24 g; Saturated Fat 7 g*

page 37 **Hot Vegetable Baguette** *Calories 286; Cholesterol 9 mg; Sodium 378 mg; Protein 9 g; Total Fat 11 g; Saturated Fat 3 g*

Index

Photo Credits

All photos not otherwise credited were taken by Gus Francisco and Allan Baillie. **Almond Board of California:** Festive Brie in Phyllo, p. 18. **American Lamb Council:** Spicy Lamb Stir-Fry, p. 51. **California Apricot Advisory Board:** Apricot Scones, p. 114. **Canned Food Information Council:** Double-Sauced Lamb Chops, p. 48. **Delmarva Poultry Industry, Inc.:** Baked Chicken with Spicy Red Sauce, p. 66. **Dole® Food Company:** Black Bottom Cupcakes, p. 126. **Florida Tomato Committee:** Pacific Chicken and Tomato Salad, p. 72. **International Olive Oil Council:** Broiled Trout with Provençale Relish, p. 54. A Casual Lunch, p. 136. **Martin Jacobs:** Kale Gratinée, p. 89. **Peter Johansky:** Herb-Stuffed Shrimp, p. 12. **Kraft Creative Kitchens, Kraft General Foods:** Exotic Fruit Platter with Honey-Yogurt Dressing, p. 2, p. 118. **Vincent Lee:** Lamb and White Bean Salad, p. 50; Grilled Chicken with Potato Salad, p. 64. **McCormick Schilling Spices:** Drunken Chicken, p. 67. **Michigan Asparagus Advisory Board:** Asparagus, Carrot, and Pasta Salad, p. 98. **National Livestock and Meat Board:** Ginger-Lime Pork, p. 47; Veal Cutlets with Tomatoes and Mushrooms, p. 52. **National Pasta Association:** Straw and Hay Fettuccine, p. 102. **National Pork Producers Council:** Pork Tenderloin with Mushrooms and Rosemary, p. 11, p. 44; Bavarian Pork Chops, p. 46; Fruited Pork Salad with Endive, p. 90. **Nestlé® Original Toll House® Chocolate Chip Cookies:** Chocolate Chip Cookies, p. 128. **Nestlé® Toll House® Baking Products:** Chocolate Raspberry Trifle, p. 124. **©1989 Ralston Purina Company:** Peppery Green Onion Muffins, 116. **Cynthia Stern:** Spaghetti Puttanesca, p. 100. **Taryn Stinnett:** Chilled Tomato and Avocado Soup, p. 20; Southwestern Corn Chowder, p. 23. **Thomas J. Lipton Company:** Goat Cheese and Herb Spread, p. 16. **USA Rice Council:** Tex-Mex Style Black Bean and Rice Salad, p. 95. **V-8 Vegetable Juice:** Puffy Pancake with Greek-Style Filling, p. 38; Beef Tostadas, p. 42. **V-8 Vegetable Juice** *Healthy Cooking Cookbook:* Peach Blintzes, p. 34. **Wisconsin Milk Marketing Board:** Blue Cheese-Walnut Wafers, p. 112. **Wylers® Bouillion & ReaLemon® Juice from Concentrate:** White Gazpacho, p. 26.